CAROLE

An Introduction to the Ḥadīth

John Burton

EDINBURGH UNIVERSITY PRESS

Edinburgh University Press Ltd
22 George Square, Edinburgh

Set in Linotron Trump Medieval
by Koinonia Ltd, Bury, and
printed in Great Britain
by Redwood Books, Trowbridge, Wiltshire

A CIP record for this book is available
from the British Library

ISBN 0 7486 0350 6 (cased)
ISBN 0 7486 0435 9 (paper)

Contents

System of Transliteration

CONSONANTS

'	ء	ẓ	ظ
b	ب	'	ع
t	ت	gh	غ
th	ث	f	ف
j	ج	q	ق
ḥ	ح	k	ك
kh	خ	l	ل
d	د	m	م
dh	ذ	n	ن
r	ر	h	ه
z	ز	w	و
s	س	y	ي
sh	ش	ة	in pause: -a otherwise: -at
ṣ	ص		
ḍ	ض		
ṭ	ط		

VOWELS

Short vowels			*Long vowels*		*Doubled*	
					uww (final: ū)	ُوّ
fatḥa	a	ـَ	ā	َا َى	iyy (final: ī)	ِيّ
ḍamma	u	ـُ	ū	ُو	*Diphthongs*	
					aw	َوْ
kasra	i	ـِ	ī	ِي	ay	َيْ

Introduction
Ḥadīth *Studies*

By *Ḥadīth* is meant the massive literature of the tradition of the Islamic community compiled from thousands of individual brief narratives, each of which is referred to individually also as a *ḥadīth*, with a small 'ḥ'. A second technical term used virtually as a synonym of *ḥadīth* is *sunna*, to which corresponds, when one is discussing the content or the theory of tradition, the term *Sunna*, with a capital 's'. Thus, where the term *ḥadīth* refers to a document, the term *sunna* refers to the usage described in such a document. The provenance of any *ḥadīth* document is intended to be attested by a list of names appended to the document, listing from latest to earliest the narrators responsible for the recording of the *sunna* or usage described. This chain of 'guarantors' by whom the document has been handed down from generation to generation is known as the *isnād*, literally the 'support' on which the document rests.

Together with the Holy Quran, the *Sunna* forms the base which supports the structures of Islamic political, legal and doctrinal thinking.

The modern reader of Islamic literature (which dates from the mid-second century AH/mid-eighth century AD) is soon made familiar with a situation in which every question of religious or legal moment is thought to have been decided on the basis of either Quran or *Sunna*. The Quran, the Book of God, revealed section by section to God's Prophet throughout the two dozen years of his public ministry first in Makka (AD 610–22) and then in Madīna (AD 622–32), can be taken for granted for the purposes of our study. It is rather the second source, the *Sunna*, as it has been documented in the *Ḥadīth* literature, which will be the focus of this investigation.

The foundations of modern Western analysis of the general *Ḥadīth* phenomenon were laid by Ignaz Goldziher in his *Muhammedanische Studien* (1889–90), and the questions of the nature and 'origins' of the *Ḥadīth* were more recently further investigated by Joseph Schacht in his *Origins of Muhammadan Jurisprudence* (1950).

Goldziher had questioned the alleged connection of much *Ḥadīth* with the age of the Prophet; and Schacht, who concentrated on one particular class of *Ḥadīth*, namely traditions employed in the discussions and debates among the jurists, announced that his studies had, in general, endorsed the scepticism expressed by Goldziher as to the historical link between the *Ḥadīth* and the person, or even the time, of the Prophet. Indeed, the significant achievement of Schacht's work was to make it clear that that link had not even been claimed in any consistent and systematic way by the Muslims until it was made the cornerstone of the polemic of the late second-century AH scholar Shāfiʿī (d. AH 204/AD 819). This discovery affects, however, only the semantics of *Ḥadīth* studies. The fact that the concept of 'the *Sunna* of the Prophet' as a consistent element in the intellectual equipment of the accomplished Muslim scholar dates only from the time of Shāfiʿī carries the discussion of the nature and origin of the '*Sunna* of the Muslims' (or, quite simply, the *Sunna*) little beyond the stage to which it had already been brought by Goldziher.

There is little to quarrel with in Goldziher's résumé of what Muslims have generally understood by the term *Sunna*:

> The Prophet's pious followers have reverently repeated the enlightening sayings of the master and have endeavoured to preserve for the edification and instruction of the community everything that he said, both in public and in private, regarding the practice of the religious obligations prescribed by him, the conduct of life in general, and social behaviour, whether in relation to the past or the future. When the rapid succession of conquests led them to distant countries, they handed on these *ḥadīth*s of the Prophet to those who had not heard them with their own ears, and, after his death, they added many salutary sayings which were thought to be in accord with his sentiments and could, therefore, in their view, legitimately be ascribed to him, or of whose soundness they were in general convinced.[1]

The material here described formed 'the basic substance' of the *Ḥadīth* which, as Goldziher notes, 'vastly increased during subsequent generations'.[2]

Undisguised disagreement on a host of detailed matters is perhaps the outstanding impression gained by the student of the voluminous *Ḥadīth* record. Seizing upon this chaotic disarray on most political, legal and religious questions discussed in the sources, and upon that 'vast increase' of *ḥadīth*s 'during subsequent generations', Goldziher proposed to explain the *Ḥadīth* as the natural consequence of divisions between innumerable groups whose rival political, theological and legal programmes had led to the exploitation of the tradition as the most natural weapon to wield in a community whose members shared a deep religious reverence for the giants of its heroic recent past. Hence the *isnād*, the technique whereby respectability could be won for any political or theological utterance by the mere expedient of attributing it to one or other of the great generation who had witnessed the revelation of the Quran and had imbibed from the Prophet's own lips the details of the Islamic practice.

Certainly, as we shall see hereafter, attribution is the aspect of the *Ḥadīth* most open to question, given both that, in many instances, one and the same form of words has been attributed to a spectrum of different eponyms in whose names information was purportedly handed down, and, more seriously, items of opposed and incompatible information have been commonly ascribed to one and the same historical personage – even to the Prophet himself. But, the attribution is itself the significant act, and is what constitutes the hallmark of the very concept of *Sunna*. That explains why attribution is the Achilles heel of the *Ḥadīth*. The ascription of mutually irreconcilable sayings to several contemporaries of the Prophet, or of wholly incompatible declarations to one and the same contemporary, together strain the belief of the modern reader in the authenticity of the reports as a whole, and led, quite understandably in the cases of Goldziher and Schacht, to outright scepticism as to the historical connection between the *Ḥadīth* and the Companions of the Prophet. Suspension of belief generated the suspicion that the information conveyed in conflicting reports (and ultimately in all reports) merely mirrored the viewpoint of some individual scholar or group of scholars now consciously fathered upon a leading figure of the past to secure the appearance of authenticity, and so enhance the likelihood of its wider acceptance. The *Ḥadīth*, in this view, was thus a weapon of debate wielded upon all sides, even, according to Goldziher, by the ruling house itself (and not only on vexed political questions). It is true that Goldziher could cite cases enough to vindicate his claim that

> among the hotly debated controversial issues of Islam, whether political or doctrinal, there is none in which the champions of the various views are unable to cite a number of traditions, all equipped with imposing *isnād*s[3]

nor does he meet any difficulty in amassing instances to illustrate the abuses of the *Ḥadīth* principle by the ruling power and by their rivals and opponents among the Shīʿa, Khawārij, ʿAbbāsids and other parties striving for influence and leadership. Examples of the kind, and other reports which emphasise the special dignity of particular towns, cities or provinces specified by name, but, unhappily, including some not even incorporated into the territories of Islam until some considerable time after the death of the Prophet or reports either lauding or damning individual persons, or religio-political groupings active (and, in the latter case, founded) only in the post-Prophetic age, have contributed to the effect calculated to be produced by the evidence selected by Goldziher from the sources.[4]

That abuse of the *Ḥadīth* form undoubtedly occurred is, however, less telling than the fact highlighted thereby, namely that, in the hope of securing wider acceptance, much inter-party propaganda assumed the garb of *Ḥadīth*. If hypocrisy lies precisely in the adoption of the external demeanour of the pious and the counterfeit testifies to the existence of the genuine coin, pseudo-*Ḥadīth* imitates real *Ḥadīth*, otherwise the exercise is pointless.

The Muslims themselves became alert to the risks they ran and the dangers they daily incurred from their very dependence upon the *Ḥadīth* and their expectation that all important information be transmitted and circulated in *ḥadīth*-form, although it is unfortunately true that the precautions which they prepared to guard against these recognised threats were slow to appear and, when they did appear, were (in being too much shaped by consideration of the importance of the *isnād*) liable to over-subjectivity in the judgments reached. It is, however, only just to add here that we shall, in what follows, find instances of the contents of *ḥadīth*s being rejected, *isnād* or no *isnād*. In cases of the sort, matter unpalatable to the scholars could be dismissed as errors perpetrated by certain of the transmitters during the course of the handing down of the *ḥadīth*s in question. Besides, the *isnād* tests that were to be introduced, were, in any event, anachronistic, since the earliest surviving works make it plain that, until the second half of the second century AH, the scholars had not attached great importance to the *isnād* and, when they first began to do so, were slow to develop the necessary skills and sophistication.

Reliance upon the *Ḥadīth* was already widespread and, to all appearances, far from being a novelty when taken up and publicly cultivated by the pietistic ʿAbbāsids, who unctuously made great show of their official support for the development of religious studies and of their favour towards those who engaged in them. For, whereas Goldziher's study opened the door for the modern examination of the *Ḥadīth* phenomenon, where it may now be said to be showing signs of its age is in his handling of the Umayyad period. Serious issue must, for example, be taken with his generous use of emotive, not to put too fine a point upon it, pejorative language. Consider the frequency with which he interlards his most penetrating analyses with the vocabulary of deception and conspiracy, using, for instance, such terms as 'fraud', 'fabrication', 'invention', 'falsification' – even 'lies'.[5]

His approach suffers also from a tone of amused condescension appropriate, perhaps, to the age of confident Western political and scientific superiority in which he was nurtured, while his personal liberal instincts betrayed him into a too-sweeping acceptance of stories of the godlessness and religious indifference imputed by their political enemies to the haughty aristocrats of the Umayyad line of 'kings'.

Doubtless justified in his assertion that, at the time of the first conquests, 'there was no ready-made system to be taken from Madīna, since the new order was only developing even there',[6] and in drawing attention to the 'otherwise incomprehensible lack of knowledge and orientation during the first century regarding religious matters in the non-Arab territories conquered for Islam',[7] Goldziher may be thought by the modern enquirer to have been much less than fair in his contention that 'the government did little for the consolidation of religious matters. The Umayyad rulers and their governors – who can hardly be said to have been Islamic-minded – were not the people to promote a religious and social life corresponding to the Sunna.'[8]

That that was not, in fact, the attitude of the devout men who gave their lives to the construction and systematisation of the Islamic sciences, will become clear from the sheer number of *ḥadīth*s which, even in our brief study, point on the contrary to the lively interest believed to have been taken in the details of religious affairs by several representatives of the ruling house, and by numbers of their high officials and functionaries.

Nor has Goldziher succeeded in concealing a romantic streak in his preference for 'free speculation' as opposed to slavish adherence to Tradition in his assessment of the contrasting trends represented respectively by the upholders of *ra'y* and the proponents of the *Ḥadīth*. As Schacht succeeded in showing, the *ra'y* group were every bit as assiduous in their collection of *ḥadīth*s as were their opponents, whom they may even, for polemic reasons, have pre-dated in unfurling the banner of 'the *Sunna* of the Prophet'.

Goldziher stressed the degree of ignorance and uncertainty prevailing in the first century in regard to ritual and legal questions. It may well be that our own investigations indicate that the same or similar evidence suggests rather a lack of broad consensus, with widespread disagreement among the Muslims over the whole range of such questions. We therefore suggest substituting 'lack of agreement' for the 'lack of interest' which Goldziher saw as underlying the fluctuation, apparent lack of decision and failure to achieve uniformity. The degree of disagreement among the Muslims, at times on matters of the minutest detail, testifies to the intense interest in the legal and ritual questions which occupied the minds of countless scholarly individuals and groups. A clearly visible lack of agreement on a wide variety of matters is, as already stated, the outstanding impression afforded the reader of the *Ḥadīth*. Disagreement on this scale presupposes the contrary of indifference. It suggests a whole series of earlier arguments each of which had thrown up different answers. Uncertainty may indicate not an inadequacy, but a surfeit of information. We may thus find ourselves 'reading the signs' differently from Goldziher.

> The preparatory work of previous generations was too scanty to afford a foundation on which to build up a system of Islamic law. There was no fixed norm for the most elementary questions of law even within a single province of Islam. The generation of the 'successors' was occasionally unsure even of Koranic law, though there had never been any doubt that this pillar of religious law was untouchable. ʿAbd Allāh, son of Abū Hurayra, asked the son of 'Umar whether fish that had been washed ashore by the sea could be eaten. The divine who was asked the question thought he must answer with a firm negative. But shortly afterwards, he asked for a Koran to be brought to him and there found a passage (5:97) from which he was forced to conclude that he had given the wrong answer to the son of Abū Hurayra.[9]

Even this matter is, however, by no means so simple. It can be seen in the source from which Goldziher derived this example that what was here involved was not a mere glance at Q 5, but the exercise of some ingenuity in arriving at an answer to the question of food-procurement when, in the sacral condition of *iḥrām*, a man is prohibited from hunting. Among the scholars whose views have, on this occasion, been listed, in addition to the son of ʿUmar, are: ʿAbdallāh b. ʿAmr; Zayd b. Thābit; Marwān b. al-Ḥakam (a prince of the Umayyad house!) and Abū Hurayra, to whom, perhaps, the son of Abū Hurayra would have done better to have addressed his query. These personages occur in *ḥadīth*s concerned not with checking the words of the Quran, but with expressing views as to its interpretation. Incidentally, Mālik (d. 179) quotes here, in addition, a purported utterance of the Prophet's, worded in such a way as to make it clear that the discussion was somewhat technical in nature.[10]

In similar vein, Goldziher concluded, since the most contradictory information was quoted on the question of whether the consumption of horse flesh was permitted to the Muslim, that even greater uncertainty was to be looked for in questions and circumstances for which no provision had been made in the Quran. 'At that time, people were ignorant even about the most primitive dietary laws.' Yet, Mālik, whom Goldziher does not, for the nonce, cite, states that the best statement that he has heard on the question of the flesh of horses, mules and donkeys is that it is not to be eaten,

> on the grounds that God, in referring to the three classes of beast, had specifically mentioned their load-carrying capacity and their ornamental qualities, but not their utility as a source of foodstuff (Q 16.8). On the other hand, in Q 16.5, in speaking of His having

> provided Man with cattle, God did include, among their several uses, the consumption of their flesh.[11]

In glossing various lexical items drawn from the same Quran texts, Mālik is here clearly to be seen engaging in the exegesis (*tafsīr*) of the verses. We note that he derived his negative conclusion from the silence of the Quran – he adduces no *ḥadīth*. At this point, Goldziher's reference is to Abū Da'ūd, and it has to be said, following what we have just seen, that the question arises as to the precise nature of Abū Da'ūd's *ḥadīth*s whose wording reproduces exactly the wording of the above Quran passage, and in exactly the same order as in the Quran passage. In short, the *ḥadīth*s are exegesis, and we must note that two opposing views are ascribed to two separate groups of Companions.[12]

Further, observing that the interpretation of Quranic texts underlay the conflict of *ḥadīth*s just noted, it may be more prudent to assume that the Mālik and Abū Da'ūd discussions represent two separate phases in the development of a purely literary tradition. Abū Da'ūd died in AH 275, almost a century after Mālik. Both men were self-evidently engaged in an entirely academic exercise.

Portraying the situation during the century of Umayyad rule, Goldziher supposed that the aims of the pious were

> divorced from reality. During the time when religious people were pushed into the background by the rulers, they, like the Jewish rabbis under Roman rule, occupied themselves with research into the law, which had no validity for the real circumstances of life but represented for themselves the law of their ideal society. The god-fearing elements of society looked upon these men as their leaders, and even some lax persons occasionally approached them for guidance *in casu conscientiae*. Without paying any attention to reality, these men founded the sunna of the Prophet upon which the law and jurisprudence of the Islamic state was to be based. The Companions and 'followers' living amongst them gave them the sacred material which formed the contents and basis of their endeavour.[13]

Exactly. These studies had nothing to do with real life.

Time and again, Goldziher returns to the theme of the conflict of information, so characteristic of the *Ḥadīth*.

> Only the assumption that in early times the most elementary questions were not the subject of normative decision can explain this uncertainty and wavering in most questions of everyday life. Without this assumption it is difficult to understand how it was possible that during the second century various teachings about ritual and legal problems sprang up in the several *madhāhib*, and

> even in the same *madhab*, with which harmonising theologists could do no more than consider them as equally justified ...[14]

and:

> even in the earliest times of its development, it is impossible to speak of a uniform *sunna* in Islam, since different contradictory *ḥadīth*s concerning one and the same question, which arose in order to support the conflicting opinions of the various schools, are juxtaposed as having equal authority.[15]

For Goldziher, *ḥadīth*s were 'invented' as required to document the differing views espoused by different scholars working together in schools. *Ḥadīth*s were also 'invented' to justify existing local usages:

> Since there was no fixed practice for most legal questions, it was unavoidable that for one and the same question contradictory *ḥadīth*s were invented according to the opinions of various theologians of various groups, or different *ḥadīth*s were selected from earlier material to be handed down. These *ḥadīth*s were then called upon to support the individual opinion or usage customary in a particular circle, since the *ḥadīth* had often only to justify existing customs.[16]

We have drawn attention to the vocabulary used by Goldziher. We shall have to conclude that he did not consider these 'inventions' the regrettable result of pious self-deception. For him, they were, rather, conscious 'fabrication', the result of deliberate fraud basely perpetrated upon the unsuspecting Islamic community with the selfish motive of gaining acceptance for the views agreed upon within small academic factions interested in ritual, legal or political issues. From this, it would appear that Goldziher was not disposed to exempt any class of *ḥadīth* from the stigma of falsehood. There was, perhaps, a core of *ḥadīth* that had come down from the generation contemporary with the Prophet. Reports had been carried from the Islamic centre at Madīna to the outlying provinces now being added to the territory of Islam following the wave of military conquests. That core had formed 'the basic material of the *ḥadīth* which vastly increased during subsequent generations'. Certain portions of that core may have been selected for onward transmission, but,

> in the absence of authentic evidence, it would indeed be rash to attempt to express the most tentative opinion as to which parts of the *ḥadīth* are the oldest original material, or even as to which of them date back to the generations immediately following the Prophet's death. Closer acquaintance with the vast stock of *ḥadīth*s induces sceptical caution rather than optimistic trust regarding the material brought together in the carefully compiled collections. We are unlikely to have even as much confidence as

> Dozy regarding a large part of the *ḥadīth*, but will probably consider by far the greater part of it as the result of the religious, historical and social development of Islam during the first two centuries. The *ḥadīth* will not serve as a document for the history of the infancy of Islam, but rather as a reflection of the tendencies which appeared in the community during the maturer stages of its development. It contains valuable evidence for the evolution of Islam during the years when it was forming itself into an organised whole from powerfully mutually opposed forces. This makes the proper appreciation and study of the *ḥadīth* so important for an understanding of Islam, in the evolution of which the most notable phases are accompanied by successive stages in the creation of *ḥadīth*.[17]

This was the brilliant discovery that Schacht so admired, and one sympathises with his deep regret that some later authors, while accepting Goldziher's method in principle, were inclined to minimise it in practice, in their natural desire for positive results. Goldziher's magnificent insight deserves the highest praise. It has certainly helped to explain many of the hitherto incomprehensible confusions and contradictions encountered daily by the student in the sources, and yet unease remains about acquiescing wholeheartedly in the suggestion that devout and pious men, conscious of the sacred nature of the source materials with which they worked, would engage in a policy of widespread deception and fraud on behalf of their own opinions while themselves sadly pointing out the approach adopted by the less scrupulous among them. For many of these scholars were men of deep piety and undoubted probity who saw themselves as engaged in mapping out in exquisite detail a statement of the revealed will of God, and charting what they viewed as the uniquely valid path to their (and their community's) eternal salvation. The very seriousness of the task on which they had embarked filled many with profound scruples and lent sharpness, at times rising to fierce acrimony, to the debates with which the *Ḥadīth* literature is crammed, as they wrestled passionately over punctilios which will strike the modern reader as intolerably pettifogging. To the Muslim scholar, every detail, however minute, might literally make the difference between eternal life or death. Properly to handle this *Ḥadīth*, we must attempt to match this high seriousness.

Now, whereas, in Goldziher's eyes,

> for cultural history, the legal parts of the *ḥadīth* are of lesser importance than those which show how the religious elements of the Muslim world came to grips with political circumstances and relations,[18]

the author of the second brilliant modern survey of the *Ḥadīth* chose to concentrate almost exclusively on the legal traditions exploited in discussions and debates among the jurists. Schacht recognised that

> the sacred law of Islam is an all-embracing body of religious duties rather than a legal system proper; it comprises on an equal footing ordinances regarding cult and ritual, as well as political and (in the narrow sense) legal rules.[19]

Notwithstanding this realisation, Schacht proposed to concentrate as much as possible on the (properly speaking) legal sphere. That, he argued, recommended itself for practical reasons, and was also historically legitimate, since, he further maintained, the legal subject matter in early Islam

> did not primarily derive from the Koran or from other purely Islamic sources; law lay to a great extent outside the sphere of religion, was only incompletely assimilated to the body of religious duties, and retained part of its own distinctive quality. No clear distinction can, however, be made,

and whenever Schacht uses the term 'Muhammadan Law', he asks the reader to bear in mind that he means it to be understood to comprise all those subjects which come within the sacred law of Islam.[20]

There arises here a major difficulty: that of what European writers mean by the use of the expression 'Islamic law'. In his references to the sacred law of Islam, Schacht was doubtless thinking of the *Fiqh* and, although showing that he appreciated the wide scope of that system which embraced topics of widely disparate natures, in deciding to limit his investigation to 'the purely legal' aspect, taking little or no account of the religious and ritual content, he has courted the danger of viewing the *Fiqh* in the inappropriate light of an exclusively rational man-made discipline. Goldziher had neatly summarised the nature of the *Fiqh*, as, indeed, did Schacht in the first of the brief passages above. Goldziher wrote:

> Fiḳh, like the jurisprudentia of the Romans, [is] *rerum divinarum atque humanarum notitia* and, in its widest sense, covers all aspects of religious, political and civil life. In addition to the laws regulating ritual and religious observances (*ʿibādāt*) as far as concerns performance and abstinence, it includes the whole field of family law, the law of inheritances, of property and of contract; in a word, provisions for all the legal questions that arise in social life (*muʿāmalāt*); it also includes criminal law and procedure and finally constitutional law and laws regulating the administration of the state and the conduct of war. All aspects of public and private life and business should be regulated by laws recognised by religion; the science of these laws in Fiḳh.[21]

'Should be regulated by laws recognised by religion' exactly brings out the nature of the aspiration that created *Fiqh*. *Fiqh* is not law. It is exegesis aspiring to become law.

The basic sense of the term *fiqh* is 'understanding'. As we find the term used in the Quran, the object of the 'understanding' is normally 'speech' and especially the speech of a prophet. *Fiqh* means, therefore, 'understanding the message conveyed on God's behalf by God's spokesman'. The implication of the term, as in the *locus classicus*, Q 9.122, is the patient endeavour to achieve a comprehensive understanding of the many duties laid upon the Muslim by God in His revelation recorded in the Book of God, the Quran. Among the most important obligations imposed upon the contemporary Arabs who agreed to make the *hijra* to join Muḥammad at Madīna was that of participating in his wars.

> Yet the believers ought not all to go out on military missions. One party of each section of Muslims should remain behind and strive to acquaint themselves with the details of the faith. They would then be better able to instruct their tribes on going home.

If, as Goldziher has also pointed out, we are to distinguish the Islamic terms *ʿilm* and *fiqh*, the former denoting, besides knowledge of the Quran and of its exposition, the accurate knowledge of the legal decisions handed down by the Prophet and his Companions (the very stuff of the *Ḥadīth*) then the latter will bear upon the effort to achieve a comprehensive systematic statement of the implications for human individual and social action of the contents of the sources: the Quran and the *Sunna*. The object of *ʿilm* is the divine input; *fiqh* is the outcome of the human contribution. Statements delivered by specialist scholars: *ʿilm – ʿulamā'*, *fiqh – fuqahā'*, as to the divine intention underlying any revealed statement of the Quran, or as to the model exemplification of its import provided in the records of the acts and sayings of the Prophet or of his closest associates, have historically been judged in the light of the closeness of the individual scholar's adherence to the twin sources. A scholar's *ra'y*, his judicious *opinio* is assessed as more or less legitimate and thus acceptable in the degree to which he has taken account of all the information provided in the Quran and the *Sunna*. Ideally, *ra'y* is exercised in strict conformity with the literary sources. Thus, the ideal scholarly approach was conceived as narrowly exegetical.

Individual private interpretation of a Quran verse, based on either linguistic or logical criteria, is invalid. That is the reprehended *ra'y*, opinion as opposed to *opinio*. Only the Prophet and the immediate witnesses of his daily acts and utterances had achieved the fullest appreciation of the divine revelations. The contemporaries of the

Prophet had been uniquely qualified by their thorough grasp of the Arabic idiom, but even more by their awareness of the precise circumstances in which the Quran regulations had been sent down, and their physical presence in the Prophet's company as he for the first time put those divine commands into practice, to pronounce upon matters of faith and *Fiqh*. The information which they have bequeathed is thus by far the surest and the safest interpretation of the sacred texts.

Denying that the 'legal' subject matter of Islam had primarily derived from the Quran, or from other purely Islamic sources, Schacht nevertheless took the importance of the Quranic element in Islamic law for granted, although wishing to qualify that for the earliest period. His work centres, in fact, upon legal theory, and, as far as *Ḥadīth* is concerned, focuses upon its role in that theory. Above all, his primary concern is attribution, and he proceeds by means of detailed analysis of both the material content of *ḥadīth*s and meticulous examination of their *isnād*s.

One of the main results of his study is that it was Shāfi'ī who was the first 'lawyer' consistently to define *Sunna* as 'the model behaviour of the Prophet'. This contrasts with the usage of his predecessors, for whom *Sunna* was not necessarily connected with the Prophet. Indeed, it was not necessarily connected at first even with the Companions, nor yet with their successors.

Schacht's brilliant investigations have shown that attribution itself was an innovation called into being at successive stages in the development of a prolonged and many-sided polemic waged between the scholarly representatives of the ancient Islamic communities of Iraq and the Ḥijāz. Summoned up to provide the accreditation of the conflicting doctrines that had become the currency of the schools of Kūfa, Baṣra, Makka or Madīna, attribution (*isnād*) consisted of the ascription of the local body of doctrine first to the immediately preceding generation, thereafter to the generation before that, and so on until, for technical reasons of legal theory, the attribution had to be eventually carried all the way back to the Prophet himself. The body of doctrine being thus attached to this or that representative of progressively more and more distant generations had originally represented the traditional – albeit ideal – usage (*sunna*) that had grown up in the various localities.

Schacht's demonstration, from the original sources, of the progressive evolution in the *isnād* of many *ḥadīth*s, and of the parallel expansion or contraction of the wording of many *ḥadīth*s, is easily the most convincing aspect of his analysis. We shall see it frequently borne out in what follows.

On the other hand, the least convincing element in his work is his hypothesis as to the ultimate 'origin' of the substantive doctrines documented in his *ḥadīth*s. Part of Schacht's aim had been to work out a method by which the 'legal' traditions might be used for following the development of legal doctrine, step by step, especially for the early period. From his detailed study of the *isnād*, and especially of *isnāds* which intersect at particular points, where more than one version is available, as is frequently the case, Schacht felt able to date many of his *ḥadīth*s. Noting that his methods, when applied to 'legal' *ḥadīth*s, carried him back to about the year AH 100 only, Schacht concluded that Islamic legal thought had begun at that time – i.e. during the Umayyad period.

For Schacht, therefore, Islamic 'legal' thought started from late Umayyad administrative or popular practice, elements of which it either endorsed, modified or rejected. But here, Schacht appends two general remarks. There are perceptible differences in doctrine between 'the ancient schools of law'. These he would explain on the grounds that legal practice in the several parts of the Umayyad Empire was by no means uniform. This would reflect the fact that, during most of the Umayyad period, the administration of justice lay in the hands of the provincial governors and, insofar as special judges were appointed, these were merely the agents of their governors. Different officials acting in different centres had dealt differently with similar questions. Second,

> although the dynasty and most of the Arab ruling class were Muslims, and although some elementary legal rules enacted in the Koran were more or less followed, the legal practice during the earlier part of the Umayyad period cannot yet be called Muhammadan law. Muhammadan law came into existence only through the application of Muhammadan jurisprudence to the raw material supplied by the practice. It will be shown that legal norms based on the Koran, which go beyond the most elementary rules, were introduced into Muhammadan law almost invariably at a secondary stage.[22]

As noted, Schacht chose to select his material from the (properly speaking) 'legal' sphere. This decision tended to channel his attention towards commercial, financial and fiscal questions affecting chiefly problems concerned with property, contract, sales, loans, revenue, exchange and the like. Doubtless, on matters of such severe practicality, it was legitimiate to anticipate a role for local customary usage and also a lively central government interest which would manifest itself in the effects upon the 'practice' – and hence upon the discussions of the learned – of official policy shifts announced in the issue of administrative and regulatory decrees. There remain the problems of attribution (and hence of dating). In assigning the origins of Muhammadan jurisprudence, which was to create Muhammadan law out of late Umayyad practice, to the later part of the Umayyad period, Schacht would not wish to rule out the possibility that that practice contained earlier elements. This highlights his recognition that the dating of *isnād*s is not the same as the dating of *ḥadīth*s. We have indicated earlier that the *isnād* itself was, at about this same time, still an innovation.

Further, Schacht's references to Umayyad administrative or to popular 'practice' are always mere blunt assertion. Not one single instance of such presumptions has been substantiated. All are attended, and rightly, by 'perhaps', 'possibly', 'probably' or 'presumably'. He readily admits that, in a number of places, the allegations by Shāfiʿī and his scholarly adversaries that certain rulings had originated merely in the decisions of local governors or their agents are patently part of regular inter-party polemic.[23] What should be noted in all such instances is that the intent underlying such allegations is always negative – that is, the decisions in question were merely those of individuals, and might not be regarded as part of the fabric of the *Sunna*. They had originated in *ra'y*, and were thus to be repudiated, certainly not endorsed. The decisions and the rulings based upon them, being man-made, had no place in a systematic exposition of the revealed law of God. In Islam, as Goldziher pointed out, all aspects of public, business or private life should be regulated by laws recognised by religion.

Of the countless issues which came within the purview of Islamic discussion, practical questions such as the level of weregeld applicable to various grades of persons; rates of taxation and determination of the classes of goods and property liable to taxation; the rules governing the division and disposal of captured enemy chattels; the organisation and regulation of internal and external commerce, supervision of markets, control of weights, measures and prices, the conditions governing the validity of sales, loans and credit; the laws governing marriage, divorce, paternity, inheritances and the like, would clearly be of concern to those ruling over the community. But, as this was an Islamic community, and those governing it were Muslims, on what basis would they make their determinations; within what limits would they feel free to make such determinations, even without the constant surveillance of the community of believers and the unremitting vigilance of their (mostly self-appointed) religious and scholarly leaders? Governments govern. On what basis did Islamic governments govern? The fact that early caliphs are reported to have pronounced on a range of questions lends a veneer of plausibility to suggestions that their reported decisions may be regarded as 'government decree' or 'administrative practice'. The caliphs were themselves either surviving Companions of the Prophet, or Successors who had met and known contemporaries of the Prophet to whom had come the momentous revelations that had revolutionised their society. It also raises the thorny problem of attribution which Schacht has elsewhere confronted courageously. Yet, we have also already pointed out that his references to 'Umayyad administrative practice', or even to 'Umayyad popular practice' are only presumed, and linked to the attribution of this or that specific measure to this or that specific date or figure in the past. But, since *Sunna* means 'precedent', the practitioners of the study of the *Sunna* are permanently looking to the past, their gaze being necessarily and by definition retrospective. Schacht has himself clearly demonstrated the general emptiness of the attribution to particular individuals of countless statements recorded in the *Ḥadīth*. Why then accept attribution to Umayyad personages? His mention of 'Umayyad administrative practice' or of the 'Umayyad popular practice' was the product of the '*isnād*-barrier', the impossibility of tracing the *ḥadīth*s back beyond the beginning of the second century. This bears, as we have stated, upon the study of the attribution appended to the *ḥadīth*, but not at all upon the substantive material content of the *ḥadīth*. Considerable achievements are thus to be registered against the names of Goldziher, who first boldly tackled the question of the 'authenticity' of the *Ḥadīth*, and of Schacht, who fearlessly took up the issue of the 'attribution' of the *Ḥadīth*. There remains the question of the 'origin' of this *Ḥadīth*. For Schacht has left unanswered the question of the ultimate origin of this 'Umayyad administrative practice' or of the 'Umayyad popular practice' – perhaps because he overlooked the wise caveat which he himself (like Goldziher before him) had issued. The 'practice' referred to by the Islamic scholars does not simply reflect the actual custom. It contains a theoretical or ideal element.[24]

Schacht had elected to restrict his consideration to the (properly speaking) 'legal' sphere. Drawing his materials from a comparatively narrow segment of the vast available *Fiqh* record – a selection dictated largely by the Western conception of law – Schacht may well have denied himself the opportunity to conceive of Islamic 'legal' literature – more correctly, the *Fiqh* – as the documentary precipitation of what we earlier described as an 'academic exercise', a paper war whose raw materials had been supplied by the exegesis of a document, the Holy Quran.

Again, like Goldziher before him, Schacht concentrated primarily upon conflicts in the sphere of the *Sunna*. His datum, like that of his great predecessor, was disagreement. His dissection of the content of his *ḥadīth*s, and especially of their *isnād*s, culminated in the hypothesis that Umayyad 'practice' had furnished the raw materials for the studies of the Islamic jurists. The application of Muhammadan jurisprudence to these raw materials supplied by the practice had brought Muhammadan 'law' into existence. Schacht's inclination to minimise the role of the Quran in this creation may perhaps have been the consequence of his concentrating heavily on a range of questions only very sketchily dealt with in the Quran. But what question is not dealt with only very sketchily in the Quran? This question goes to the very heart of the nature of the *Sunna* itself. It is true that the discussion of the questions pursued by Schacht developed mainly in the sphere of the *Sunna*. But, not only those questions – every question discussed in the *Fiqh* developed mainly in the *Sunna*. It must not be overlooked that, here, we speak of 'development'. That the Quran's reference to a topic may be perfunctory to the point of obscurity does not alter the fact that the Quran, in referring to the matter in the first place, initiated its discussion, throwing down a challenge which no self-respecting scholar could refuse to take up.

We have noted Schacht's references to the 'practice'. In his view, the *Ḥadīth* discussion of problems paralleled – even originated in – some Umayyad practice. When on the other hand, the detailed discussion of one topic drawn from the law on marriage is accompanied in the *Ḥadīth* by numerous references to the Quran, including frequent appeals to the so-called 'variant reading' (in reality, merely a sub-form of variant *ḥadīth*) of a relevant Quran verse, said to have been shared by several major figures of the Companion generation, thus placing beyond all doubt the Quranic origin of this particular dispute, Schacht's insistence upon the 'practice' makes him here presume an ancient Arab institution. That the 'practice' in question has been linked with one of the sources bestows, for Schacht, 'reality' upon the 'practice'; since the source mentioned is the Quran, the 'practice' must be pre-Islamic and it must be 'sanctioned' by the Quran.[25] He apparently deems it unnecessary to submit the *ḥadīth*s in this case, and especially their *isnāds*, to the kind of searching scrutiny which he elsewhere applies so fruitfully to the *ḥadīth*s employed as weapons in other debates which rage around what precisely constitutes the *Sunna*.

Schacht's most valuable contribution to our knowledge focused upon 'legal' theory, or Islamic jurisprudence. So far as the role bestowed upon the *Sunna* in the development of that theory is concerned, his work is unlikely for the foreseeable future to be equalled. It is improbable that it will be surpassed, especially in regard to the problem of attribution, where he showed a masterly grasp of his materials. If we imagine that we have detected a weakness in

Schacht's study, this is because his very concentration on only one series of documents, the *Sunna*, contrasts so strongly with the procedures adopted by the scholars engaged in the actual creation of the *Fiqh*. Those men leave their reader in no doubt that they were simultaneously having to cope with two series of documents, since they saw themselves (and frequently to their considerable embarrassment) having to take account of two sources: the Quran and the *Sunna*. Schacht discussed the role of the Quran in the evolution of Islamic 'law' only very briefly, and again from the angle of the development of legal theory. Failing to extend his penetrating insight on matters of attribution (*isnād*) to the Quranic element of these Islamic discussions, he inclined to restrict consideration of the contents of the revelation and to minimise the pressure that they may well have exerted on the thinking of the Muslim savants.

Schacht presents the evolution of the *Fiqh* as proceeding within a literary tradition to be placed within a framework of 'law'-creation, whose starting point was actual historical custom and practice.

Islam was the most literate culture in the Middle Ages, and the following studies will suggest the possible alternative of placing the same lengthy literary tradition within a framework almost wholly exegetical in inspiration. The search for an answer to the 'origin' of the *Sunna* must involve the study of *ḥadīth*s which agree, as well as *ḥadīth*s which disagree, and seek to identify a common factor underlying both types. It will be suggested that that common factor was the obscurity of the Quran's expression which provoked a human determination to unlock its secrets.

NOTES

1. Goldziher, *Muhammedanische Studien*, English trans. *Muslim Studies*, C. R. Barber and S. M. Stern, George Allen and Unwin, 1971, vol. 2, p. 18.
2. Ibid.
3. Ibid., p. 44.
4. Ibid., ch. 3.
5. Ibid., pp. 44, 51, 78 – 'falsification(s)'; pp. 49, 81, 106 – 'fabrication(s)'; pp. 44, 49, 52, 78ff. – 'invention(s)'; p. 54 – 'forgeries'; p. 55 – 'lies' (p. 44); p. 87 'fictions'; p. 126 – 'fake'.
6. Ibid., p. 38.
7. Ibid.
8. Ibid.
9. Ibid., pp. 77–8.
10. Mālik b. Anas, *Muwaṭṭa'*, 2 vols, Cairo, 1348/1929, vol. 1, p. 326.
11. Ibid., p. 327.
12. Sulaimān b. al-Ash'ath, Abū Da'ūd al-Sijistānī, *Sunan*, 2 vols (in 1), Cairo part 2, p. 142.
13. *Muslim Studies*, loc. cit., p. 42.

14. Ibid., p. 78.
15. Ibid., p. 85.
16. Ibid., p. 81.
17. Ibid., p. 19.
18. Ibid., p. 89.
19. J. Schacht, *Origins of Muhammadan Jurisprudence*, Oxford, 1950, Preface, p. v.
20. Ibid.
21. *Encyclopaedia of Islam*, 1st edn, Leiden, 1913– s.v. *Fiḳh*.
22. Schacht, *Origins*, p. 191.
23. Ibid.
24. Ibid., p. 68.
25. Ibid., pp. 266ff.

1
The Mission of the Prophet

For twenty-three years, AD 610–32, the Prophet Muḥammad, already forty years old at the time of his call, attempted to gain a hearing for a warning and a promise. The warning was one of impending doom; the promise, life everlasting. Tirelessly, he preached a programme of religious and social reform in a mission which falls neatly into two phases: the Makkan period and the hijra.

THE MAKKAN PERIOD

In the face of general indifference, the earlier, Makkan period, AD 610–22, was a comparative failure. Engaged in importing rare, luxury goods from Africa and the Far East and re-exporting them to the rich markets of the north, his peers were much too preoccupied with the business of amassing profits to have time for far-fetched preachings about the perils of an imminent Judgement Day when each man would be sternly judged on the record of his daily activities and then be assigned either to an eternal life of inexpressible bliss, or to an unending existence of indescribable misery and pain. It was not that they had to be convinced of the existence of God.[1] They already believed in a creation and a Creator, but this was something dating back to some distant past and was of no real significance for their busy daily routines. He who had created the earth and all its inhabitants, and the skies above with all their stars and planets, was too distant a figure to concern himself with the warehouses and the counting-houses of Makka and too far removed for any present-day communication to be conceivable. Why would He suddenly wish to communicate now; and, supposing He did, why with Makka; and would He not in any case have chosen some more prominent citizen than the obscure and scarcely noteworthy Muḥammad?[2]

Over the generations, intermediary figures had been inserted between the too-remote Creator and men. If properly propitiated and their intercession won, they might speak to God and He might be prepared to listen and remove some sudden natural disaster or the more personal misfortune of a deterioration in trading conditions. The hazy notion had grown up that certain heavenly beings, 'the daughters of God', could be won over by offerings of rich sacrifices brought to them at the periodic ceremonies held in their honour at a number of shrines in or near the towns and other trading-posts of Arabia. Measures needed also to be taken to placate other supernatural beings that hovered around unseen, ready to work mischief on a man's health or that of his offspring or of the draught animals on which he depended for his livelihood. A class of specialists were in communication with these spirits and, if consulted, could convey messages from them on the probable outcome of a proposed commercial undertaking, or advise on how to remedy the infertility of a wife or of a valuable beast. By a combination of natural temperament and acquired skills, the seers and soothsayers were able to relay to those bearing gifts relevant oracles provided by familiars who, being spirits, could loiter near and eavesdrop upon the deliberations and decisions of the Heavenly Council. This they regularly did, at the risk of being detected and pelted with shooting-stars by the ever-vigilant celestial guards.[3]

Measures also had frequently to be taken to propitiate a host of jinn, ifrits and hobgoblins that entered houses by night to annoy the inhabitants by overturning pots, spoiling stored food, turning the milk in the jug or the udder sour, stirring the embers of unguarded fires or upsetting lamps, and causing serious damage or even loss of life.[4] These demons could also be recruited by an enemy to use their powers to upset an individual's health or cause miscarriages. One had to be on guard constantly against their malevolence, as one had to be aware of the dangers of the evil eye that could be applied by jealous neighbour or business competitor.[5] Religion did thus have serious repercussions on everyday living. But it affected only this life. There was only this life. On his death, a man simply ceased living and all existence ended.[6] The best that one could hope to do, therefore, was to avoid the multiple dangers that surround one in life and, by energy, ingenuity and guile, make for oneself and one's household as comfortable and prosperous a living as one could contrive.

For other difficulties, the encroachment of powerful neighbours, undue pressure from greedy competitors, or quarrels and disputes leading to physical violence, a man had the backing and support of his clan, ready to close ranks and act in solidarity to protect the life, limb and property or the honour of its members, who shared and gloried in a common ancestry. Any threat or insult to a clan member would be met by the concerted act of the entire clan, which would spring to his defence, offering advocacy and negotiation if that were sufficient, but armed intervention if it were not. Each clan member was conscious of the benefit of belonging to a body that would provide its most outstanding orators to plead every argument in his favour and would not hesitate to avenge insult or injury to one of its own number. It was not at all necessary to identify the culprit. Action against any member of the offender's clan would satisfy honour, while the certainty of wider consequences and dread of a prolonged inter-clan feud would cause older heads on both sides to press for a negotiated settlement and cessation of hostile action, even if that meant restraint of a clan member, should he be judged to have acted intemperately. The wilder, more reckless spirit could usually be contained by the mere threat to withdraw the clan's protection. In the extreme cases in which an undisciplined clansman was expelled from the clan, that was as good as a death sentence, since no-one else owed him the duty of protection. The outlaw was truly exposed, since all could assault, even kill him with impunity. Such clan-centred thinking proved infertile soil for Muḥammad's concept of an afterlife and judgment seat before which each individual was alone answerable for his every act.

The Makkans had difficulty in taking Muḥammad seriously. He had already spent a lifetime among them without showing any signs of the clairvoyance which he now appeared to be claiming to possess.[7] They saw him as a moderately prosperous merchant, one of their own kind. What he now alleged about an afterlife was to them a clear absurdity. All knew that life is snuffed out by death. In a short time, the buried corpse decomposes and crumbles to dust. It was mere madness to suggest to hard-headed businessmen that some sort of trial could be held at which the arraigned was a handful of dust indistinguishable from the dirt in which it lay and with which it would soon merge. Mouldering bones had never been seen to rise again from the grave.[8] Nor did it forward his cause to threaten that at any moment God might overturn their city by earthquake, or consume it with fire sent down from the sky. Well might he try frightening the women and children with his chilling tales of long-ago floods that had engulfed man and beast, save for the few invited to embark in a ship constructed just in time; or of the sea parting to allow the passage of Israelites and their prophet-leader, only to close over the armed might of Egypt. Those and the rest of his stories were old wives' tales, fables that had been repeated until they had now lost their power to scare grown men.[9] If Muḥammad really believed in the rising of dead bodies mouldered to dust, let him provide a demonstration. He should produce some of the ancestors so that they could be questioned about conditions beyond this life. If he really feared that God was about to rain down fire and brimstone wiping out all of Makka, but for Muḥammad and the few deluded creatures who followed him, he could convince the more intelligent by praying to his God to mount a brief demonstration.[10] His talk about messages coming from Heaven would be more convincing if he could be seen actually mounting up to Heaven and bringing down a parchment that men could touch and feel, examine the script and read with their own eyes.[11]

Muḥammad was regarded as not merely disordered. He was probably also dangerous. His subtly crafted versions of the stories of the prophets of old usually showed them as demanding obedience to themselves as a sign of true belief.[12] In his public preaching, Muḥammad always contrived to extend the same moral to include himself. He claimed to be a prophet and alleged that God invariably demands obedience to the commands and prohibitions of His prophet and to nobody else, promising rich rewards to those who believe and threatening the destruction of those who do not believe and who defy the prophet to do his worst. This claim to be a prophet and the demand for obedience to himself suggested that Muḥammad had social and political aspirations in addition to – indeed, arising from – his religious reflections. That could threaten the balance of social and political forces that Makkan society had by now achieved. His denunciations of the commercial ethos as materialistic, ungodly and self-centred, and his accusations that it subordinated all other considerations to the detriment of the welfare of all less fortunate members of society, was mere humbug.

What kept the city fed, if not the industry of its merchants? In its barren, rocky valley, where agriculture was totally inconceivable, what kept the city alive, if not its commerce and its enterprise? Makka and its inhabitants could not have survived if its merchants, bankers and investors had not had the courage to take risks with their capital. Without its energy and the deserved rewards of hard work, Makka would not have enjoyed the high reputation that its citizens had won among the Arabs. To criticise these efforts and their results was nothing but ingratitude. Muḥammad's talk was dangerous and simply fed the dissatisfaction of the feckless and the less enterprising, as witness his pernicious notion that those who believed in him were all equal in the eyes of his God. His preaching implied also that the noble ancestors of the clan, including his own parents and grandparents, languished in Hell, not having had the advantage of hearing his message, and that all who paid homage to other supernatural beings besides God would be eternally damned. These were gross insults to the pride and honour of the tribe that ought not to go unpunished.

Faced with growing hostility in his own community, Muḥammad attempted to interest the citizens of a nearby settlement in his warnings and promises, only to be met with a similar lofty aloofness in their chiefs and the stones and insults of the mob. So bleak seemed the prospect that he encouraged a group of his followers to set sail and seek refuge in the neighbouring Christian Kingdom of Ethiopia, in the hope that there they might find the freedom to live in peace and to worship God undisturbed by daily insult and prejudice.

The final blow that almost drained Muḥammad of hope and which heralded the end of his Makkan mission was the near-simultaneous deaths of his uncle, the chief of the clan under whose protection he had hitherto been safe, and of his wife. The Lady Khadīja had been fifteen years his senior when, at the age of twenty-five, he had wed her. Perhaps the first to believe in Muḥammad's call, she had stoutly stood by him and borne his children, and he remained monogamously faithful to her as long as she remained alive. Although he had never consented to convert, the uncle, Abū Ṭālib, had fulfilled his duty to his nephew as clan chief. He was, however, now to be replaced by a new chief who had never hidden his hostility to Muḥammad, whom he regarded as an incorrigible and dangerous impostor.

God moves in a mysterious way. Shortly after suffering this double tragic loss, Muḥammad found himself being approached by representatives of several clans from a township to the north who had arrived to participate in the religious rituals associated with the annual pilgrimage to the ancient temple of Makka. Having heard, or at least heard of, his passionately-held beliefs, these men thought that they might find in Muḥammad a solution to their political and civil disorder. Unlike Makka, with its comparatively homogeneous population, the majority of whom were members of a single tribe, Quraysh, the other township, Yathrib, had been settled by elements of unrelated clans belonging to a number of different tribes and, in consequence, was regularly disturbed by quarrels and disputes over land-ownership and water rights which led not only to private vendettas but also to periodic bouts of more general blood-letting. No single grouping had ever had the strength or the numbers to gain an undisputed victory, so the pattern of alliances between the clans was constantly changing. Uncertainty, instability and fear threatened the entire economic and political life of the community.

Since several of the Yathrib clans were Jewish, the members of the delegations sent to interview Muḥammad may well have been more familiar with, and hence more responsive to, his ideas and idiom than the heathen Makkans had proved. His thinking and vocabulary may have resembled part of what they could already have heard from their Jewish neighbours. Certainly, when scoffed at by his own people for suggesting that God made a habit of sending messengers, revealing books for prophets to recite to their listeners, it had been the Jews whom Muḥammad suggested they consult.[13] They should ask those who already possessed their own scriptures whether what he alleged was true or false. The People of the Book, he was confident, would confirm his claims.

This Yathrib delegation had come seeking a wholly disinterested outside party to undertake to propose impartial solutions to the numerous causes of dispute and division rending their community. To invite any outsider to act in such a capacity would be to expose him and anyone who chose to accompany him to the gravest personal danger. In a tribally-organised society where a man feels safe only within the reach of his own blood kin-group, he dare not venture beyond the radius of its protection, as no-one else owes him the duty of protection. What was suggested to Muḥammad amounted to what nowadays would be called 'defection'. It was only during the sacred pilgrimage season, when there was a strict traditional taboo on the shedding of blood, and only within the sacred enclave around the Makkan temple, where there was a strict traditional taboo on carrying weapons, that the Yathrib delegation had ventured to seek out Muḥammad. He, for his part, would have to demand and be assured of obtaining the most solemn and binding undertakings to protect life, limb and property for himself and for any of his followers who agreed to accompany him, before he could contemplate considering the invitation to go to Yathrib. Following detailed consultations with the leaders of the clans at Yathrib, the delegation were at length empowered in their further negotiations with Muḥammad, which spanned several pilgrimage seasons, to offer Muḥammad the guarantees that he and his followers needed. It was thus agreed that they would be protected, but only within the boundaries of Yathrib.[14] They had to devise for themselves the means of getting there.

Following prayer and grave consideration, and having put the matter in secret to his own small following, Muḥammad took his momentous decision. It was true that the atmosphere towards himself had altered with the coming of a new clan chief; yet he had now to carry responsibility for asking his followers to renounce clan and tribal affiliation, abandon home, relatives and property and, placing their trust only in an unseen God, set out on the perilous ten-day journey, exposed throughout each of the 200 miles to the constant danger of being overtaken and attacked by Makkan or stranger with complete impunity.

THE *HIJRA*

The defection from Makka occurred in AD 622, and the event came to be regarded in later generations not merely as an act of unprecedented faith and courage but also, from its results, as marking the true beginning of the realisation of the Prophet's God-given mission. It was for these reasons that, in a later time, perceiving the extreme significance of the event, the Muslims selected the year in which Muḥammad had quit Makka for Yathrib to be the first year of the calendar of the new Islamic dispensation: AD 622 became AH 1.[15]

Having safely reached Yathrib without misadventure, the Prophet arranged for his followers to be accommodated in the homes of his new

Yathrib sympathisers. For the help and hospitality that they offered the refugee Prophet, they would henceforth be known as the Helpers, the Anṣār. The Makkans accompanying Muḥammad and sharing with him the renunciation of home and family, the *hijra*, would be known henceforth as the Muhājirūn. Between these two groups, Muḥammad formed a formal bond of brotherhood: all together would henceforth be 'believers', muslims, those who had thrown their very lives into the safekeeping of their God and had subordinated their personal wills to the wishes of the Prophet.

Promptly addressing the problems which had brought him, he issued a series of decrees constituting the different groups within the township, including the new immigrants and the several Jewish clans, a single, exclusive community, or *umma*.[16] Each of the groups would continue to regulate its own affairs under its own chieftain on the basis of its own clan tradition, but relations with other, outside communities and questions of war and peace were retained in Muḥammad's hands. Against all external threats to Yathrib, the newly-established federation would react with one voice and with one hand. In the same way, united action would meet any internal breach of the general peace, while quarrels and disputes between the clans forming the new union would be referred to God, through his representative, Muḥammad. From the outset, it would appear that his determination to reserve to himself sole control of external relations may have had chiefly the Makkans in mind, while it equally obviated the old dangers of divided loyalties that had plagued the Yathrib clans. It is, however, the case that the texts of these decrees, which are one of the two sets of contemporary documents to have reached us, specifically prohibit all members of the federation from offering protection, aid or comfort to any Makkan or to any of his property.

Muḥammad's new responsibilities offered him the opportunity to demonstrate that, in addition to his religious interests, he possessed considerable political and diplomatic skills. His band of Makkan followers had arrived at Yathrib with neither possessions nor immediate prospects. The generous hospitality shown them by their hosts had been essential in the first days of their new life, but it was clearly advisable that it be drawn on for the shortest time possible. Resentment might sooner rather than later arise spontaneously from their novel additional burden, or be fostered by those with political aspirations and interests not wholly sympathetic to the arrival of Muḥammad and his group. That had thwarted some ambitions, and bitterness could create an atmosphere inimical to the Prophet's activities and plans, threatening the promising start that he had made in his role of peacemaker.

Yathrib lay astride the trade routes linking Makka with its lucrative northern markets. To provide an immediate means of income for his supporters, Muḥammad organised them into small raiding parties and set them to intercepting and plundering the caravans of the rich Makkan trading-houses. Early success seemed to vindicate the policy, while Muḥammad exploited each successful foray as evidence of divine support and approval of his claims to represent the will of Heaven. By a combination of raiding and trading in the Yathrib markets, his associates soon made themselves independent of their generous hosts. The Prophet made astute propaganda use of these initial successes,[17] taunting the unbelieving Makkans and, beyond them, addressing also the leaders of those Arabian tribes with whom the Makkans had built, over generations of skilful negotiation, a network of mutual non-aggression and co-prosperity ties. He wooed Arab onlookers and aimed to win them over eventually to his side in the struggle against Makka that must come.

The arrival of Muḥammad and the Muhājirūm had not been universally welcomed at Yathrib. But so desperate had been the situation preceding his invitation that those who looked to him for the resolution of age-old instability would not long brook political manoeuvring or dissident grumbling that he was leading them into a war that was entirely of his making and served only his ends. The internal opposition, of which we hear something, was not organised, was indifferently led, lacked clear alternative policies and proved no match in any case for Muḥammad's iron determination, acuteness of political sensitivity and clarity of vision. Nor did it match the wholehearted backing which he received from his Makkan group, who shared his perilous exile and who had no other focus for their loyalties. The Prophet's faith in his call was absolute, and had already been demonstrated by his stubborn persistence in publicly proclaiming it throughout twelve barren years at Makka. Allied to the strength that Muḥammad had found to continue in Makka, to an unshakeable faith in the rightness of his claims and of his cause and to the courage and determination that he showed to bring it to a successful conclusion was his practised talent for persuasion. These qualities made Muḥammad a magnetic leader and a formidable manipulator of situations.

When scoffed at for claiming to receive guidance and regular communications from Heaven, he had appealed, in confirmation of his claims, to the information already in the hands of the Jews. At first, that had been a general abstract riposte restricted to the question of the historical fact of prophethood and of revelation, of which he now alleged that his mission was the continuation and renewal. Arriving at Yathrib with the guarantees won by his tireless negotiations, he began in his new surroundings on reasonably satisfactory political ground. The early decrees which he had issued had included the Jewish clans in the political undertakings by which he had bound the numerous clans to his own émigré group. The recognition of the traditions of the clans included, in the case of the Jews, freedom to continue their religious practices. If, in addition to these political undertakings, Muḥammad entertained hopes that in the religious aspect of his activity he would soon be joined and supported by the Jews when they saw the similarities between his beliefs and their own, he was soon to be disabused. The leaders of the Jewish groups, no less than the leaders of other groups, especially those opposed to his arrival, regarded him with suspicion as an unwelcome intruder into their society.

Together with the texts of the agreements already mentioned, the texts of the Holy Quran complete the only body of documents to have reached us from the days of Muḥammad. The latter consist of the transcripts of Muḥammad's public statements and preaching in both periods of his mission. During the course of each of the two phases, in addition to the instruction given by the Prophet on the significance of human actions both for the life of society in this world and for the personal fate of the individual in the next, the objections raised by his audiences and the responses to their mockery or arguments suggested by God are all recorded. Preserved both by being memorised by the faithful and by being instantly recorded in writing at the Prophet's order, the texts provide the onlooker with a window onto the progress of the mission, its reception and the changing relations between Muḥammad and a variety of audiences. In the recension in our hands today, the texts have not been organised in the chronological order of their delivery. But, insofar as his relations with the Jews are concerned, this is compensated for in that many of the passages are addressed directly to 'the sons of Israel', or to 'the People of the Book'. From such sections, a gradual transition may be detected from a feeling of warm relatedness, through a growing impatience with carping criticism, to a devastating series of angry denunciations culminating in the brilliantly simple and telling solution to the embarrassing conundrum that those to whom appeal had so often been made for confirmation of the reality of prophethood proved the most stubborn in not recognising the reality of Muḥammad's Prophethood. This was the accusation that the realisation that their power was waning and being placed in the hands of others had tempted the religious authorities of the Jews to withhold the vital information that the appearance of the Prophet Muḥammad had been foretold in the texts of their own scriptures.[18] From envy and rancour at the realisation that God grants authority to whom He pleases, and withdraws it from whom He pleases, they denied that there were any such texts in their sacred Book. Since the God who is informing Muḥammad of this treachery is the same God who had written the previous scriptures, who is more to be believed – the author, or the rabbis who find they must now take second place in God's plans to His latest prophet?

In this latest act of revelation, the Quran, God insists that Muḥammad is indeed His Prophet and His spokesman, sent to renew the mercy of divine communication and to rid the religion of men of all unwarranted accretions to which, in the intervals between prophets, revelation tends historically to be exposed when left in the keeping of humans. In His former revelations and especially in the Covenant which He had exchanged with Israel, God had formally bound His previous prophets, in the name of their congregations, to expect the coming of subsequent prophets and, on their appearance, to acknowledge and proclaim them before all men.[19] Both in the Tora and in the Gospel, God had formally announced the coming of this latest prophet, who would also be God's last prophet to Earth.[20] If the rabbis challenged this, they did so wittingly and from base motives. They would have chosen to deny the Covenant, although God had chosen the Jews above all others to be His people and the repository of His most holy Word.

A detailed record of their national history presented in the Quran is designed to demonstrate how often previously and how far they had fallen below the standard of faithful fulfilment of their side in the Covenant.[21] Those who most loudly boast the greatness of Moses had regularly treated even him and the office which he represented with contempt. Today they no longer consult the Tora which had been granted them. They prefer instead to apply a book that they themselves had concocted for the sake of the paltry income that it brought them, thrusting the Book of God out of sight behind their backs, as though they had never heard of it.[22] In effect, they rejected Moses. They rejected Christ. It should surprise no-one that they rejected Muḥammad, since they reject any prophet who does not agree to sanction their cynical attitudes. In rejecting Muḥammad, they elevate him into very noble company – the company into which God through His mercy had admitted Muḥammad. The Prophet's consolation lay in God's informing him that those to whom God does not wish well, He renders deaf, blind and quite incapable of recognising a true prophet when they hear and see him. Those who believe and follow this, His latest prophet, are the new chosen of God for whom He created His paradise.

Makkan reaction to Muḥammad's interference with trade, slow at first, began to gather pace. Much was at stake. The mounting casualties and growing financial loss were grievous. Equally important was the effect that the harrying of their trade had on the reputation and political and religious prestige of their city, while their disgruntled Arab partners and the uncommitted tribes looked on the struggle and wondered what the outcome might be.

Yathrib had initially pledged itself to defend Muḥammad and protect his group only within the confines of their township. The rich prizes won in his early successes brought fresh recruits to his force from the Yathribites themselves, greatly improving the potential to intensify what the Quran began to project as the struggle between the party of God and the forces of infidelity.[23] Every success enhanced the Prophet's power and prestige and increased the attractiveness of the 'cause of God'. Setbacks could be blamed on the people who were not yet sufficiently persuaded of Muḥammad's claims, who, lacking faith, hesitated to give him total control over their lives and their resources.[24] He had assigned to himself, it will be remembered, sole prerogative to determine when to make war and when to call a halt to hostilities and offer peace. As, in a short time, the enmity between the Prophet and the Makkans blossomed, as the pessimists at Yathrib said it must, into full-scale war between the two cities, to question the wisdom of Muḥammad's policies not merely called for outstanding courage but could be represented as treason or, even worse, as defiance of the will of God Himself. In the circumstances, the voices of dissent grew weaker until they were heard no more.

Three major confrontations between Makka and Yathrib had punctuated the continuing armed raids on trading caravans. The first, unexpected clash between the forces of the two sides ended in a crushing defeat for the Makkan force. Following the encounter, Muḥammad used his followers, flushed with victory, to expel one whole clan of Jews from the town, on the grounds that they had given inadequate support to the Prophet's campaign.[25] The second meeting of the two sides led to a defeat of Muḥammad's army, content with which the Makkan force withdrew, failing to follow up their advantage. A second Jewish clan was now forced out of Yathrib.[26] Realising their former error, the Makkans mounted a third, more dangerous campaign, besieging Yathrib to try to starve it into submission and finish Muḥammad and his allies once and for all.[27] The Prophet had had the foresight to gather in the harvest before the enemy arrived, leaving them with no fodder for their animals, while the population, with plenty of supplies and water, sat behind the heavy fortifications, which proved too strong for the Makkans to overcome. Differences and arguments among the Makkans and between them and their allies led to long periods of military inactivity, until, growing bored with the entire enterprise, group after group of Makka's Arab contingents withdrew from their camp and went home. In the end, the Makkans themselves, realising the failure of their plan, abandoned the siege and returned to Makka. Alleging that, in this hour of Yathrib's greatest peril, his Jewish opponents had been in treacherous communication with the enemy, Muḥammad urged the elimination of the last remaining sizeable Jewish clan. The males were executed and the females and children sold off into slavery.[28] The embarrassment of Jewish opposition to the Prophet that could not be overcome by intellectual argument was thus finally silenced by military violence. As the last remnants of Jewish opposition were extinguished, there faded at last also the last shreds of internal opposition to Muḥammad.

Six years of warfare had failed to resolve matters effectively between Muḥammad and Makka. New policies in both the political and the religious aspects of the Prophet's mission seemed to be called for. The Makkans had regarded Muḥammad's teaching among them as consisting largely of matter alien to their culture and tradition. It has also been suggested that the astute merchants had feared the diminution of additional revenues that had accrued to the town from the annual influx of pilgrims to Makka's ancient temple and the surrounding shrines, with a corresponding reduction in the transactions at the trade fairs associated with the sacred period, should Muḥammad's denunciation of their goddesses and religious rites lead to the abandonment of the old religion and its cult.

Muḥammad's severe reaction to the opposition of the Yathrib Jews marks the outward sign of his final dissociation with their tradition, which he had not been able to exploit. Their stubborn failure to rally to his support showed that they had failed to preserve the apostolic tradition in its true form. In the time after Moses and Aaron, they must have betrayed the Law. The Quran speaks reverently of Christ and of a few who had remained faithful to his teaching. But, for the rest, the main body of the Christians had shown themselves no less guilty than the Jews. The Christian doctrine of the sonhood of Christ was an absurd blasphemy. It was as perverse as the Jewish belief in the sonhood of 'Uzayr, while the Christian belief in 'three' was no advance on the misguided Makkan faith in 'the daughters of God'.[29] It was nonsense to speak of God's offspring when it was clear to all that the Deity had no consort.[30]

To strip away these false and unworthy ideas that men had developed concerning God, it would be necessary to overstep the accretions and distortions of centuries and reach back to the revelations granted to and exemplified in the blameless lives of the great patriarchs. Supreme among them had been the prime monotheist Abraham, 'who had been neither Christian nor Jew' but heroic protagonist of simple, pure, unadulterated belief in the oneness and the singleness of God.[31] That stout champion of the uniqueness and the unicity of God had never once, whatever torment and torture was visited upon his person, wavered in his belief in and total submission to the will of the one, true, only living God. Abraham's obedience to God had known no bounds. He had demonstrated as much by his preparedness to sacrifice his own son when challenged to give proof of his faith and trust.[32] Abraham had been the common ancestor of Jew and Arab. His eldest son, who immediately submitted to his father's report that he had been invited to offer him up as a holy sacrifice and, indeed, urged his heartbroken parent to do as he had been asked, permitting himself to be trussed up and offering his throat to the knife, had been redeemed by a grateful Deity and spared to father the Arab race.[33] He had been settled by his father in the valley of Makka where, on arrival, he had assisted his father in the foundation and construction of the first temple on earth dedicated to the exclusive worship of the one, true, living God. The Kaʿba, the ancient 'house of God', still stood in the valley bottom.[34] Ismāʿīl, with his father, had instituted the ancient rituals and ceremonies of the pilgrimage that should hereafter be made each year. It was to the Kaʿba that the Prophet, in earnest of his final break with the Jews, ordered his followers to turn and face as they performed the daily ritual prayers[35] That has the additional merit that, to do so, it is necessary to turn one's back on Jerusalem, the direction traditionally faced by the Jews.

The policies pursued throughout the previous six years were suddenly reversed. All efforts to modernise the biblical religions were abandoned. The Arabs were supplied with a new national myth, and the religion of Islam was set on the firmer ground of reviving the ancient, simple, strict monotheism of Abraham. In a move to effect a rapprochement with the city of his birth, Muḥammad made it publicly known that the rites of the ancient pilgrimage to Makka were henceforward to be incorporated into the growing system of religious practice of Islam.

Moving on Makka at the head of some 1,400 followers, he announced his intent to perform an *ʿumra*, or visitation to pay his respects to the owner of the ancient house. The Makkans hesitated to permit their arch-enemy to enter the town, knowing that the eyes of Arabia were keenly watching to see what would happen. The Arabs would conclude that he was now grown so powerful that Muḥammad could move wherever he pleased, even into the Makkan capital itself, when it suited him. The Makkans managed to delay Muḥammad and draw him into prolonged negotiations. They eventually saved face and preserved peace by offering the Muslims entry into the city the following year, but only for three days. The main clauses of the agreement hammered out between the two sides included the suspension of all warlike activities for ten years and permission to third parties to accede to the agreement by declaring their alliance with the side of their choice. Certain provisions of this treaty caused some dissatisfaction in Muḥammad's camp. One was the Makkans' stubborn refusal to accord to Muḥammad the dignity of 'the Prophet of God', so that he was obliged to sign the treaty in his usual style, 'Muḥammad, son of ʿAbdallāh'. One clause recognised the right of anyone at Yathrib to return and resume residence and full citizen's rights at Makka with no right on the part of Muḥammad to seek to retain him. Any person, however, leaving Makka to join Muḥammad at Yathrib without the consent of his family and clan must be returned forthwith to Makka on request. Despite this vexatious clause which would be honoured in the breach, Muḥammad might well feel content with the outcome of his negotiations. Some of his followers thought he had been bested by his enemy, but the fact spoke for itself. Under the gaze of Arabia, Muḥammad had manoeuvred the Makkans into treating him as a political equal, which was victory enough for the moment.[36]

As provided for, the tribes in the region now began to ally with either Makka or Muḥammad for protection in the final struggle that must yet come. To assuage some of the criticisms among his own party and, perhaps, occupy them with other things, Muḥammad bypassed his base on the return journey and led his force to besiege and reduce the neighbouring Jewish settlement at Khaybar. This was the first land acquired by Islam, its first 'foreign conquest', and the terms agreed between Muḥammad and the Jews of Khaybar would continue to interest the scholars for several generations. The Prophet is said to have accepted the Jewish proposal that they be allowed to retain possession of their land and to continue to cultivate it against payment to Muḥammad of an annual tribute of half the produce. It is also emphasised in the relevant accounts of this agreement that it had set no time-limit on this arrangement .

The following year, the Muslims were led back to Makka to perform the *ʿumra* provided for in the treaty. It is called in the sources *ʿumrat al-qāḍā'*, 'the "made-up" *ʿumra*', or *ʿumrat al-qaḍiyya*, 'the *ʿumra* mentioned in the treaty', according to whether the scholars viewed it as the obligatory 'making-up' of the abortive *ʿumra* of the previous year, or merely the fulfilment of a politically negotiated bargain. That it spited the Makkans is also one interpretation of the alternative name, *ʿumrat al-qiṣāṣ* (the tit-for-tat *ʿumra*).

Shortly after the *ʿumra* had been thus consecrated as a valid Islamic act of worship, one group that had in the interim allied with Makka treacherously attacked a second group that had declared for Muḥammad. Despite desperate Makkan diplomatic attempts to conciliate the Prophet, he chose to interpret the incident as a deliberate challenge to the treaty and so as a casus belli. Last minute appeals from Makkan leaders failed to appease him. The most that he would concede was that no-one who remained indoors and offered no resistance would come to harm when he marched into the city.

Only eight years after the Prophet had given up all hope of winning his native city by preaching, he made himself its master in a virtually bloodless military conquest.[37] Summoning the city elders and clan chiefs, he magnanimously confirmed them in office and pleaded for their willing cooperation. Within weeks, he found himself at the head of a joint Makkan-Muslim army in a desperate and finally successful defence of the city against a great, armed Arab confederation.[38] Once more, much vocal dissatisfaction greeted Muḥammad's generous treatment of his latest defeated enemy. He is portrayed as silencing the outcry that this latest show of magnanimity provoked by promising the people from Yathrib that he proposed to return with them and continue to make his home among them. He is reported as telling them: 'These people may have been given the spoils of battle – mere baubles of this world's wealth. Does it not please you that you are taking home with you the prophet of God?'[39] From now on, we should become accustomed to referring to Yathrib by its new, proud title, Madīnat al-nabī, the seat of the Prophet of God – in short, Madīna.

The year AH 9 was occupied with the usual show of force to overawe the Arab tribes and with the reception of delegations sent in by other tribes to profess allegiance to Muḥammad and receive instructions as to the rights conferred and the obligations incurred by offering fealty to the prophet.[40] Hitherto, it would appear that what had been expected of the tribes making terms with Madīna was rather more than neutrality, if somewhat less than conversion – *islām*, submission, rather than *īmān*, total commitment. They undertook not to aid and comfort the enemies of Muḥammad and to be prepared, when called upon, to furnish levies and subsidies, in cash or in kind, such as mounts or weapons, and generally assist in promoting 'the cause of God'.

That year's pilgrimage, it was said, was presided over by the Prophet's father-in-law and long-time lieutenant, Abū Bakr, who announced to the assembled throng the solemn warning that those who had treaties with Muḥammad but had shown themselves lukewarm had a grace period of four months in which to decide to be more serious about the terms of their agreements or risk facing the Prophet in battle. That did not apply to those who had scrupulously kept to the letter of their undertakings by eschewing all other alliances. Their treaties would run for their appointed duration but, on the expiry of the holy months, that is, after some seven weeks only, all other Arabs should consider that a state of war existed between them and Muḥammad. From that point on, only adoption of the religious principles and practices of Islam would save them. Excluded from this ultimatum were those with whom Muhammad had exchanged treaties at Makka, as long as they faithfully fulfilled the terms. If they did that and if they assumed the religious duties of the Muslims, the prophet would regard them as 'brothers-in-religion'. This open declaration of war on all unfaithful allies and on unbelievers is preserved in the ninth section of the Quran, the Dissociation.[41] War in the name of God was elevated into a religious obligation binding upon every Muslim, while the same passages exclude for the future all except the believers from the visitation of the sacred mosque and all duties associated with its care and maintenance. Henceforward, the house of God would be an exclusive Muslim shrine, its rituals and ceremonies reserved only to believers. Having recently acknowledged the *'umra* and the pilgrimage as valid acts of Muslim worship, Muḥammad now appropriated both, making them acts of exclusively Muslim worship.

In AH 10, Muḥammad himself presided over the one and only pilgrimage that he ever made. None but Muslims were present, and the numbers of the concourse surrounding him have been put in the tens of thousands. It has since come to be known as the 'Farewell pilgrimage', when the Prophet took his leave of the believers; for, within the year, Muḥammad was dead. Minute descriptions abound of every act that he performed on that occasion and of every word that he then uttered, some quite lengthy and detailed. They have been treasured for every crumb of precious information that they are thought to convey of precisely how God's Prophet had approached the performance of each of the complex of numerous acts that constitute this central act of Muslim worship.

2
The Islamic Tradition

Like Christianity, Islam is a religion of the revelation. For the Christian, the divine revelation resides in a person, the Word made flesh. The book, or Gospel, represents merely the personal reminiscences of its human authors, in the form of anecdotes told years later about the life and work, the acts and perhaps the words of the man whom they believed in and whom they followed in the hope of finding salvation. Also included in the Gospel are reports about the infancy and early organisation of the movement founded to continue Christ's work and teaching, stories of the acts and experiences of his disciples, and some correspondence from early Church leaders to groups of fellow believers in different lands. By the fourth century, it had been decided which writings should form part of the authentic Gospel, while other books regarded as pseudo-records were left aside as apocryphal.

For the Muslim, the revelation is deposited in the Book. The Quran did not result from divinely-inspired human authors recollecting past events. It was composed by God Himself. Its texts preserve the precise words spoken by God, who told Muḥammad exactly what to say throughout the course of his mission to those among whom he lived, whose Arabic idiom God had selected for use in His address to mankind, so that it should be understood, they should be in no doubt, and they would be unable to plead ignorance.[42] Muḥammad was a mere mortal who was chosen to be the conduit of this divine revelation. Being a mortal, he could not be expected to perform miracles. The age of miracles had passed. They had been useful in bringing men to believe, but had proved useless in preserving the purity of belief and doctrine. Let the fact of revelation be miracle enough. The Quran text is wholly and exclusively the Word of God. Every sentence, every word originated in Heaven and was imparted to Muḥammad by Gabriel, the angel chosen to deliver it to him.[43] Thus, as Christ is to Christians, the Quran is to Muslims, the Word made Arabic.

What Christianity finds in the Gospel – details of the birth and life of its founder, stories of the evidentiary miracles granted to him, instruction and explanation he provided for his followers, the record of the model they saw in him of the perfect human life lived in accordance with the will of God, which they aspire to apply in their own lives and hope to bring others to imitate – the Muslim seeks in a literature additional to, parallel with and thus lying wholly outside the Holy Quran. This is the literature of the Islamic Tradition, the *Ḥadīth*, which had its origins in the life of the community which strove to pattern the life both of the individual and of the group on its understanding of the implications of the Book presented to them by their Creator, and attempted to fashion from that understanding a private and a corporate mode of life most pleasing to Him who had sent it. At the very heart of that Tradition, as it is now known and revered by the Muslim of today, is the figure of Muḥammad. What, however, distinguishes the Muslim from the non-Muslim examination of that Tradition is the question of whether Muḥammad has always, from the dawn of Islam at the turn of the sixth to the seventh century AD, occupied that central position, or whether that is a later development. By a series of arguments, the Muslims were convinced by the beginning of the third century of their era that that necessarily was and always had been the case. The non-Muslim scholar argues a number of considerations that put a large question-mark over that conviction. The evidence and arguments marshalled on both sides of the divide ought to be reviewed as neutrally as possible, for a matter of such human consequence deserves the most sober and impartial scrutiny that ordinary logic and emotion will permit.

The literature of the Islamic Tradition is vast. The language can be difficult, at times impenetrable, and the mode of presentation adopted by authors usually writing to convince others as expert as themselves in the minutiae of arguments normally spanning several generations can frequently take for granted knowledge of the Islamic sources as wide or as profound as their own, though not always possessed by the modern Muslim or non-Muslim reader. The texts are frequently allusive, suggesting reference to other contexts familiar to their authors and to those whom they address, not all of which, however, have reached our day, or, where they have survived the whim of medieval literary fashion, not always fully recognised by us. There are many vexatious gaps in the record. There are also misrepresentations, intentional or inadvertent. Above all, there are serious confusions and, what is worse, downright contradictions, especially in the attribution to named persons of views and opinions supposedly uttered by them, making an already difficult enough task the more perplexing. On a large number of topics, the hope of reaching certainty is still often frustrated, given the obscurity of many of the details. But much seems to be clear enough to enable a broad account of the Tradition to be attempted.

In the West, our modern study of the *Ḥadīth* can be taken to have begun with the publication in 1889–90 of a book by the Hungarian scholar Ignaz Goldziher, now available in English translation. The book has not, to my knowledge, appeared in Arabic, but a familiarity with the main thrust of Goldziher's thesis (although unaccompanied, it must be said, by his detailed reasoning and the battery of references to original sources which he scrupulously provided) soon reached some Muslim intellectuals. The book provided useful lecture notes for a few academics trained in German or other European centres of learning, and thus able to read it, while some of his ideas filtered down to others who, finding them attractive, sought to influence their own students into taking the 'progressive' line in the internal debate then developing.[44] The modernists, eager to introduce into their own society 'the best of the West' as a key to some of the advances which they wished for their own community, and as a weapon in their struggle to free it of 'the tyranny of tradition' which they blamed for all the social and economic or political ills around them, adopted what they thought were the latest ideas. The conservatives, mistrusting the 'heathen European' who continued to harbour imperialistic aspirations, and genuinely fearful for the cultural and spiritual heritage of the Muslims and anxious for the effect that the undoubted attractions of the contemporary West might have on the spiritual and intellectual development of the nation's young, fiercely oppose all Western intrusions into *Ḥadīth*.[45]

Since early medieval times, the Muslims had portrayed the Islamic Tradition as stemming directly from the Prophet's untiring and solicitous instruction of his immediate group by word and example, as he patiently initiated them into the knowledge of the details of every doctrine and ritual practice of the new religion. A vast corpus of individual narratives, consisting of supposed eye-witness accounts of Muḥammad's every act, his orders, prohibitions, recommendations, approval or disapproval, covers every conceivable aspect of personal, private, domestic, public, political, commercial, military, fiscal and administrative, as well as strictly religious, activity undertaken hour by hour, day by day, week in, week out, year after year of the twenty-three years of his public ministry. All that he had ever been seen to do, or heard to say, or reply when questioned had, it was claimed, been reported by one or other of his inner circle and immediately taken up, talked about, analysed, checked, stored, memorised and preserved and then handed on to any who had been absent by those who had been present to see, hear and record.[46] Muḥammad's immediate followers were portrayed as constantly observing, endlessly discussing, avid for every scrap of information which they regarded as indispensable to the salvation of their immortal souls. No act, no word of this remarkable man who was in regular receipt of Heavenly guidance and direction had been thought too trivial to be stored away in the human memory, discussed with one's family at home and with one's colleagues in the market or in the mosque, repeated time and time again and pondered for every ounce of significance that could be gleaned from it. Such eagerness for this essential religious information was held to account for the fact that the minutest details were engraved on the capacious memories of the Prophet's contemporaries and to explain how so much detailed knowledge had been garnered that Muḥammad's could be projected as the most thoroughly documented life in the entire history of humanity. If anyone enquired how one should hold one's little finger when engaged in devotions; how to dress the hair, whether to dye the hair or the beard, and, if so, what was the proper colour for a Muslim to use; how to perform the complex major ritual purification process; which foods were lawful and which unlawful, which beverages might and which might not be enjoyed; whether there were certain preferred garments, or materials, or colours and a preferred mode of wearing them; what to say on entering or leaving the water-closet, how to sit and in what direction, once installed there, and how to cleanse oneself on completion of the natural functions; what to say on going to bed and which was the preferable side to lie on; what to say before and after relations with one's wife, and precisely what was permitted during the days of her menstruation: on these and a host of other questions, he would be assured of receiving an answer, since the Muslims had information on what the Prophet had done in every waking and sleeping moment of his life. Pride in this unusual accumulation of information on even the smallest trifle is reflected in one Muslim's report: 'Your man', scoffed the outsiders, 'teaches you everything, including how to relieve yourselves.'[47]

We learn of the Prophet's dislike of onions, carrots and, above all, garlic; we are told the most private details of his conjugal life in the privacy of the bedroom. We know all this because the Muslims thought they needed to know and to be certain of getting every detail right. If, as is reported, the Prophet had once declined a dish of lizard meat, that had to be probed to ascertain whether his refusal indicates that the flesh of the lizard is not lawful, *ḥalāl*, or whether that had been merely a matter of personal taste. His intervention, on one occasion, on agricultural methods resulted in a much-diminished crop, leading to his telling his followers: 'I merely expressed a personal opinion on that business of pollination. But take heed of whatever I say on any matter affecting religion.'[48]

This represents someone's attempt to place a limit on the incessant collection of detail on the Prophet's supposed views on every subject under the sun. We shall see in due course that that attempt was doomed to failure, given the serious anxiety that many Muslims felt for the eventual fate of their souls. Muḥammad has been reported, although a Prophet, as having been capable of, on occasion, forgetting a verse of the Holy Quran when reciting it in the ritual prayers. Later, noticing his error, he asked a man who performed that prayer with him why he had not prompted him. 'I thought', said the other, 'that that particular passage had perhaps been withdrawn.' 'No,' was Muḥammad's reply, 'had it been withdrawn, I should have informed the believers of that fact. I just forgot it at that moment.'[49] This and similar reports was taken to indicate that Muḥammad had always been conscious of the importance of his example and his teaching role.

On another occasion, to the confusion of the congregation, Muḥammad miscounted the constituents of the ritual prayer and led the faithful in an irregular devotion. When asked about this later, two varying replies have been reported, one of which is that he admitted his error and completed the part of the prayer which he had inadvertently muddled, adding: 'I am human and, like you, I sometimes forget, so when I do forget, remind me'.[50] That he had miscounted the elements of the prayer might mean that his prayer on that occasion had been either too long or too short. To cover either eventually, we have reports on two events, one when he prayed too long a prayer and another when his prayer had been too short. The exchanges between the Prophet and the congregation are identical in both reports. The second reported reply[51] that he may have made is: 'I am sometimes made to forget, in order to establish a practice that you should adopt in the event that you similarly forget'. This report stems from quarters that would deny that a Prophet can forget, especially on so sacred a topic as the ritual prayer but prepared to admit that a prophet might be made to appear to forget, in order to establish a pattern of behaviour for those whose forgetting would be nothing unusual.

Thus, in the Muslim view, the very remarkable character of the man and the singular nature of the events that surrounded him, allied to a constant anxiety about their own personal fate in the Hereafter, would explain men's determination to uncover absolutely every possible scrap of information that they could about him. Their heightened moral awareness and their shared sense of gratitude for the richness that he had brought into their lives imbued in them a vocation to spread their information on this very remarkable person and his celestial teachings as far as they possibly could. When death suddenly removed the Prophet from the midst of his Companions, they are said to have found that collectively they possessed what might serve to fill the void that his departure might be thought to have left. The significance of the Tradition is thus the sense that it preserves the Prophet alive in the midst of the believers, available still to be consulted on any and every question. In this light, Muḥammad's death became irrelevant.

Consciousness of the grievousness of their loss nevertheless made his associates the more dependent on each other's information and spurred them to greater determination to share the privileged knowledge among them, the greatest not disdaining to be instructed by the least among them. Some had to assume the burden of governing the religion and the infant state which the Prophet had fashioned. Others, unburdened by the responsibilities of office and decision-making, could devote their time and energy to the equally important task of setting in order the welter of seemingly unimportant detail on religious and civil matters that their group had acquired, to provide a reservoir of counsel and information available for the guidance of those who did govern, but also for those who would come after them.

> The Companion, ʿAbdallāh b. Qays, sought an interview with the caliph ʿUmar. He was not, however, allowed to enter, the ruler being at that moment too busy to be interrupted. After ʿAbdallāh had gone, the caliph said, 'Did I not hear ʿAbdallāh's voice? Bring him in', but was told, 'He's gone'. ʿUmar summoned him and ʿAbdallāh said, 'I was just doing what we were ordered to do'. ʿUmar demanded proof of what ʿAbdallāh had said. So ʿAbdallāh called on a group of the Anṣār to whom he explained his predicament. They said, 'None shall be sent to confirm your statement but the very youngest among us'. They sent Abū Saʿīd to ʿUmar with ʿAbdallāh to confirm what he had alleged. ʿUmar said, 'I didn't know the Prophet had given that particular order. I was too busy with my transactions in the market to hear that.'[52]

This report is characteristic of the *Ḥadīth*, in that it alludes to a parallel report without knowledge of whose fuller text it would be difficult to appreciate the point of the story.

> Abū Saʿīd reports, 'I was sitting in a group of Anṣār when ʿAbdallāh came in looking very frightened'. He said, 'I asked to be allowed to see ʿUmar three times, but was not allowed in, so I went away. Later, ʿUmar asked me why I had not waited, and I said that I had asked three times to be allowed to see him and each time I was denied permission, so I went away, since the Prophet said once, "If you ask permission three times to enter and are not permitted to do so, go away". ʿUmar rather strenuously insisted that I bring him confirmation of what I reported. Did any of you chance to hear the prophet say anything to this effect? 'Ubayy b. Kaʿb said, in response to ʿAbdallāh's plea, 'By God! only the youngest will accompany you'. Abū Saʿīd said 'Being the youngest present, I got up and went with him and informed ʿUmar that the Prophet had, indeed, said that'.[53]

A further characteristic of the *Ḥadīth* to which it is by no means fanciful to draw attention is that there is a verse in the Holy Quran which warns the believers to order their slaves and minors that they must not enter a room without first seeking permission to do so at three particular times: 'before the dawn prayer; when you undress at noon; and following the night prayer – three times when you are uncovered'.[54] Thus, if someone says that the Prophet had said that the Muslim must seek permission three times, he would be perfectly truthful, although the Abū Saʿīd story can be seen to have generalised this instruction and taken it out of its context.

The value of the stock of information in the hands of the Companions and how it might be applied was thought to have been demonstrated in the very moment of the Prophet's death. The more remote tribes of Arabia, failing to understand that their treaty relations with Madīna had been entered into with God Himself, rather than with His earthly representative, deemed the treaties to have automatically lapsed on Muḥammad's decease. They therefore withheld further payment of the taxes he had imposed. Muḥammad's immediate successor, his elderly father-in-law, Abū Bakr, was determined to snuff out the first signs of abandonment of what Muḥammad had laboured to create, and so decided to use military force to oblige compliance. His decision was challenged by the second most powerful figure in Madīna, the forceful ʿUmar, who asked the caliph how he could contemplate making war against other believers when the Prophet had declared that any who uttered the formula of allegiance, 'There is no god other than God and Muḥammad is indeed His Prophet', had rendered thereby their persons and their property inviolable. Correcting ʿUmar's imperfect reference to the Prophet's dictum, Abū Bakr completed it: 'except what is due to God'.[55] Time and again, God in His Book conjoins mention of the financial levy (*zakāt*) with mention of the ritual prayer (*ṣalāt*). Time and again, the Prophet, in setting out their obligations to the newly-converted, is reported similarly to have conjoined reference to the levy with reference to the prayer. What God and His Prophet had joined together, Abū Bakr would permit no man to separate. He therefore proceeded with his war, which occupied most of his brief reign. During that of his successor, the Arabian civil war, called when viewed through an Islamic perspective the War of the Apostasy, merged into the great Muslim wars of conquest which, within scarcely a dozen years of Muḥammad's death in AD 632, brought under the rule of Madīna and Islam one after another the surrounding lands of the former Persian and Eastern Roman Empires: Syria, Egypt, Iraq and Iran.

Having conquered these vast territories, the Muslims set about governing them and, in time, converting their peoples. The first generation of field commanders, provincial governors, financial administrators, judges and a host of minor officials were drawn from the ranks of Muḥammad's contemporaries, many of whom had known him, some for longer and some more closely than others. They were thus, from the outset, not all equal in terms of their stock of information about the Prophet and, given the distances and the difficulties of communication, could not be in regular contact either with each other for guidance and advice, or with the centre of the administration at Madīna.[56]

Islam, born at Madīna, continued, in the years following Muḥammad's death, to evolve and mature along the lines that its Arabian environment would determine. Simultaneously, Islam now embarked upon its provincial growth in a variety of newly established centres remote from and very different from its original home, each with its own social and cultural past, distinct population and language, mode of life and customs. The provincial growth of Islam would now parallel its Arabian growth, supplementing it, enriching it and, in time, competing with it.

The Muslims settled in the various centres, when in doubt, might consult those Companions now settled in their midst. Often the same questions arose, but the answers received were not uniform.[57] We have already seen one instance in which, within days of the Prophet's death, a fresh circumstance had led to a difference between two of his oldest associates, each of whom retained a different remembrance of what Muḥammad had said on a single topic and with significantly differing implications. Greater distance in time and place could not but lead to the multiplication of such instances of difference:

> Anas b. Mālik, who had known Muḥammad since his childhood, and who, after the death of the Prophet, had settled in Baṣra, returned home for a visit to Madīna. He was visited by two old comrades, like himself early converts. Anas offered them a meal, at the conclusion of which he rose and performed the *wuḍū'* ablution. His two comrades thereupon enquired, 'Is that some Iraqī custom, Anas?' The other two rose to perform the ritual prayer without making any kind of ablution at all.[58]

In cases of disagreement, when Muslims failed to reconcile their differences by discussing them, it might be thought appropriate to consult in the first place the Holy Book. In one celebrated clash concerning a matter that must have been witnessed during the Prophet's lifetime on thousands of occasions, the ritual ablution to be performed before one embarks on the performance of the ritual prayers, reference to the Quran proved wholly ineffective. Brief consideration of this one case will show the progressive nature of the *Ḥadīth* when used as a weapon of debate. The verse relevant to the dispute, Q 5.6: 'When you rise to pray, wash your faces and your hands up to the elbows and wipe over your heads and your feet up to the ankles', signally failed to settle the issue. It must be emphasised that the English translation given here may obscure the nature of the difficulty facing the Muslims. The highly inflected and rhetorical language of the Quran was alleged to have been read in the past in two incompatible senses. 'Wash', being transitive, has a direct object in the accusative; 'wipe' is intransitive and governs by a preposition with its object in the genitive. If the argument depended on one reading, the meaning is 'wash the feet'; if on the other reading, the meaning is 'wipe over the feet'. The conflict was irresolvable, and remains so to this day. Those who insisted on washing the feet had two main arguments. They showed that they could tolerate the genitive reading by alleging, first, the linguistic phenomenon acknowledged in the native grammatical tradition, of 'case-vowelling by attraction'. 'Feet' may well be read in the genitive, but that does not indicate the intention of the divine speaker. It shows merely the acoustic effect of the positioning of the words 'and the feet' in that particular sentence, after the instruction to 'wipe over the head'. Alternatively, it was also argued that the Book had suggested 'wiping', but the Tradition had always favoured 'washing'.[59] To avoid the appearance of a clash in this instance between the Book and the Tradition, scholars reverted to consideration of the text. Each side drew up lists of those Companions who had been reported to have actually recited the verse in the accusative or in the genitive, and their practice adduced in support of their reported reading. The lists of 'readings' that the two sides had drawn up for this purpose themselves called for justification. It was now said that several of the more prominent of the Prophet's Companions had adopted varying versions of the texts of the Quran, and that the Prophet had known of these variant readings but had not been so pedantic as to seek to impose upon them a single uniform reading.[60] This effect was achieved by having Muḥammad adjudicate a number of quarrels over textual details and showing him declare each of his quarrelling Companions to be in the right, for 'this Quran was revealed to me in multiple versions, so *recite whichever you find easiest*'.[61] The italicised words are not Muḥammad's own, but derive from Q 73.20, a verse on a quite different topic which has been applied elsewhere in this literature to the quite separate arguments on the precise number of ritual prayers to be performed daily, on the obligatory or non-obligatory character of the night prayer, and on its timing and its preferred duration.[62]

We shall have more to say in due course on the topic of the versatility of the *Ḥadīth*, another of its striking characteristics.

Cumulatively, reports on the different 'readings' of the Quran attributed to some of Muḥammad's senior Companions, preferably those who had been engaged in the actual written recording of the sacred texts in the course of their revelation, or those who were thought to have contributed to the preservation and dissemination of the texts following the Prophet's death, matured into the developed allegation that each Companion had prepared for his personal use an individual codex of the entire Quran text. This was a claim that had then to be reconciled with the observed fact that the Muslims everywhere and of whatever centre, sect or party were now in possession of a single, uniform and universally agreed text of the Holy Book which alone might furnish the Quran recitation constituting an indispensable part of the valid daily ritual prayers. Reports on official caliphal initiatives undertaken as a state responsibility to provide that single agreed text had next to be constructed to show the steps leading from a supposed multiplicity of texts in use in the time of the Prophet, to this unique text in the hands of the entire Muslim population of the Empire, only fifteen years later.[63] That was, however, only one of the purposes served by such reports on the collection of the Quran texts. A second, even more crucial motive underlying the same reports will be considered in its proper place.

The preparation and promulgation of an officially approved definitive text of the Quran from which no deviation would ever be permitted, said to have disposed of all other rival Companion codices, did not, however, put an end to arguments about the details of the pronunciation of the verses, nor to the accompanying disposition to allege evidence from Companions in favour of this or that 'reading', as has just been seen in the case of the shared text of Q 5.6. For the possibility of prolonging the same arguments, although on a more restricted scale, was offered by the actual condition of the texts in circulation among the early generations. A later generation of Muslims was driven by such disputes to seek to ameliorate a primitive script by the introduction of much-needed signs to distinguish the written symbols representing two, three or sometimes as many as six quite unrelated consonant sounds. It was also necessary to invent various techniques for distinguishing the three short vowels of the language and to indicate the presence of the long vowels, which play so important a role in Arabic morphology as to be absolutely crucial to the comprehension and interpretation of any words presented solely in writing.[64] Older reading traditions survived the improvement of the script. Where they continued to show differences, this generally affected only single consonants of similar appearance in writing, although capable of being pronounced differently. Such cases had no effect on the meaning, being restricted to disagreements over whether to read certain words as 'you' (plural) or 'they'. Short vowels, on the other hand, when interchanged, can have a significant effect on the meaning, such as has happened in the case of Q 5.6. There, the problem arose from the old absence of vowel-markers.

The method of transmitting the Quran from one generation to the next by having the young memorise the oral recitation of their elders had mitigated somewhat from the beginning the worst perils of relying solely on written records, and thus obviated all but the least significant occasions of difference. Any greater differences that emerged later among the Muslims can certainly not be blamed on the Quran texts. Rather, as will be seen, they are to be traced to the interpretation of the texts, in our investigation of which different deposits laid down in different periods can, as will be shown, be detected.

Thus, the reading differences over Q 5.6, which affected only a single short vowel, must have been very old. As stated, it has not been solved to this very day, for the majority of Muslims, the so-called Sunnīs (a name we shall investigate), wash the feet, while the minority, the Shīʿa, prefer that the feet be wiped. Noteworthy for our purposes is that each group can call to its aid reports on the Prophet's own practice and that the reports precisely mirror their own distinct views.

A second category of so-called 'readings' survived the supposed removal of opportunities to appeal to alleged codices of Companions. This class of report is represented, however, by obvious attempts to interpolate extraneous matter into the texts that could be ignored by all except those so wedded to reports from previous generations as to have made themselves quite incapable of throwing off that reliance and to have become unable to read the Quran texts without mentally supplying these additions. Q 5.6 is a case in point. The verse speaks of 'rising' to pray. 'Rise' may mean 'stand'. It was therefore concluded that prayer may be performed solely in a standing position. Ritual ablution appears to be an indispensable requisite to the validity of each of the prayers, 'When[ever] you rise to pray' – and one rises to pray five times a day. It is reported that the Prophet performed the ablution five times a day.[65] Ritual ablution renews ritual purity. We have other reports that ablution is required only if the ritual purity has been breached. That means that many read: 'When you rise to pray [and are not in a state of ritual purity], wash your faces and your hands up to the elbows ...'.[66] Asked what the prophet did, Anas replied: 'He renewed his ablution for every prayer'. Asked what the Companions had done, he replied: 'We performed the ablution only once a day unless we had breached the ritual purity in the meantime'.[67]

But the raison d'être of *Ḥadīth* is imitation of the Prophet. Would his Companions act differently from Muḥammad? But, as Prophet, Muḥammad regarded the prayers with such reverence that he would insist on renewing the ablution even when it was not at all necessary that he do so. What explains the Companions' practice was that the word 'rise' actually means 'get up out of bed'[68] It suffices to perform the ritual ablution only once daily, on first rising in the morning. But would the practice of the Companions actually vary from that of the Prophet? On one of his campaigns, the Prophet is reported to have performed several prayers in the course of a day without once renewing his ritual purity by performing the ritual ablution. One of his soldiers mentioned to the prophet: 'I saw you doing something today you have never done before'. Asked to what he was referring, he said: 'I saw you perform several ritual prayers without once renewing the ritual ablution'. The Prophet replied: 'That's true, and I did so deliberately'.[69]

The Prophet had done so deliberately to demonstrate to his followers that their understanding of the matter was correct. Another characteristic of the *Ḥadīth* reports is the frequency with which the significant elements in a report are deliberately emphasised by being repeated, to make sure that none will miss the point. This has had an interesting consequence for the literary style of the *Ḥadīth* in which dialogue plays an important part. Here, the point is made that the practice of the Companions did not vary from the occasional practice of the Prophet.

Those who claimed that 'rise' means 'get up out of bed' had unwittingly introduced the notion that sleep must, therefore, breach one's ritual purity. More than one word in Arabic refers to sleep, and some of the commoner synonyms imply 'to lie on one's back'. A variety of sleeping postures became the subject of consideration, until the factor that breached the ritual purity was finally identified as sleeping lying down.[70] This appeared to gain some confirmation from advice given by the Prophet: 'Before you renew your ritual purity, first wash the hand separately, before you embark on the ablution proper, since you never know where the hand has spent the night'.[71] This, too, did not always apply to the Prophet himself, but 'a prophet's eyes may sleep; his consciousness, however, never does'.[72]

The Companion Anas had been criticised by his Madīnan comrades for renewing the ritual purity after he had eaten a meal. The story formed part of the documentation of the wide-ranging discussions on this matter. Since, for the ritual prayer, one must be ritually pure, it had been natural to ask what would make one ritually impure. Rejection of the notion that eating did so gave rise to the aphorism that ritual purity is breached not by what goes into the body, but by what comes out.[73] Eating and drinking has no such effect, but the natural functions of urination, defecation and, perhaps, the shedding of one's own blood might undo the ritual purity. Once turned in the direction of enquiring what might breach ritual purity, the fertile human mind showed a capacity for compiling differing lists of polluting activities. The check-lists prepared in the different centres inevitably expanded under the pressure of religious scruple. There being a host of such activities, the compilation of the lists led to undisciplined casuistry, as item after item was first suggested, considered and then traced to pronouncements alleged to have been uttered by one or other major personality of the past. Precisely the same scholarly activities led, in the case of fasting, to the emergence of a second aphorism, the contrary of that just cited, namely that fasting is breached not by what comes out of the body, but by what goes into the body.[74]

Casuistry of the type just alluded to was a principal factor in the search for reports on the words or actions of the prominent personalities of the past. Evidence for their words or actions formed the raw materials of the *Ḥadīth* as its mass grew both in the centres in which Islam had grown up in Arabia and, following their conquest, in the provincial centres also.

THE *ḤADĪTH*

The word *ḥadīth* has both a technical and a non-technical sense. Non-technically, it refers to any utterance, be that a simple conversation, a communication or report, whether written or oral. The significance of the *ḥadīth* as a technical literary form is shown by its ubiquitous use in every form of Islamic literature. In such varied fields as history, biography, Quran commentary, theology, law, politics, literary criticism and even linguistics, authors display a constant predilection for casting any statements that they wish to make into the form of brief narratives to demonstrate that another had informed them of what they assert. From external appearances alone, one could judge that Islamic culture showed a reverence for authority. To name one's authority is 'to prop up' one's assertions. The Arabic for 'prop', *sanad*, gives the technical term for 'propping up', *isnād* . The *isnād* is the list of names of those who one after the other transmitted the information until it reached him who currently reports it. The typical appearance of an *isnād* is: 'A informed B who informed C who informed D who informed me'.

To receive the serious consideration of scholars, all information was expected to be transmitted in the form of a *ḥadīth*, which consequently consisted of two parts: the *isnād*, without which the information would be regarded as merely the expression by the latest speaker or writer of his purely personal opinion, and the *matn*, the content of the report.

In its technical sense, the word *ḥadīth* more usually refers to a special class of narrative of relevance to more particular religious concerns, although, even here, it will still be found that the *ḥadīth* fulfils many roles and has been employed for numerous purposes. In relation to the Quran, for example, every single statement on detailed textual matters, such as the rival 'readings' for Q 5.6 considered earlier; any account of the history of the text, whether referring to the date and the circumstances of its first being collected into book-form, or identifying who was thought to have taken the first initiative to result in that collection; every story attached to an individual verse which relates its contents to an event external to the text itself – the so-called *asbāb*, or 'the circumstances which allegedly provoked the revelation of the verse'; each and every attempt to interpret a single word or phrase occurring in the Quran, must be accounted a *ḥadīth*. But very much more than even direct connection with the Holy Book is involved in the *Ḥadīth*, as will be seen.

Since it was known to every Muslim that the Quran had been divulged gradually to the Prophet throughout the entire period of his public ministry, there was an understandable propensity, especially as next to no material was available from any other source, to seek to extrapolate the events of the Prophet's remarkable career from statements in the Quran which appear to refer to events. The procedure is fraught with hazard, since it is to seek to make one thing – exegesis, a strictly literary process – determine quite another thing – biography or history – which purports to be a statement of 'fact', that is, a happening in the external world. The insatiable curiosity of the Muslims drove them to extract, from as many Quran passages as possible, pointers to happenings in the Prophet's life. One natural question, for example, would be to ask: 'How did it all start? Which of the revelations had been the very first to come to him?'

> A widow of the Prophet, 'Ā'isha, informed her nephew, 'Urwa, an assiduous collector and disseminator of *ḥadīth*, of events that had occurred before she was born, but concerning which the Prophet had spoken to her.
>
> a. Muḥammad would spend periods praying in seclusion in a cave. Suddenly he was alarmed by the appearance of an angel who commanded him to recite. Muḥammad sought to make excuses, but each time he tried to do so, the angel seized him and squeezed the breath out of him, obliging him in the end to repeat: 'Recite in the name of your Lord who created ...' [the

opening of Q 96]. Fleeing home in terror, Muḥammad called out, 'Cover me! cover me!' [*zammilūnī*], which they did, and gradually his fear subsided.[75]

b. Yaḥyā b. Abī Kathīr asked Abū Salama, 'Which was the first revelation Muḥammad received?' Abū Salama replied that it had been Q 74 [*al-muddaththir*]. 'But I have been informed, persisted Yaḥya, 'that it had been Q.96.' Abū Salama patiently explained that he had asked Jābir [the prominent Companion of the Prophet] the same question and, receiving the same reply, had made the same objection that Yaḥyā was now making to him. Jābir had said 'I am telling you only what the prophet told me. Muḥammad said, "I was coming down off the mountain when someone called me. I looked right, I looked left; I looked ahead and I looked behind but I could see nothing. Then I looked up and saw something and rushed home shouting, 'Cover me! cover me! [*daththirūnī*], and pour cold water over me!' They did so, and Q 74 was revealed."'[76]

These two stories would appear to have been generated in discussions on the odd words *muddaththir* and *muzzammil* that occur at the openings of Q 74 and Q 73 respectively, and later used as the titles of the sections. Among the several versions of the Jābir report, we find:

a. There he was, seated on a throne between Heaven and Earth.[77]
b. There was the angel *who had come to me previously* on the mountain, seated on a throne between Heaven and Earth.[78]

The second version shows awareness of a rival account and consciously bridges and reconciles the two conflicting *ḥadīth*s. That gave rise to the harmonising motif occurring in other versions: 'Jābir said, "The Prophet spoke of an interruption [*fatra*], in the revelations which were then resumed after a break".'[79] Q 73 is addressed to 'the one wrapped in a garment', *muzzammil*. Q 74 is addressed to 'the one wrapped in a garment', *muddaththir*. Q 74.2 reads: 'Arise and warn!' Q 96, we have seen, commands Muḥammad: 'Recite' – or 'Proclaim' – 'the name of Him who created'.

Either could plausibly be taken to have been the first order to undertake public preaching. Or, one could mean that and the other be seen as a command to resume preaching after an interval.

a. Masrūq asked ʿĀ'isha, 'Did Muḥammad actually see God?' She replied, 'You've made my hair stand on end. Whoever tells you that Muḥammad saw God is lying: "Human eyes cannot attain to sight of Him, but He can see them. God is insubstantial, all-knowing"' [Q 6.103].[80]
b. ʿĀ'isha asserted that anyone who said that Muḥammad had seen God was lying, so Masrūq said, 'What about this verse?

"He then approached and descended until He was a mere bow's length away, or even nearer, and He revealed to His creature that which He revealed".' She replied, 'But that refers to Gabriel. He used to come in human guise but, on this occasion, coming down in his own form, he blocked the entire horizon.'[81]

According to the leading Companion, 'Abdallāh b. Mas'ūd, the Prophet had seen Gabriel twice in his angelic form. He had 600 wings.[82] It can be seen from the wording of Q 53 how some might take the passage cited by Masrūq as an account of a meeting with the Almighty Himself.

A *ḥadīth* may have a more technical purpose such as, for example, 'proving' an earlier exegesis by documenting from the Prophet's supposed conduct the linguistic assumption underlying the earlier interpretation. Argument raged, for instance, in what may appear to be merely a squabble among etymologists, but has much more complicated implications, over whether a word, *naskh*, means 'to replace' or, whether, as others insist, it means 'to suppress'. Evidence needed to settle the dispute was supplied in a bizarre anecdote, now familiar to all.

> Despairing of weaning his fellow-Makkans from devotion to 'the daughters of God', Muḥammad had attempted a compromise by finding room for their local deities in his pantheon, although placing them in a position subordinate to God's. Once, when publicly reciting Q 53, 'Have you considered al-Lāt, al-'Uzzā and the third, al-Manāt?', he added on his own initiative, 'Those are the high-flying cranes on whose intercession you may rely'. Noting the unwarranted interpolation of these words, God immediately dispatched Gabriel with a severe admonition to His Prophet: 'We have sent no previous messenger or Prophet but that, when he decided to launch out on his own initiative, Satan smuggled false words into the man's utterance. But God *naskh*s that which the Devil insinuates and God reinforces His own signs.'[84]

Although the story was rejected as absurd by some of the greatest figures in medieval exegesis, it continues to find a ready hearing among non-Muslim scholars on the grounds that 'a story which portrays Muḥammad in such a poor light could scarcely have been invented by a believer, or foisted upon the Muslims by a non-believer'.[85]

It is therefore thought that it must contain a grain of truth. Plausible as that may sound, plenty of other stories abound among the believers determined 'to prove' that the Prophet had been seen to forget portions of the revelations, and not merely momentarily, but *irrecoverably*. Once forgotten, they were lost forever, so that the revelations now in the hands of the Muslims have never represented the entire Quran.[86] These are merely some instances in which the imperious need of one theory or another has driven the believers into making what appear to the outsider to be very dangerous suggestions. Exegesis has its own logic and its own imperatives. Its function was to explain to the congregation every nuance and detail of the meaning of each of the Quran's verses. It was thought that that could be best achieved by introducing stories from Muḥammad's 'experiences', frequently with scant regard to Muḥammad's reputation or even, as we have just seen, to his most basic beliefs and impassioned teachings. It has also been maintained that he made similar attempts to conciliate the Jews by adopting some of their customs and practices. Thus,

> on the day he arrived at Madīna from Makka, Muḥammad saw the Jews observing a fast. Asking what the fast represented, he was told that it had been instituted to commemorate God's deliverance of Moses and the Israelites from bondage in Egypt. Declaring that, as a prophet, he could claim a closer relation with his brother Moses than Jews could, Muḥammad required his followers to observe that fast.[87]

But some Muslims found it intolerable that Muḥammad should have had to depend on unbelievers for any item of religious information. They determined to sever this link with the Jews, imitation of whom could only detract from Muḥammad's prophethood, which was sustained by direct communications from Heaven. They therefore projected this fast back into the days before his call. It had been the Makkans who had observed the one-day fast of 'Āshūrā' which the Prophet, approving it as one pious custom of his tribe, had observed and had continued to observe after his transfer to Madīna, where he had imposed it on the Muslims as part of the fabric of Islamic devotions.[88]

This second attitude is reflected in what I should call a 'second order' *ḥadīth*. That is, it stemmed from dissatisfaction with an already existing story. It does not appear to have occurred to anyone to question this attribution of a pious custom to the Makkan heathens, who are normally denounced as immersed in superstition, idolatry and depravity and who otherwise provide a foil for all that is held true and good in Islam. Neither of the two *ḥadīth*s, in fact, has any kind of historical grounding. Both were entirely literary in origin, springing from knowledge of Q 2.183: 'Ye who believe! There is hereby imposed upon you the obligation to fast, as it was imposed upon those before you.'

Two sets of stories differ merely in the identification of those who were before Islam. Whereas ʿUmar b. al-Khaṭṭāb, the Prophet's second successor, is reported to have commanded the Muslims of his day to observe the fast of ʿĀshūrā',[89] his own son, ʿAbdallāh, is pointedly said never to have observed it:[90] '"People of Madīna," thundered Muʿāwiya, the fourth [or fifth] caliph after the Prophet, "where are your scholars? I heard the Prophet say, 'God never imposed this fast on the Muslims'."'[91] Divided on whether Muḥammad had ever actually seen God; divided on whether he had, or could have, uttered the 'Satanic verses'; divided on whether he had or had not imposed the fast of ʿĀshūrā' and, if so, how and where it had originated, the Muslims will be found to be equally divided on a host of questions. Almost every issue that arose for discussion in working out the implications for human conduct of the momentous revelations that they had inherited divided the believers into opposing groups, each equipped with an imposing battery of evidence traced to one or other of the great personalities of the community's past. Whether the argument concerned a ritual, a legal, a political or a commercial topic, the all-pervasive *ḥadīth* demonstrates a constant reaching back in debate for support from past authority. Dispute and disagreement encompassed every branch of the social and intellectual life of the Muslims, which the *Ḥadīth* cannot but faithfully reflect. The disarray of opinion and a confusing welter of proposition and counter-proposition, ideas, suggestions and views promoted in the different centres and in the different generations are all so faithfully reflected in the *Ḥadīth* that it is understandable that, failing to locate clues to an agreed core of Tradition, which might indicate a record of continuity of life and praxis, non-Muslim scholars ended by regarding the entire Tradition as the mere offspring of disunity. That had been the position reached by Goldziher, whose immense learning and command of a vast range of Islamic literature brought him to a pessimistic outlook on the sensitive issue of the 'authenticity' of the *Ḥadīth* in general. Aware of the acute, at times acerbic quarrels among the Muslims themselves on a host of topics, he was emboldened to conclude that the disarray among the scholars spoke of a lack of regulation on the entire range of questions over which they endlessly bickered. There had been no ready-made system established at Madīna available for export to the conquered territories following the death of the Prophet. On the contrary, many of the *Ḥadīth* reports testify to the most profound ignorance on many elementary questions of Islamic faith and practice.

> In the absence of authentic evidence, it would indeed be rash to attempt to express the most tentative opinion as to which parts of the ḥadīth are the oldest original material, or even as to which parts of them date back to the generations immediately

following the prophet's death. Closer acquaintance with the vast stock of ḥadīths induces sceptical caution rather than optimistic trust regarding the máterial brought together in the carefully compiled collections. ... we ... will probably consider by far the greater part of it as the result of the religious, historical and social development of Islam during the first two centuries.

The ḥadīth will not serve as a document for the history of the infancy of Islam, but rather as a reflection of the tendencies which appeared in the community during the maturer stages of its development. It contains invaluable evidence for the evolution of Islam during the years when it was forming itself from powerful mutually opposed forces. This makes the proper appreciation and study of the ḥadīth so important for an understanding of Islam in which the most notable phases are accompanied by successive stages in the creation of the ḥadīth.[92]

3
The Political Dimension of the Ḥadīth

In mentioning Muʿāwiya above, I hesitated between calling him the fourth or the fifth in line of succession to the Prophet. A Muslim would not hesitate to call him the fifth. The fourth successor had been the prophet's cousin and son-in-law, 'Alī. A later, important minority, the Shīʿa (from *shīʿat ʿAlī*, supporters of the claims made on ʿAli's behalf), would insist that, despite having been designated by the Prophet to be his immediate successor, ʿAlī had been elbowed aside and denied the right to fulfil the Prophet's expressed wish by the jealous machinations of the Prophet's close inner circle of Makkan Companions. This usurpation showed that, as Muḥammad himself had allegedly feared, he was no sooner dead than the old Makkan hubris re-emerged. Pride and arrogance drove his associates back into their old Arab ways of thinking. They became 'backsliders into worldliness, treating the succession as a group possession to be handed around among themselves'. The Prophet reportedly said that the thing he feared most for the Muslims after he was gone was that they would struggle among themselves in a scramble for the things of this world.[93] He had had to re-assure the Anṣār on several occasions, when they did not understand his politic sharing-out of the spoils of victory, that he really virtually considered himself one of them, and to pacify them had promised, even after the conquest of his own birthplace, that he proposed to end his days among them in their city which had become his city. He did, however, warn them that, after him, they would see others preferred above them.[94] They should be patient until they met him again at his cistern in Heaven.[95] The Anṣār would have been justified in claiming a greater say at the head of affairs after the Prophet's death. The succession was, in fact, procured in what nearly amounted to a coup d'état engineered by the forceful ʿUmar, in favour of Abū Bakr, Muḥammad's elderly father-in-law, who, it is said, in his inauguration address, told the Anṣār: 'We Makkans are the rulers and you are the lieutenants'.[96]

Despite their role as the real creators of the conditions which had made the success of the Prophet's mission possible, the Anṣār, whose patient, self-denying services to His cause God recognised in His Book:

> Those who prepared the home and established the faith before the Muhājirūn, who love those who sought refuge among them, feeling themselves in no need of that which the refugees are being given, who, indeed, put the interests of the refugees before even

> their own, great as their own need is – those who guard against the greed of their hearts, will certainly be successful [Q 59.9]

were to be by-passed in the matter of the succession and the control of the polity of Islam. Their city would remain for a while the capital of the new regime, but the power would be exercised by others. This is self-consciously mentioned in a number of *ḥadīth*s.

> Seeking the counsel of the Muslims on one problem, 'Umar consulted a group of the earliest converts, but had to dismiss them, since they could not agree among themselves. Similarly, he had to dismiss the Anṣār on whom he had called for advice, since they too, could not agree. It was only the Muslims of the Conquest [of Makka] who were agreed on the advice they offered him. Later, it was discovered that their recommendation had, in fact, been what the Prophet had decided on that very matter.[97]

> Jābir b. Samura reported the Prophet as having said, 'There will be twelve princes'. Not catching the rest of the Prophet's words, he had to ask his father, who said that the Prophet had concluded, 'They will all be from Quraysh'.[98]

> 'Abdallāh b. 'Umar reported the Prophet's words, 'This polity will always remain with Quraysh, as long as two of them remain'.[99]

After his brief, war-filled reign, Abū Bakr, like the Prophet, died peacefully in his bed. He would be the last leader of the Muslims to do so for a number of years. Abū Bakr is said to have nominated as his successor the redoubtable 'Umar, like himself an early convert to Muḥammad's movement and, like him also, a father-in-law of the Prophet. It was he who oversaw the first wave of the great Islamic conquests and established the bases of a new imperial administration which, at first, concentrated mostly on the division of the spoils of victory and their distribution among the warriors for the faith, and instituted the principles of the fiscal policies and a rudimentary judicial administration that would govern the newly-won external territories. Falling victim to the dagger of a non-Muslim assassin, a Persian, it is said, who had some grievance about his tax assessment, the caliph lingered long enough to give thanks to God that he had not been slain by a believer, and then to appoint the members of a six-man electoral college charged to select his successor from among their own number. He is reported as having said about this: 'If I were to nominate my own successor, a man better than I did that; if I do not specify my wishes concerning the succession, a man better than I did that too'.[100]

The choice fell on 'Uthmān, like his two predecessors an early convert to Islam from the old pre-*hijra* days, and a son-in-law of the Prophet. Of another branch of Quraysh, 'Uthmān had stronger clan and family links with the rich mercantile oligarchy who had long held sway in Makka, who had suppressed the Prophet and the believers and who had become converts, not from any profound conviction but, it was said, when there was nothing else left to do, as their city fell to the armed might of nascent Islam.

During his reign, the Islamic conquests continued to bring Islam untold and undreamed-of wealth while carrying the Muslims further and further from their Arabian homeland into lands far to the east and the west. ʿUthman, in his turn, met a violent death (AD 656), but at the hands of disaffected believers stirred up by widespread discontent at the distribution of the spoils of continuing victories, complaints of maladministration of the new provinces and dark hints of nepotism in the allocation of lucrative state appointments. The murderers of the aged ruler had come from Egypt, but a similar restiveness had affected the Muslims of Iraq, some of whose leaders, at this critical juncture, are thought to have invited ʿAlī to fill the vacuum and accept their support in his bid to secure for himself at long last the succession which, as father of the Prophet's only surviving male descendants, some thought ought to have come to him. Other Companions of the Prophet, resentful of Iraqi intrusion into what they regarded as the prerogative of Madīna to decide the succession, marched into Iraq accompanied by a widow of the Prophet's, the lady ʿĀ'isha, daughter of Abū Bakr, to pre-empt the Iraqi designs on the leadership. ʿAli, who had recruited support in Baṣra, was the initial victor. Two Companions of the Prophet, Ṭalḥa and al-Zubayr, fell in what has been called 'the Battle of the Camel' in reference to the white camel ridden by ʿĀ'isha, who was now respectfully escorted back to her home in Madīna, which now faded from the political forefront. A new, more formidable adversary took up the challenge presented by ʿAlī's and the Iraqi presumption.

Appointed Governor of Syria in the time of ʿUmar, Muʿāwiya now led the army of his province into Iraq. It may have been an unheard-of thing for Muslim to engage in armed conflict with fellow-Muslim, as was now happening, although the Quran appears to address such a contingency:

> If two parties of believers fall to fighting, reconcile them. If one party aggress against the other, fight the aggressing party until it returns to God's affair. If it return, reconcile the two sides with justice and equity. God loves the equitable. The believers are brothers, so reconcile two groups of your brothers and fear the Lord, and perhaps you will be shown mercy.[101]

What seemed to many a novel situation proved a fertile field for the appearance of *ḥadīth*s.

The Prophet is said to have foretold that the Day of Judgment would not appear until two groups of Muslims took up arms, against each other, both claiming precisely the same thing.[102]

In a sermon, the Prophet had foretold several instances of future civil dissension. 'But', he said, 'whoever gives an *imām* his hand in token of his allegiance, let him obey him, if he can. Should another come along and dispute the leadership, kill the later one.' A listener questioned the narrator, 'I entreat you by God! did you really hear that from the Prophet?' The man replied, 'I heard it with these two ears and I stored it in my breast'. The other persisted, 'but here is your kinsman, Muʿāwiya, asking us to spend our wealth vainly and recommending that we kill each other – both procedures that God Himself has prohibited'. After a short silence, the other replied, 'Obey him in what is obedience to God and disobey him in what is disobedience to God'.[103]

Jābir reports that the Prophet once made a man cover his arrows on entering the mosque in case he accidentally scratched a Muslim.[104]

The Prophet also said, 'Whoever takes up arms against us is not one of us'.[105]

'To insult a brother-Muslim is sinful; to kill him is unbelief.'[106]

Al-Aḥnaf b. Qays set off with his weapons. Meeting him, Abū Bakra asked him where he was heading. 'I am going to the help of the Prophet's cousin', he said. 'But', rejoined the other, 'I heard the Prophet himself say,"Any two Muslims who take up arms against each other will both land in Hell". Understanding that that might well apply to the killer, the audience asked, "Why should that apply to the victim?", to which the Prophet had replied, "He intended to kill his opponent, didn't he?"'[107]

Following a series of half-hearted, indecisive engagements, it was agreed between ʿAlī and Muʿāwiya to make the attempt to patch up some political solution. Readiness to negotiate proved ʿAlī's undoing. Some elements among his supporters argued with legalistic pedantry that his agreeing to participate in the proposed parleys suggested that there was something to negotiate. That might be seen as ʿAlī's admitting in advance that there was some question over his claim to succeed the Prophet, for which Muslim blood had already been spilled, but which he was now apparently prepared to place in abeyance until the outcome of the negotiations. On the view that a caliph did not possess any right of abdication, these men declared that, in introducing doubt as to his God-given trust, ʿAlī had forfeited his sacred office. Others in his camp, represented as adopting a more 'biblical' view of the situation, denied that mere political deliberations could settle a holy issue so delicate as that of the leadership of 'the cause of God'. They demanded that God Himself be called upon to decide the issue between ʿAlī and Muʿāwiya, whom they regarded as in rebellion against the lawful leader. They now clamoured for the matter to be settled by the ordeal of battle. Denouncing ʿAlī as a backslider into unbelief, different groups withdrew their pledge of support and declared war on both contestants. That plunged ʿAlī into confrontation with two sets of determined opponents, Muʿāwiya and the Syrians, and now his own former most fervent supporters. His strength was weakened by a series of desertions brought about partly by these internal wranglings in his camp and partly by the discouragement which some may have felt at his lack of immediate military success, which may have said something to the more pious among his followers about the degree of divine support for his claims.

Events fortuitously turned in favour of Muʿāwiya and the Syrians when ʿAlī was murdered at the instigation of his own erstwhile supporters in revenge for the harshness of the measures that he had taken against the regular desertions (AD 661). Killing his own men had created among their comrades and kinsmen an obligation to seek retaliation.

Each of these quarrelling groups and their figureheads would attract favourable and unfavourable comment from later generations of Muslims who, in taking sides retrospectively in the old divisions, would form the nuclei of the sects and factions that began to appear. The views which they expressed long continued to reverberate in the shape of their *ḥadīth* reports, which may still be read in the voluminous literature. Eloquent testimony to the depth of feeling created in the community as it looked back on the earlier struggles, reflecting on who had been in the right and who had been in the wrong, and evidence of the utility of the *Ḥadīth* in advancing the interests and opinions of the several factions and sects descended directly from the protagonists in these ancient battles, is stamped into the reports in which they addressed each other and the wider community of the faithful. In the endless arguments about who should rightfully have succeeded the Prophet, which is how the unsuccessful express their dissatisfaction with history, it was natural that they would involve the authority of the Prophet himself. He is, for example, said to have foretold the death of ʿAmmār, the devoted supporter of ʿAlī, at the hands of 'the aggressing party'.[108] Coded as the language of the *ḥadīth*s may appear to be, the vocabulary and references would be understood by all to hark back to the ancient ruptures.

The initiative could well have been taken in many cases by those who sought retrospectively to plead ʿAlī's cause.

> The prophet is supposed to have said to ʿAlī: 'You are of me and I am of you'.[109]

On one occasion, amid a throng of his followers, the Prophet is said to have declared:

> 'He whose patron I am, ʿAlī is also his patron'.[110]

> When Muʿāwiya attempted to incite Saʿd to insult ʿAlī, Saʿd said, 'Don't you recall the three things the Prophet said? He had left ʿAlī behind on one of his expeditions and ʿAlī protested at being left with the women and children. The Prophet said, "Aren't you pleased to be to me as Aaron was to Moses – although there will be no prophet after me?" Then, at Khaybar, the Prophet said, "I shall give command to one who loves God and His Prophet and whom God and His Prophet love". We all hoped it would be given to us, but he said, "Call ʿAlī". ʿAlī came, suffering from ophthalmia which Muḥammad cured by spitting on his eye. He then gave him the flag and God granted him victory. Thirdly, when the verse, "Let us call our sons and your sons" [Q 3.61] was revealed, the Prophet summoned ʿAlī, Fāṭima, Ḥasan and Ḥusayn, saying, "These are my family".'[111]

A similar story tells of the attempt of the representative of a later caliph seeking to suborn a different Companion to insult ʿAlī, with a similar negative result.[112]

Muḥammad is reported as addressing his followers at the Pool of Khumm:

> 'I am but mortal and soon the messenger of my Lord will call and I shall accompany him. But I shall leave you two solidities, the Book of God in which is guidance and light. Take the Book of God, hold fast to it. I shall also leave you my family. I remind you of God in respect of my family and commend them to you.'[113]

Mālik had heard but can produce no *isnād* for the following:

> The prophet said, 'I have left you two things which, if you embrace, you will not go astray – the Book of God and the *sunna* of your Prophet'.[114]

Of his grandson, Ḥasan, the Prophet said: 'Lord God! I love him, love him too, and love those who will love him.'[115] He also said of him: 'This son of mine is a leader. Perhaps through him God will reconcile two great forces.'[116] Following the death of ʿAlī, Ḥasan marched against Muʿāwiya with a huge force. Muʿāwiya sent two men of Quraysh to assuage him. They were eventually able to make him enough promises to satisfy him.[117]

> The Prophet whispered something to his daughter Fāṭima and she wept bitterly. He whispered to her again and she laughed. She had wept because he told her of his impending death, and when she wept, to console her, he asked, 'Does it not, however, please you that you will be the first of my family to join me and that you will be the first lady of Heaven, and chief of the female believers?'[118]

That this was supposed to have been reported by ʿĀ'isha would not be lost on the listeners.

As death approaches, the Muslim is required to set his affairs in order by appointing an executor to see that his dying wishes are respected. Thus, there are reports to the effect that the Prophet had appointed ʿAlī to be his executor. They were pointedly challenged by other reports in which ʿĀ'isha asks:

> When would there have been time or opportunity for the Prophet to do that? I nursed him in my arms day and night and he breathed his last in my embrace.[119]

There is a close conceptual link between leadership in the communal prayer (*imāma*) and leadership in the governance of the entire community (*imāma*), ready to be exploited in the reports on the Prophet's last few days of life. Several of these feature ʿĀ'isha, said to have been Muḥammad's favourite wife. She was the daughter of the man who, in fact, had been the first to succeed the Prophet. When no longer capable of leading his community in public worship, Muḥammad had told her to ask Abū Bakr to deputise for him. To reinforce this point, ʿĀ'isha is shown in the narrative making a series of excuses. That obliges the Prophet to keep repeating his request – a favourite narrative technique often employed in the *Ḥadīth*.

> Abū Bakr worships in such a humble, devout manner that the congregation would be quite unable to hear him and to follow his lead. He was inclined to be so emotionally overcome when reciting the Quran that his sobs and pious groans would obscure from those behind him the wording of the holy texts. It would probably be better to send for ʿUmar. ʿĀ'isha prevailed upon her co-wife, Ḥafṣa, daughter of ʿUmar, to make the same arguments. Exasperated by their female wile, the weakened Muḥammad denounced both wives as 'just like the women in the Joseph story'. Repeating his insistence that Abū Bakr be called, 'since God and the Muslims will have no other,' the Prophet eventually succeeds in having his wishes respected.[120]

On another occasion, consulted by a woman, Muḥammad told her to come back later, adding: 'if you don't find me, ask for Abū Bakr'.[121]

It was easy to represent here that, thinking of his own death, the

Prophet was expressing a view on the succession. He is regularly reported, when adjudicating on any legal matter, to have called the evidence of the older witnesses before that of their juniors. He stated his preference for the *imāma* of the oldest present in the communal worship in the district mosques. Where more than one elder was proposed, the office should fall to the one more familiar with the Quran and, in the event that they shared an equal knowledge of the texts, preference should be shown to him whose conversion to Islam and adherence to the Prophet had been earliest.[122] This explains the quite large number of reports declaring now Abū Bakr, now ʿAlī, to have been the first to believe in Muḥammad's claims. The outcome of that debate is still apparent in Abū Bakr's honorific title, al-Ṣiddīq, 'he who firmly believed' and endorsed the claims.

None would miss the drift of the words attributed to the son of ʿUmar when questioned by one of the faithful.

> He replied: When the Prophet was still among us, we compared no man with Abū Bakr and, after him, with ʿUmar, and then ʿUthmān. We made no distinction between the remaining Companions.[123]

It proved worthwhile to transfer this sentiment to ʿAlī.

> Asked by his son, 'Which is the best Muslim after Muḥammad?', ʿAlī replied, 'Abū Bakr'. To the further question, 'Then who? ʿAlī replied, ''Umar'. Fearing to ask the next question, lest his father mention ʿUthmān, the son suggests, 'Then yourself?' ʿAlī replied, 'No. I'm just another ordinary Muslim.'[124]

> Sufyān exclaimed, 'I don't think that the religious acts of one who alleges that ʿAlī had a stronger claim to succeed the Prophet than Abū Bakr or ʿUmar can commend themselves to Heaven. For that would be to accuse Abū Bakr, ʿUmar, the Muhājirūn and the Anṣār of having committed an error.'[125]

> The Prophet described waiting at the cistern in Heaven for the arrival of his Companions. As they draw near and are about to join him, they are suddenly seized and swept away to a fate other than he or they had anticipated. 'Those are my dear Companions', he complains. 'Yes,' comes a voice, 'but you do not know what innovations they introduced after you left them.'[126]

A prophet and hence privy to the unseen, Muḥammad was thought to be able to foresee the future. 'Don't', he is reported as saying, 'revert to unbelief after I'm gone, striking each other with the sword.'[127]

> Ascending Madīna's Mt Uḥud one day in the company of Abū Bakr, ʿUmar and ʿUthmān, the Prophet was angered when the

> mountain quaked. Stamping his feet, he called out, 'Be quiet! a prophet, a true believer and two martyrs!'[128]

> A man asked ʿAlī about the action he had taken: 'Was that something the Prophet told you to do, or was it something you just thought up for yourself?' ʿAlī assured him that it had not been something the Prophet had told him to do, merely something he thought he would do.[129]

The idea that the patriarchal rule of 'the rightly-guided caliphs' at Madīna had been a smooth and legitimate succession was fostered in the words attributed to the Prophet. 'The apostolic succession, then God will grant authority to whom He pleases.'[130] The forgiving, harmonising effects of the *Ḥadīth* are apparent in the inclusion of Ṭalḥa and al-Zubayr alongside ʿAlī in the list of the Companions allegedly foretold by the Prophet as the men destined for Paradise.[131] The power of the *Ḥadīth* to sway general attitudes is, however, clear in a variant to the above.

> The Prophet foretells that the apostolic succession will last only thirty years, after which God will grant authority to whom He pleases. One scholar checked this dictum: Abū Bakr, two years; ʿUmar, ten years; ʿUthmān, twelve years, then ʿAlī – informed that the present rulers asserted that ʿAlī never had been caliph, the man exploded in a torrent of expletives.[132]

In the report that 'the rightly-guided caliphs' had been five in number, Abū Bakr, ʿUmar, ʿUthmān, ʿAlī and ʿUmar b. ʿAbdul ʿAzīz, the exclusion of the dynasty established by Muʿāwiya was designed to make an undisguised political point.[133]

Following the murder of ʿAlī, to the inconsolable chagrin of some Iraqis, who had been too divided by their own internal bickering to be of any real assistance to him or to remain constant to their promises to support him, power had passed to 'the latecomers'. Muʿāwiya's skilful diplomacy had enabled him to come to an accommodation with ʿAlī's son Ḥasan, and his astute assessment of the situation led to the transfer of the capital to Syria, where his main support lay. For the next ninety years, Islam would be governed from Damascus, and it was all too easy to accuse the new dynasty of the Umayyads of ruling the Muslims by force rather than by consent. They presided over a still-expanding empire and, beset with serious internal opposition from other groups, were forced to govern the provinces with a firmness that many would find inconvenient. The descendants of those who had failed ʿAlī in his confrontation with the Syrians kept up a ceaseless barrage of propaganda of an increasing bitterness and fomented a series of uprisings against the new regime in the name of the house of ʿAlī, the *ahl al-bayt*, or 'holy family', one after another of whose hapless members were sacrificed on the altar of conscience and in the name of Iraqi separatist aspirations in a series of hopeless revolts suppressed with ruthless Syrian efficiency. Most tragic of all these events had been the slaughter of the Prophet's grandson Ḥusayn, who, together with a large number of his family and relatives, had been slaughtered on the field of Karbalā' by the army of the Umayyads' viceroy. Surrounded by the government forces and denied food and water until they could no longer offer any effective resistance, they had been butchered like cattle. Dramatic descriptions of this appalling act provided poets and musicians with the materials for countless elegies and dirges, many of which were brought together into a passion play which to this day is still movingly enacted in towns and villages on the anniversary of the massacre, retaining its power to reduce the audiences to shuddering and tears. As the lists of Shī'ī 'saints' and 'holy martyrs' swelled, even more shrill excoriation of the 'impious regime', 'the dogs of unbelief' and 'enemies of God', born of repeated frustration and a sense of impotence, flowed into the *Ḥadīth*. A man who consulted ibn 'Umar on whether the pilgrim plagued by a gnat would incur the penalty for shedding blood if he crushed it drew from the venerable sage the withering shout: 'Listen, will you, to this Iraqi. His people slaughtered the Prophet's grandson and he asks me about the blood of a gnat![134]

Nor was the party that most vigorously kept alive the claims of the house of 'Alī the only group that cursed and execrated the Syrian rulers. The chorus of vituperation was amplified by the voices of the secessionists, the Khawārij (from *kharaj*, 'to desert'), now formed into numerous raiding parties recruited from the fierce warriors of the desert which rampaged up and down the border land between Iraq and Syria, killing and looting in the name of purity of belief and the rule of the most faithful to the laws of God and the Quran. All Muslims who failed to respond to their call to make 'the new *hijra*' to join them in their camps were denounced as unbelievers, denizens of the abode of faithlessness whom God in His Holy Book had urged the true believers to root out without mercy. This failure to join them showed indifference to the general evil emanating from 'the godless' rulers at Damascus who had turned 'the affair of God' into another hereditary monarchy and who, misguided themselves, were misguiding the people of God and using them to keep hold of the leadership which they had impiously seized. Worse, failure to make the *hijra* might expose these villagers or townsmen as supporters of those who also thought they had family claims on the leadership of the Muslims, the accursed Shī'a, who were engaged with the Umayyads in a base struggle for the trappings of temporal power and pelf. The Khārijites declared war on both Umayyads and Alids. In their view, both parties, no better than each other, were backsliders and apostates who had betrayed the Book of God and His Prophet. Both were the enemies of God upon whom Heaven had declared unremitting war until God should decide the issue and His rule alone prevailed.

The Umayyads, in the interests of good order, stability of the state and the preservation of the immense gains that Islam had made, saw no alternative to retaining power in the hands of their own clan as they strove to maintain the unity of the Muslims.

> Muʿāwiya recalled in the course of one of his sermons that he had heard the Prophet say: 'This polity will remain with Quraysh. None will show them enmity but God will cast him down on his face – as long as they uphold the religion.'[135]

Also reported from the Prophet were his words:

> 'He who obeys me, obeys God; he who disobeys me, disobeys God. He who obeys the ruler, obeys me; he who disobeys the ruler, disobeys me.'[136]

> 'Israel', said the Prophet, 'was governed by prophets. As one died, he was replaced by another. There will, however, be no prophet after me, but there will be caliphs and they will be numerous.' His Companions asked him, 'What do you advise us to do?' He replied, 'Faithfully fulfil your oaths of allegiance to them, one after the other. Give them their due. God will question them about their stewardship.'[137]

> Muḥammad informed Ḥudhayfa that he must cleave to the unity of the Muslims and uphold their *imām*. 'What', asked Ḥudhayfa, 'if there is no unity and no *imām*?' The Prophet warned him, 'In that case, avoid all factions'.[138]

> A man complained to ibn ʿAbbās, cousin of the Prophet, about the manner in which Muʿāwiya performed a particular prayer. 'Let him be,' said ʿAbdallāh, 'he is a Companion of the Prophet and a man who understands the religion.'[139]

The idealistic view adopted by the Khārijites that the people of God be governed only by the purest of faith and the most scrupulous in his observance of the ordinances of the faith, 'even if there be set over you an Ethiopian with a head like a raisin',[140] soon led, given the different degrees of rigour possible in defining both 'belief' and 'piety', to their splintering into numerous smaller camps, each swearing allegiance to its own chosen 'Commander of the Faithful' judged to measure up to their severe criteria. That of course, made them the more difficult to pursue and to destroy.

A man had once accused the Prophet of acting unfairly in the distribution of booty and advised him to act more scrupulously. When the man had gone, the Prophet said that there would be descended from him people 'who would recite the Quran, although it would get no further than their throats. They would depart from Islam with the speed at which an arrow leaves the bow. They would kill the people of Islam, while sparing the unconverted heathen.'[141]

'If I should be spared to encounter them,' said Muḥammad, 'I'd kill them.'[142]

The same man had associates with whom none of the Companions of the Prophet would deign to pray or to fast ... Their sign will be a black man one of whose upper arms will resemble a female breast ... They will appear at a time when the Muslims are divided. 'I swear', says the Companion, 'I heard the Prophet say this. I further swear that I was with 'Alī when he fought those people. A search was made for the man and when he was found, I examined him and found him to be exactly as the Prophet had described him.'[143]

The fearless raids and ceaseless depredations of the Khārijites proved a severe trial to the unarmed villagers, a scourge to the traveller whom they would examine in detail to ascertain the purity of his theology, and a thorn in the flesh of the Umayyads who had to mount countless campaigns to counter their lawlessness. They may even have contributed their share to the weakening and eventual downfall of the regime. But they served Islam incidentally by opening up, in addition to the political issues which they raised, the question of the definition of 'sin' and the effect that it might have on 'faith', thus provoking some of the earliest theological discussions among the Muslims.

The questions having once been raised, the different theological attitudes being framed and given expression in *ḥadīth* form prompted among the general body of the Muslims the need to confirm their own positions vis-à-vis the welter of *ḥadīth*s with which they were being bombarded from all sides. They showed an inclination to challenge some of the views expressed and to counter them with their own *ḥadīth*s expressing their own point of view. The chief drawback of the Khārijites in the eyes of ruler and ruled alike was the destructive effect which their activism was having on public order. Passivity and resignation were now drummed into the public mind in *ḥadīth* after *ḥadīth*.

The Prophet foretold, 'There will come after me governors who will not be governed by the guidance I have provided, nor proceed on the path I have laid down. Among them will arise men with the hearts of devils in human bodies.' 'What shall we do if we live to see that?' he was asked. 'You will hear and obey the prince, even if he beats your back and steals your property. Hear and obey.'[144]

'Whoever abandons obedience [var.: the ruling power] and separates from the general body of believers, then dies, dies a pagan. Whoever enlists under a flag whose objectives are not clear, from anger against one party, or whoever summons others to one party, or responds to the call for assistance to one party against another and kills, kills as a pagan. Whoever rebels against my people, striking pious or impious, making no distinction in favour of those who believe, whoever does not faithfully keep to the oath of allegiance that he freely gave, has no connection with me, nor I with him.'[145]

To those who complained of the evil of the times, consolation was offered in:

'You will not live through one period, but that the one after it will be even worse. Bear patiently until you meet your Maker.'[146]

Whoever withdraws his hand from allegiance will meet God on the Day of Judgment and will have no defence. Any man who dies owing allegiance to no ruler will die a pagan.[147]

Even rulers who insist on receiving their due but who deny the believers their due are to be obeyed. 'They will be judged for what they do, and you will be judged for what you do.'[148] It is not the business of the individual Muslim to make snap moral judgments on his rulers, deciding which of them is evil and bound to go to Hell. God will judge these rulers in due course; only He knows the true innermost condition of men's hearts.

Furious with one of his generals (it might have been Khālid, or it might have been his adoptive grandson, Usāma), the Prophet had stormed at being informed that, in the heat of battle, ignoring the enemy's calling out, 'I believe that there is no other god besides God', the Muslim had cut the man down. 'He had confessed to the faith,' thundered Muḥammad. 'But he just said that to save his skin.' 'How do you know that? Did you tear the heart from his breast and peer at it to find out if he was sincere or not? I am not commanded to look into men's hearts. I am commanded to summon them to belief, and if they say that they believe, to accord them all the benefits of their belief, and to honour their lives and their property as inviolable.'[149]

The business of the ruled is to render unto Caesar the things that are

Caesar's and to render unto God the things that are God's – as long as the ruler upholds the religion and as long as he provides the conditions in which the practices of the religion may be observed both in public and in private without constraint. Providing the ruler is at the very least a nominal believer, it is the duty of the Muslims to obey and to eschew, in the interests of the unity of the Muslims, any seductive call to judge the morals of the de facto authority as an excuse for legitimising rebellion.

Those who do not take up arms against the ruling power are distinguished from the implacable foes of the Umayyads, the Shīʿa and the Khārijites, by the title 'people of the *sunna* and unity'. We have already seen the term '*sunna* of the Prophet' used consciously in contrast to the *ahl al-bayt*, the family of the Prophet, the rallying-call of the Shīʿa. This term, *sunna*, is intimately intertwined with the concept of the Tradition of the community embodied in the term *Ḥadīth*, with which it shares the concept of 'continuity of practice', the 'way of the ancestors', or the pious forebears. Some writers consider the two terms *Ḥadīth* and *sunna* to be synonymous and therefore interchangeable. That, however, did not become the case until the late second/eighth century and then only for a specific technical reason that remains to be examined. The term *sunna* retained its original general sense until well into the literary phase of the history of the *Ḥadīth* ,was still in current use in the second half of the second Islamic century and can still be distinguished from the term '*sunna* of the prophet' which was just beginning to appear alongside it. The semantic transition was already under way but not yet complete in the time of Mālik b. Anas of Madīna (d. 179/795), as a few examples from his classic work on Madīnan legal opinions will make clear.

> Discussing a legal restriction on an owner's freedom to sell his property, and mentioning a ruling said to have been given by the Prophet himself, Mālik says, 'and the undisputed *sunna* with us on this question is in conformity with that'.[150] Mālik had heard that the early Madīnan legal expert, Saʿīd b. al-Musayyab, being asked whether there were any *sunna* on this same question, had replied, not, however, with a *ḥadīth*, but with a statement of the legal principle involved.[151] Of a particular commercial transaction, Mālik himself says, 'that is not the way Muslims do things'.[152] Describing certain arrangements made between investor and agent, he speaks of the *sunna*, the past practice of the Muslims.[153] Of another transaction, he says that it follows the ancient practice, *sunna*, in this type of transaction.[154] Certain marriage restrictions he describes as 'following the ancient way', *sunna*.[155] Anyone proposing to perform one of the major Islamic

rituals of prayer, fasting, pilgrimage or religious retreat has only to follow 'the ancient way of performing them', the *sunna*, which is known by the Muslims. He may not introduce any innovative practice [*muḥdath*], but must follow 'the way of the Muslims'.[156]

The caliph Abū Bakr had been unaware of a ruling on a legal question in either the Book of God or 'the *sunna* of the Prophet'. He consulted the Companions and one of them recalled a ruling that the Prophet had given in just such a case.[157]

This claim being confirmed by a second Companion, the ruler accepted it and acted upon it. In his day, ʿUmar, in a development of the same case, declined to vary his predecessor's decision.[158] The judgment which he gave in the new case arising out of the earlier one is elsewhere projected back as having, in fact, been delivered by Abū Bakr.[159] 'That', says Mālik, 'is a ruling not known to have been departed from "since Islam began".'[160] Of another ruling, he says that it 'has persisted from the Prophet's time until today'.[161] But, another ruling is not adopted, since 'it is not the way of the Muslims'.[162] One particular practice 'has always been disapproved of in our region, owing to the Prophet's having prohibited it.'[163]

On the other hand, in one question professional adjusters have to be engaged to advise, 'since nothing has come down from the Prophet, *nor is there any past practice, sunna*, to guide us'.[164] ʿUmar had warned the Companions about their conduct, 'since the people imitate what you do.'[165] ʿUmar himself explains his refusal to act in a certain way that had been suggested to him by a Companion, 'for, if I did, that would become a *sunna*'.[166] Consulted on a matter of personal hygiene and asked 'whether any report had come down', Mālik replies, without naming names, 'I have heard that some of the earlier Muslims used to do that'. It is not, however, he stresses, what he himself does.[167] Commenting on a feature of the ritual prayer, Mālik says he had not heard that it had been done 'in the ancient period'.[168] He has, indeed, heard that ʿUmar had been responsible for certain innovations in relation to the prayer.[169] Finally, he reports that ʿĀ'isha recalled, when mentioning the story of a case concerning her freedwoman, Barīra, that the *ḥadīth* conveyed three *sunnas*.[170]

The distinction is therefore made that, while the *ḥadīth* is the story or document itself, the *sunna* is the practice or ruling that is to be inferred from the story. In the following century, a scholar found, in one *ḥadīth* about a man who died while on the pilgrimage, as many as five separate *sunna*s.[171]

Setting aside his normal attitude of sceptical reserve towards the *ḥadīth*, Goldziher allowed himself to be duped into accepting that the Umayyads really had been 'the godless regime' that their enemies depicted. For him too, they were the worldly 'race of kings', materialistic in outlook, little interested in matters of religion, the bitter opponents of the pious religious party whom they suppressed with cruel tyranny.

> Religious people were pushed into the background by the rulers ... Like the Jewish rabbis under Roman rule, they occupied themselves with research into the law, which had no validity for the real circumstances of life, but represented for themselves the law of their ideal society.[172]

Using their great power and the wealth which they expropriated from the state finances, the rulers succeeded, in Goldziher's view, in seducing a number of prominent scholars into defending their position and illegitimate policies by inventing and spreading *ḥadīth*s in their favour, putting into the mouth of the Prophet statements condemning their enemies as unbelievers, and consigning their opponents to a fearful fate in the Hereafter. Including in his sweeping condemnation the great father of Arabian *ḥadīth* studies, Zuhrī, 'a pliant tool' of Umayyad ambition, Goldziher even managed to misconstrue a remark attributed to this scholar: 'These emirs forced us to write *ḥadīth*s'. That, he concluded, could be understood only on the assumption of Zuhrī's willingness to lend his name, which was in general esteemed by the Muslim community, to the government's wishes.[173] The full statement makes a quite different impression: 'We did not originally approve of the written recording of religious knowledge until these princes obliged us to do so. Then we decided we should withhold it from none of the Muslims.'[174] This has nothing to do with the formation of a ministry of propaganda where, behind closed doors, officials engaged in concocting false *ḥadīth*s to be disseminated among the public to further the regime's public relations. The remark occupies its own place in the academic quarrel over the legitimacy or otherwise of preserving and transmitting the *Ḥadīth* in writing. The interest of the rulers in opening up what had hitherto been the preserve of a few specialist scholars in order to spread the knowledge of the religion beyond their confined circle makes an impression quite opposed to that intended by Goldziher. The princes of the ruling house were themselves either Companions or Successors – the founder of the dynasty, Muʿāwiya, had been the Prophet's brother-in-law – and the names of several members of the family occur in the *isnād*s of the pious as frequently as those of their contemporaries from the house of ʿAlī, the *ahl al-bayt*, in, for example, Mālik's *Muwaṭṭa*'.

Professor Abbott has shown the interest of several members of the Umayyad dynasty in acquiring for their libraries copies of the written collections of several prominent Companions' *ḥadīth*s, an interest which preceded in date that attributed to the most revered member of their house, ʿUmar b. ʿAbdal ʿAzīz.[175]

More recently, Professor Schacht took up for reconsideration Goldziher's general thesis that much of the *Ḥadīth* had been the result of widespread fabrication.[176] Schacht, however, not merely chose to restrict his investigations to the *ḥadīth*s adduced in the disputes between the coteries of scholars in the several regional schools of law, and in the quarrels between the 'lawyers' and the devotees of the *Ḥadīth*, but he also chose to confine his analyses to *ḥadīth*s of more strictly 'legal' application, showing less interest in those relevant to the strictly 'religious' matters of cult and ritual. Crucially, he showed little interest in the Muslims' handling of *ḥadīth*s on matters regulated in the Quran. His studies concentrated rather more on legal theory, that is, jurisprudence, than on the underlying phase of law derivation from both Quran and *Ḥadīth*. Schacht had a special interest in the attribution of statements relative to law to specific individuals in the first Islamic generation (the Companions) and in subsequent generations (the Successors). He thus focused on the *isnād*s of the *ḥadīth*s, and it is in this field that his most perceptive insights lie. For Schacht has shown that the *isnād* had a tendency to grow both vertically, that is, backwards, and horizontally. Statements adduced in one context from Successors tend to reappear regularly elsewhere either in identical statements from Companions or as counter-statements attributed to other Companions. The same relation can be seen to obtain between statements attributed in one context to Companions which reappear elsewhere as statements or counter-statements from different Companions, or from the Prophet. This tendency of the *ḥadīth*s 'to grow backwards' shows, Schacht suggests, a movement natural in scholars who, taking their information at first from the lowest source available to them, gradually make, under the pressure of dispute, the transition to tracing it to ever higher and higher authority.[177] In this development, the role played by the *Ḥadīth* specialists was of significance. We have seen that the *isnād* is a list of names intended to identify and so guarantee the successive stages through which information passed down. Frequently, *isnād*s branch off after a particular point into several alternative lists: thus, A – B – C – D can become: A – B – E – F, or A – B – G – H, and so on. The last common link in all these cases is B. This phenomenon suggested to Schacht the possibility of dating the first appearance of an item of information, in the present case to lifetime of B, or immediately after, if the information were first put into circulation either by B or by someone using his name.[178]

We shall meet instances in which scholars, invited to consider *ḥadīth*s alternative to their own, will be seen to declare that they had never heard these alternative reports. Similarly, in the literary phase of the *ḥadīth*, it frequently happens that a master is silent, while a particularly relevant *ḥadīth* appears in the writings of one of his pupils. On the argument that a scholar would have used in debate a particular item if he had known it, this observation is also used to determine the approximate date of that *ḥadīth* in the interval between master and pupil, or between one writer and another, slightly later.[179]

A characteristic feature of many *isnād*s is incompleteness. One or more links in the chain of authority may be absent. If found elsewhere with a complete *isnād*, the *ḥadīth* may be said to have been 'improved'. Schacht thus draws a series of conclusions:

> Companion *ḥadīth*s are later than Successor *ḥadīth*s; prophet *ḥadīth*s, it follows, are later still. *Ḥadīth*s with perfect *isnād*s are later than *ḥadīth*s with faulty *isnād*s. The *isnād* is the most arbitrary part of any *ḥadīth*.[180]

In common with other scholars, Schacht experienced the *isnād* barrier. The further back one reaches, the more unsatisfactory the *isnād* until it is discovered that, on the basis of the *isnād*, one cannot proceed further back than about the year AH 100. Faced with this problem, Schacht made his most radical proposals. Although, like all who study the *Ḥadīth*, Schacht realised that there was a considerable ideal element in the statements of the Muslim scholars, and that expressions like 'our practice', 'our generally agreed practice' and 'our practice on which there is no disagreement' can equally well mean[181] 'the practice, in our view, ought to be such-and-such', Schacht nevertheless proceeds on the assumption that what is being described is actual behaviour which he refers to as 'the living tradition' of Madīna, Kūfa, or whatever the case may be. In the great debate between those who confined their vision to the study of traditions only and those who were attempting to codify the law, this 'practice' can be seen to come into conflict with the content of *ḥadīth*s. From the date at which the discussions known to us were being conducted, both between the 'lawyers' of the different regions – to be determined by those whom they cited as their main authorities – and between the 'lawyers' generally and the cultivators of the specialist study of the *ḥadīth*, Schacht decided that the origins of Muslim jurisprudence were first being laid down about the year AH 100 by legal specialists whose raw materials were being furnished by actual practice, whether official enactments instituted by late Umayyad rulers and their officials or 'popular practice' current among the people.[182] To this, it was cogently pointed out that that is to abandon the whole of the period between the death of the Prophet and the end of the first century, and especially the entire period of the Madīnan caliphate (AD 632–5).[183] This telling criticism raises the need for a continued search for the origins of the substratum behind the lawyers' 'practice' which perhaps will not be located without taking more account of the role of the Quran in its contribution to the thinking of the intelligent Muslim of the earliest and most crucial period as to how the 'practice' ought to be fashioned.

4

The Study of the Ḥadīth

The student about to embark on the study of the *Ḥadīth* may well feel as daunted as the novice mariner navigating a chartless ocean. But there are ways to 'tame' the waves of what even the Muslims think of as 'this raging sea'. First, one organises the *Ḥadīth* into categories according to the main topics. Political, ritual, legal, theological, technical or exegetical themes tend to be recognisable. In dealing with the last group, it can be convenient to divide it into 'pure exegesis' and 'applied exegesis'. By 'pure exegesis' is meant here a type of report which can most easily be explained as originating direct from a Quran text. 'Applied exegesis' is more complicated. Discussions in a later generation led to a serious split in opinions: the quarrels over how to read Q 5.6, whether to wipe the feet or to wash them, illustrate the activity. A dispute was thought to be resolvable by going back to the Quran to seek out texts that could be claimed to support one view of the matter over the other. We shall take the categories in turn.

PURE EXEGESIS

In many Muslim countries, it is still today preferred that a non-Muslim should not possess a copy of the Quran, an attitude that arises from an ancient notion that none may even touch the sacred Book who is not in the state of ritual purity (*ṭahāra*) required of one about to embark on the ritual prayer. It may easily be supposed that the idea derived in turn from Q 56. 77–9: 'It is a noble quran; in a concealed book which none may touch but those who have been purified [*muṭahharūn*].'

The celebrated *Ḥadīth* expert, 'Urwa,

> discussed with Marwān various acts which breach *ṭahāra* and require renewal of the ablution [*wuḍū'*]. Among the acts Marwān listed was touching the genitals. 'Urwa protested that he had never heard that. 'Well,' said Marwān, 'a woman told me she had heard the Prophet say so.'[184]

'Urwa must have accepted what Marwān had told him, for 'Urwa's son reports that that had been his father's teaching.[185]

> Muṣ'ab reports that he used to hold the holy text while his father recited from it. Once he fidgeted and Sa'd asked, 'Did you by any chance just touch your gentials?' When Muṣ'ab said he thought he might have, his father told him to go and renew his *wuḍū'*.[186]

> The son of ʿAbdallāh b. ʿUmar tells us that that had also been the teaching and practice of his father. Sālim had seen him one day perform the minor ablution [*wuḍū'*] after having just completed the major ablution [*ghusl*]. 'I'd have thought that the *ghusl* would enable you to dispense with the *wuḍū'*?' said Sālim. 'It does,' said ʿAbdallāh, 'but occasionally I find that in doing it, I touch my genitals, so I perform the *wuḍū'* for that reason.'[187]

The Marwān-ʿUrwa exchange had been reported by a distinguished member of the family which still retained some of the Prophet's papers. He states that among these documents were Muḥammad's written instructions to his great-grandfather that none except the ritually pure (*ṭāhir*) may touch the Holy Quran.[188] Malik explains that one may not even carry the text on a cushion if not in a state of ritual purity (*ṭāhir*). This rule has nothing to do with whether or not one's hands are clean or, if dirty, liable to stain the holy pages. The matter is wholly abstract, one of consideration for the great sanctity of the Word of God, for which one must always show the greatest reverence. As to the verse, the best thing he had heard was that it resembles Q 80.11–16: 'Nay! it is a reminder; whoso wishes may recall; on honoured sheets; elevated, purifed [*muṭahhara*]; by the hands of scribes noble and pious.' Words are treacherous. *Ṭāhir* refers to humans in a state of ritual purity; *muṭahhar* refers to Heavenly beings intrinsically pure, having been made so by divine action (Q 2.25). That reminds Mālik of a report about

> ʿUmar, who had been with a group who were reciting Quran when he broke off to go and relieve himself. As he emerged from the privy, ʿUmar was still reciting Quran, at which one of the company, scandalised, pointed out to the caliph that he was reciting the holy text without having first renewed his ritual purity. 'Who was your teacher,' asks ʿUmar, 'was it perhaps Musaylima?', referring to Muḥammad's arch-rival, execrated by the Muslims as 'the false prophet'.[189]

One need not be in a state of ritual purity to recite Quran. Ritual purity is demanded only of those about to pray.

Q 75.1–19 presents a dramatic scene at the Last Judgment. It depicts the arrival of the individual soul before the tribunal to be shown the record of its earthly deeds. It will then realise that all its days it has been under surveillance. A record kept by an ever-watchful angel will be read out. Should the soul begin to proffer excuses, it will be told not to seek to anticipate the reading of the charges. It is the divine responsibility to keep the record and to read it out. The soul is commanded to follow in silence the reading of the charges. It will be for the judge to expound the details. The passage is in the form of direct address. It is easy to understand how it might be taken to have been spoken to the Prophet, and, once that identification had been made, the Muslims thought they were in possession of one further item of biographical information. (Double quotation marks enclose actual Quranic citations; single quotation marks enclose commentary.)

'The Prophet used to keep repeating the revelation over and over again as the sections were being delivered, for fear of forgetting them.'[190]

'When Gabriel brought a revelation, Muḥammad would have to wrap himself in a garment, so oppressive was the weight of the revelation. Before the angel had completed a communication, Muḥammad was already repeating to himself the beginning of the passage, for fear that he might forget it. Gabriel asked, "Why do you do that?" Muḥammad replied, "I am afraid I might forget it", so God revealed Q 87.6–7, "We shall empower you to recite the Quran and you will not forget – except what God wishes". This new revelation relieved the Prophet's anxiety about his powers of memory.'[191]

'As revelation was being delivered, the Prophet moved his tongue, so God revealed, "Do not be impatient, do not move your tongue" [Q 75.16]. He feared it might escape him.'

'We it is who must assemble it and recite it.'	Assemble it in your breast and fix it there
'and recite it'	so that you can recite it.
'When We have recited it'	when it has been revealed to you,
'follow the recitation'	it is for Us to clarify it, i.e. 'to provide the clarification through the elucidation that you will provide [cf. Q 16.44]'.

'When We have recited it, follow the recitation' – base your practice upon the revelation.[192]

After this, whenever Gabriel came, Muḥammad would bow his head and, when the angel departed, Muḥammad could recite, as God had promised him.[193]

A similar passage on the Last Judgment occurs at Q 20.109–14: 'Do not hasten to recite [quran] before its disclosure [*waḥy*] is completed'. But this passage is complicated by uncertainty as to whether the terms it uses – 'an Arabic quran', 'do not rush its quran' – are intended as verbal noun, 'recitation', or proper noun, Quran. The native commentators assume that the Quran is meant, and one has drawn attention to the similarity between Q 20 and Q 87 (as opposed to Q 75).[194]

I describe these discussions as 'pure exegesis', since that is how they would have begun. But it can be seen how quickly, as a result of comparing verse with verse, they also became *sabab* comment, that is, assertions as to the circumstances that had prompted the revelation of particular Quran passages. This type of comment helped to fill out details of the 'life of the Prophet'.

APPLIED EXEGESIS: ʿUMAR'S 'READING'

'Believers! when summoned to the Friday prayer, hasten [*isʿaw*] to worship' [Q 62.9]. The Muslims were expected to leave off what they were doing and make their way promptly to the communal prayer. Taking the word *isʿaw* literally, some would run to the mosque. We hear, for example, that ʿAbdallāh b. ʿUmar, on hearing the call to prayer, would make all speed and might arrive flustered and out of breath. In order to make the point that the Muslim should come to prayer in the composed frame of mind that befits the ritual, his father, the caliph, recited not the word *isʿaw*, but *imḍū*, 'make your way to the mosque'.[195]

> In reporting this, for which he has no *isnād*, Mālik comments: In the Book of God, the root *saʿy* implies merely 'doing', nothing more. Citing a number of appropriate verses, he feels that he can demonstrate that the term does not imply 'running', certainly not 'rushing'. He thinks that ʿUmar had reacted to a false interpretation of the verse and so had substituted the other word in order to establish his view of the meaning.

ʿUmar's alleged view was taken up in an instruction from the Prophet himself, as reported by Abū Hurayra: 'When the ritual prayer is called, do not run, but come to prayer in a seemly and dignified manner'. Apparently Mālik had not heard this *ḥadīth*, or he might have cited it, for he had nothing against the Abū Hurayra reports. This particular Abū Hurayra report from the Prophet may then, be taken to date from after Mālik's time. Mālik's pupil, Shāfiʿī, knew a more generally worded *ḥadīth* and was able to interpret it as including the Friday worship at the mosque.[196] In a second report,

> hearing another man recite the Quran in an unfamiliar version, ʿUmar brought him before the Prophet. Having listened to both versions, Muḥammad pronounced both correct, 'for the Quran has been revealed in several versions for the convenience of the Muslims'.[197]

This *ḥadīth* laid the foundations for a host of assertions that this or that Companion had recited this or that verse of the Quran in this or that way. The allegation was the essential preliminary for any departure from the strict letter of the holy text in all arguments which involved matters addressed in the Quran. Clearly, for such debating procedures, the approval of the Prophet was a prime desideratum. It provided the Muslims with adequate room for manoeuvre whenever, in the course of discussion, the actual wording of the Quran might prove inconvenient. The allegation that the Prophet had raised no objection to the circulation of variant Quran texts in his day among his followers had an even greater attraction to the Muslims, who all knew that they shared an identical Quran text in the period following the Prophet's death. That alone showed that the unique Quran text which the universal body of Muslims now shared had been supplied not by the Prophet but by one of his successors. Indeed, the Prophet's failure to do so had prompted the impulse behind another's initiative to 'unify' the texts.[198] We shall have to revert to this important point.

PRAYER

The Prophet's widow ʿĀ'isha is purported to have described the original imposition of the daily ritual prayers. According to this report, when first introduced, each of the five daily prayers had consisted of only two *rakʿa*s, or cycles of Quran recitations accompanied by bowing and genuflection.

> That situation had endured throughout the Makkan period. When the Prophet came to Madīna, the form of the prayers was reorganised. The ancient two-*rakʿa* prayer was now declared to be valid only for travellers. For the settled Muslims, prayers were to be made longer. The dawn prayer would continue to be one of two *rakʿa*s, but the noon, afternoon and night prayers were all increased to four *rakʿa*s each.[199]

The report, which makes no reference to the sunset prayer, a ritual of three *rakʿa*s for traveller and non-traveller alike, came from the hand of one who knew that it was alleged that there was a difference in respect of prayer between travellers and non-travellers, and set out to 'explain' the difference. Unhappily, the difference has been wrongly accounted for. No such dispensation rules in favour of travellers. Q 4.101 does, indeed, discuss the prayer obligation of the warrior fighting in 'the cause of God'. In times of war, when the time for the ritual prayer comes, the fighting men may apprehend the danger of coming under attack in the course of their devotions. If such is the case, they will be entitled to avail themselves of the special concession to decrease the length of their rituals. It is clear from the terms of the verse that the operative condition is actual fear of imminent enemy attack. In the absence of such real fear, the concession would not apply.

A Counter-Ḥadīth

ʿĀ'isha exhorted the Muslims to complete their ritual prayer when travelling.

> When reminded of reports as to the Prophet's supposed observance of shortening the prayers when travelling, she insists, that, of course, in his day, the Prophet and his group had every expectation of hostile action whenever they ventured forth from their base at Madīna. Those days had gone and gone forever. Following the pacification of Arabia, a Muslim could travel the length and breadth of Arabia with no fear of encountering hostility from any quarter. Circumstances in which a Muslim traveller might avail himself of the divine concession to abbreviate the ritual prayer no longer existed.[200]

When ʿĀ'isha's nephew, ʿUrwa, relayed to the great *Ḥadīth* expert, Zuhrī, ʿĀ'isha's account of the original imposition of the prayers, later to be extended to four *rakʿas* for non-travellers only, Zuhrī asked him to account for the other reports that, even when travelling, ʿĀ'isha had invariably performed the four-*rakʿa* prayer. ʿUrwa surmised that she had probably regarded the right of the traveller as a concession which one was free to accept or not. She may have sought the greater merit that would accrue from performing the longer ritual.[201]

Much more convincing, however, is the thought that the latter *ḥadīth*s, circulating also under the aegis of ʿĀ'isha's name, had occurred in the minds of those who could see the reference in the Quran to fear of enemy attack and who, on that account, now might acquiesce in the historical 'reality' of a shortened prayer in war conditions, but reflected that that had applied in the time when Islam was struggling against powerful forces.

> A man is reported as saying to ibn ʿUmar, 'I can find in the Quran a "fear-prayer" and the references to the prayer of the sedentary. But there is no trace of a "travel-prayer".' ʿAbdallāh replied, 'Cousin, God sent us Muḥammad when we knew nothing, and we merely do as we saw him do'.[202]

Thus, the 'travel-prayer' is non-Quranic. It is a *sunna*.

> A second man pointed out to ʿUmar that the very wording of Q 4 stipulated actual fear of enemy attack as the condition of the concession to abbreviate the prayers. Following the pacification of Arabia, there no longer existed any such apprehension. ʿUmar admitted that he had been as surprised as the other and had asked the Prophet about this very point. Muḥammad said, 'It is a free gift that God has bestowed upon the Muslims. Accept God's gracious gift.'[203]

These frank admissions that the source of the 'travel-prayer' had not been the Quran did not appeal to all, or did not reach all. The Quran text remained, and it seemed to state a condition for the abbreviation of the prayer. This potentially embarrassing fact could be neutralised in a number of ways. One might, for example, offer to punctuate the passage. A report, handed down in the name of

> ʿAlī, alleges that a group of peaceable merchants had consulted the Prophet on their prayer obligation in the course of their commercial travels. Through His Prophet, God had answered their query: 'When you travel, you will incur no moral guilt in abbreviating the prayer'. At this point, revelation ceased.
>
> A year later, as Muḥammad was about to lead those accompanying him on one of his expeditions in the ritual prayer, they were confronted by an armed force who, familiar with the forms of Muslim worship, determined to attack the believers as they were engrossed in worship. To frustrate the enemy ploy, God intervened at this critical juncture, revealing: 'If you fear the assault of the unbelievers, they have ever been openly hostile to you', whereupon the Prophet divided his force into worshippers and guards, in accordance with the instructions provided in Q 4.102, by which he was now guided.[204]

The consequence of this type of report was that the Muslims could assert that, from the Quran, one may distinguish three categories of ritual worship: the prayer of the peaceful traveller; the prayer of the warrior; the prayer to be performed by the non-traveller at home. Arising from this, ʿAbdallāh b. ʿAbbās is credited with the view that

> non-travellers perform the four-*rakʿa* prayers; the traveller's prayer is of two *rakʿa*s, and the warrior's is one of one *rakʿa* only.[205]

The caliph ʿUmar allegedly maintained that the 'travel-prayer' is not an abbreviated form of the ritual but an independent form of worship, complete in all respects.[206]

We have seen that, in the days of the Prophet, several of his senior Companions were said to have compiled personal codices of the sacred revelations for their own use and that the Prophet had not been so pedantic and bookish as to seek to impose a single uniform text on all. The idea is useful in cases such as the present where an inconvenient Quran verse appears to impose conditions on the right to shorten the prayer. It was now recalled that the Companion Ubayy, who had served Muḥammad at Madīna as secretary of the revelations, had preserved Q 4.101 in his private copy in the following terms: 'When you travel abroad, you will incur no guilt in shortening the prayers, lest you be attacked by the unbelievers'.[207] That was intended to excise the troublesome condition of 'fear' and to reassert a Quranic sanction for the 'travel-prayer'. The intent has, however, not been fully executed, since the allusion to unbelievers and the possibility of assault both persist.

Dreams

The dreams of prophets are regarded as structurally part of the means of revelation. That had been how Abraham had been ordered to sacrifice his son. Among the dreams bestowed on Muḥammad was one in which he was informed that he would enter the sacred precinct of Makka in perfect safety, accompanied by persons with shaven heads and others with trimmed locks.[208] In an autobiographical anecdote, the Basran Abu 'l-ʿĀliya recounts his journey to Makka. As he proceeded, he was asked by the scholars at various points how he was performing the prayers.

> Stating that he was abbreviating them, he was asked if that were Quranic. 'Both Quran and *sunna*', he replied, and reminded his questioners of the verse: 'God has granted His Prophet a veracious dream: "Your party will enter the sacred mosque. God willing, in perfect security, some with shaven heads [*muḥalliqīn*] and abbreviating the ritual prayer [*muqaṣṣirīn*], while fearing none"'.[209]

The use of the exegesis of one verse (here, Q 48.27, but based on a dubious etymology) to bolster the exegesis of another verse (Q 4.101) is a commonplace procedure in this literature, as is the creation of one *ḥadīth* to reinforce another.

Prayers at Makka

Also prevalent in the literature is the motif that certain of the ritual prayers are abbreviated in the course of the rites of the pilgrimage at Makka. Following his establishment at Madīna, Muḥammad made only one pilgrimage to Makka. The reports on this event, the 'farewell pilgrimage', are replete with references to his shortening of the ritual prayers. To go to Makka involves an arduous journey of several days. The prophet-pilgrim was ipso facto the prophet-traveller. The motif that he shortened the prayers at Makka was extended into that of his shortening the prayers both on his way to Makka and on his return journey. Several of the reports lay heavy stress on the point that Muḥammad had shortened the prayers on this occasion when any thought of enemy attack was inconceivable.[210] It is emphasised that what is being described is not a 'fear-prayer' but a simple 'travel-prayer'. Further, the concept of 'the continuous practice of the Muslims' is intentionally also heavily underlined. Abū Bakr, 'Umar and

ʿUthmān are all said to have based their performance of the shortened prayers, both at Makka and on the way thither and thence, on what had been reported – indeed, on what they themselves had witnessed – to have been the practice of the Prophet.[211]

> Abbreviating the prayer, Muḥammad turned and said to those he had been leading in the ritual, 'People of Makka, now complete the rest of the prayers by yourselves, for we are travellers'.[212]

Identical words are reported as addressed to the Makkans by ʿUmar on the occasion of his own pilgrimage.[213]

The perfect, unbroken continuity of the Muslim practice in this regard was not, however, sustained. We hear of breaches in this *sunna* in the days of ʿUmar's successor, ʿUthmān. A man reported to ʿAbdallāh b. Masʿūd who, together with ʿAlī, features in the literature as one of the chief eponyms of the teachings of the school of Kūfa in Iraq, much as ʿUmar and his son ʿAbdallāh fill the same role in the school of Madīna, that he had just seen ʿUthmān perform a four-*rakʿa* prayer, although at Makka. ʿAbdallāh had some harsh words for ʿUthmān. Later, however, praying behind ʿUthmān, ʿAbdallāh compliantly followed his lead in completing a four-*rakʿa* prayer. Taken to task by those accompanying him,

> 'You criticise ʿUthmān, then do exactly as he does', ʿAbdallāh exculpates himself by insisting that division in the ranks of the Muslims would be an evil, adding, however, that of the four-*rakʿa* ritual prayer he had just completed behind the *imām*, he fervently prayed that two *rakʿas* would find a gracious acceptance in the eyes of God.[214]

'Travel Prayer'

As already seen, ʿĀ'isha too had broken rank by completing the four-*rakʿa* prayer when travelling. She had been excused on the grounds that, perhaps, she had exercised *ta'wīl*, that is, interpretation, as, doubtless, ʿUthmān had done. Prodigies of rationalisation were applied to these reports on ʿUthmān's reported conduct. It is alleged that

> he had been approached by a beduin from whose conversation ʿUthmān had gathered that the man had continued to perform the two-*rakʿa* prayer the whole year round, having seen how the caliph had performed the prayers at the previous year's pilgrimage. Bethinking himself of his caliphal role as instructor of the Muslims, ʿUthmān thought that, to disabuse this man of his misunderstanding, he should this year perform the complete four-*rakʿa* prayer. To this, it was objected that the Prophet had had an even more elevated teaching role, yet he had not seen fit to perform the complete four-*rakʿa* prayer at Makka.

In that event, possibly on that occasion, ʿUthmān had been accompanied by one of his wives, which would have lessened the degree of isolation that characterises the situation of any traveller. But, had not the Prophet been in the habit of having some of his wives accompany him on his journeys and expeditions?

Well, then, perhaps ʿUthmān had taken a Makkan wife, or had bought some property at Makka. That, however, could be dismissed. Neither was permitted to a *muhājir*.

More probably, as Commander of all the Faithful, ʿUthmān in exercise of his office was 'at home' wherever within the realm of Islam he might alight. The caliph can never be considered a stranger, an outsider, a traveller.

The same charming consideration has been applied to ʿĀ'isha. The Quran declared the wives of the Prophet 'the Mothers of the Faithful'. ʿĀ'isha would always be among her children wherever within the realm of Islam she might alight. She, too, could never properly be described as a 'traveller'.

Or, as ʿĀ'isha is also thought to have done, ʿUthmān might have supposed that abbreviation of the ritual prayers was a gracious concession and not a peremptory requirement. It was thus something he was free to avail himself of or not, as he chose. This shortening of the ritual prayer must therefore be optional.[215]

The detail of ʿAbdallāh's remonstrating with ʿUthmān, then of his later reported following of ʿUthmān's lead in the four-*rakʿa* prayer, acquires an added piquancy from one's hearing that the later Iraqi school which traced so many of its teachings to reports on ʿAbdallāh's words or actions was to take the view that to shorten the prayer was not the traveller's option but his inescapable obligation.[216] In their view, the ritual prayer of the traveller who completes four *rakʿa*s is ipso facto invalid.

Combining Prayers

Certain of the ritual prayers are reported as having been combined by the Prophet at Makka. Unsurprisingly, for the scholars, a further concession extended to all travellers is that of combining ritual prayers. More surprising, however, is the further report that the Prophet had combined ritual prayers when not travelling. The great Madīnan expert, Mālik, presents such reports in a chapter curiously entitled: 'On combining ritual prayers when not travelling and when travelling'.

Reproducing from ibn ʿAbbās the report to the effect that

the Prophet had combined ritual prayers in peacetime conditions and when not travelling, Mālik ventures to presume that, on that occasion, it was probably raining.[217]

Observing that the report describing Gabriel's descent to demonstrate to Muḥammad the hours at which the five daily ritual prayers are to be *separately* performed, and the present report on the Prophet's performing two prayers jointly at the hour appropriate to one of them, both stemmed from one and the same person, ibn ʿAbbās, Mālik's great pupil, Shāfiʿī, constrained to accept both reports, and attempting to tease out the circumstances that might account for the difference makes no advance on the explanation of his teacher. It might have been raining.[218]

Muḥammad, according to the *ḥadīth*s, had made much of the social character of worship. The reports show him constantly and consistently exhorting the Muslims to engage in communal prayer, said to be twenty-five degrees more meritorious than private worship.[219] Regularly he spoke of the superior merits of group prayer, and he is shown repeatedly (therefore, it must be said, with little sign of success) pleading with his followers to come out to the mosque at the hours stipulated for the prayers.[220] Muḥammad was also, in the descriptions of him in the *Ḥadīth*, portrayed as a caring and loving leader, understanding and sympathetic to the difficulties and hardships frequently met by his devoted followers. Thus, he is shown in cold, inclement conditions, instructing the insertion into the call to prayer of the additional phrase, 'Pray at home.'[221] The common factor, in Shāfiʿī's estimation, that links the reports on the concession to the traveller to shorten the ritual prayer and the second concession to combine two of the prayers, and the advice to the faithful that they need not venture out of doors on cold, windy, rainy winter nights, is that of hardship. There is hardship involved for the traveller in constantly stopping and having to dismount and remount. Shāfiʿī thus enunciated the principle that whoever is entitled to shorten the ritual prayer is entitled to combine two ritual prayers.[222] Coming out and going home, only to have to come out again to the mosque, would seriously inconvenience worshippers in bad weather. So that, he suggests, must explain the Prophet's combining ritual prayers even when not travelling.

A further version of the ibn ʿAbbās *ḥadīth*, which now reports that Muḥammad had combined two prayers when at home in Madīna when it was not even raining, proved too much for the scholars, who abruptly dismissed it.[223]

Mālik's teacher,

Zuhrī, consulted Sālim, son of ʿAbdallāh b. ʿUmar, on the question of combining two ritual prayers when travelling. Sālim

> could see no harm in that, since that is what the pilgrims do at ʿArafa.[224]

Mālik's second great pupil, the Iraqi Muḥammad al-Shaybānī, commenting on Mālik's report that

> ʿAbdallāh b. ʿUmar would do as the *imām* did, if he combined prayers on account of rain, states: 'We do not accept that. We do not combine any two prayers at a single hour, with the sole exception of the prayers at ʿArafa and Muzdalifa, during the pilgrimage.'[225]

The Iraqis thus declined to extrapolate from the pilgrimage to mere journeys, that is, on the question of combining prayers. Illogically, they countenance the shortening of the prayers on mere journeys. A report had reached Shaybānī according to which

> the caliph ʿUmar had written to the Muslims in all the provinces prohibiting the combining of two ritual prayers at the hour appropriate to one of them and describing that as a most heinous sin.[226]

When

> challenged by Zuhrī, ʿUrwa went back to ʿĀ'isha to ask her why she completed the ritual prayers on all her journeys. 'My dear.' she said, 'I find no hardship in performing a complete ritual prayer.'[227]

The traveller may be fit and able-bodied, yet he is allowed to combine two ritual prayers. For Mālik,

> the sick are even more deserving of consideration. Surely this concession should be extended to the sick.[228]

His pupil, Shāfiʿī adamantly refused to grant this extension in favour of the sick.[229]

FASTING

One concession to travellers which one would not expect to occasion contention was that granted by Q 2.184–5 to postpone the fast until one arrived. Notwithstanding expectations, all aspects of the question were vigorously debated, with every standpoint finding a champion among Companions and Successors. Division must be laid at the door of the Quran's expression:

> those who are ill or on a journey, a number of alternative days, and incumbent on those who can, the ransom of feeding one of the poor; and he who voluntarily does good [*khayr*], it will be counted as a good deed [*khayr*], and that you fast will be counted as a good deed [*khayr*], did you but know.

Some took the words 'and those who can' to refer to the sick and the traveller who, notwithstanding their special condition, are nevertheless physically capable of sustaining the fast. If they claim the concession to postpone the fast, they incur the penalty of supporting one of the poor.[230] Others took them to be a general address. Those who can fast but choose not to must support one of the poor. That makes the fast an option, a view that is almost universally defended, although cast back into 'early Islam'.[231] Fasting became obligatory only with the revelation of Q 2.185: 'those present during the month shall fast'. The term *khayr* may mean, as translated here, 'a good deed'; but it may also mean 'better'.

> 'He who voluntarily does better' was thought to indicate the merit of feeding more than one poor person; others thought it meant 'he who, although entitled to postpone the fast, volunteers to fast';

that was then reinforced in 'and that you fast is better',[232] that is, than claiming the concession to postpone one's fast. The most radical proposition was that neither sick nor traveller had any option. Their obligation was to postpone the fast. If either attempted to fast when sick or travelling, that fast would be quite invalid and would require to be repeated. Their obligation was the fast of 'a number of alternative days'.[233]

Each of the above positions has been attributed to certain Successors, or Companions, even to the Prophet himself. But, as we are informed in harmonising *ḥadīth*s that the Prophet had both fasted on some journeys and broken his fast on others, some could conclude that the matter was optional.[234] Others earnestly continued to track down every detail that could be unearthed in the forest of *ḥadīth*s on this topic, in the hope of locating which had been the Prophet's indubitably latest attitude on the question. They supposed it absurd to maintain that a prophet sent to guide mankind would have left any element of the praxis obscure. Zuhrī, on this matter of fasting when travelling, is credited with the dictum: 'They used to follow the latest of the Prophet's enactments',[235] judging that to have abrogated all other reports on the subject.

TEMPORARY MARRIAGE: *MUTʿA*

A further concession, allegedly made to the warrior or the traveller bereft of female company, had been the facility to enter into a temporary or quasi-marriage, claimed to have been once, in 'early Islam', a legally valid procedure. The men would make arrangements with the women of the villages which they passed, striking a bargain normally consisting, it is said, of a handful of dates, flour or grain, or perhaps an outer garment, in consideration of their anticipated enjoyment. They would stipulate a time-limit of, say, three days, on the expiry of which the compact spontaneously expired, unless by mutual consent they agreed to extend the time-limit. The institution had a distinct name, being known as *mutʿa*.[236]

There are a host of *ḥadīth*s in the literature on this topic. What must be underlined as most significant is that wherever such reports are conveyed by scholars of the Sunnī persuasion, or attributed by them to Successors or Companions, great pains are taken to append to each report the deliberately worded rider that, of course, in the end, the Prophet prohibited the 'practice', declaring it outlawed until the Day of Judgment. As all Sunnī Muslims express extreme loathing for the *mutʿa*, the question naturally arises as to the source of these reports. Why should they take the trouble to mention that, at one time, the Prophet had recognised, some say recommended, this *mutʿa*?

The most interesting fact about these reports is that an impressive proportion connect *mutʿa* not with just any journey, but with a journey to Makka. Regrettably, that led one Western scholar to muse about the possibility of temple-prostitution associated with the pilgrimage.[237] Another, equally prominent Orientalist more recently saw in *mutʿa*

> presumably a pre-Islamic institution adopted into Islam and even given a measure of Quranic sanction.[238]

The supposed institution owes its existence, its name and its very discussion to the use of the term by the Quran in one context that is concerned with marriage, as it owes its supposed connection with the pilgrimage to use of the term in a second context concerned with the pilgrimage.

Q 4.23 lists the women of forbidden degree with whom no Muslim may ever contemplate marriage. One indispensable element in the validity of any Islamic marriage contract is the dowry. Making that clear, Q 4.4 permits the woman the freedom to remit part of the promised dowry if she so chooses. Q 4.24 states that, apart from those just listed in Q 4.23, the Muslim is free to use his wealth in seeking a wife.

> Apart from that, it is declared lawful that you seek out with your wealth – intending to accommodate them, not mere physical gratification – and, in consideration of what you enjoy from them [*istamtaʿtum*], give the women their obligatory payment. You will incur no moral guilt in renegotiating the amount of this obligatory payment, on the basis of mutual consent.[239]

In context, 'apart from that' clearly refers to the foregoing list of ladies who are not eligible to be marriage-partners.

ʿAbdallāh b. ʿAbbās, who is supposed to have acquired his knowledge of Quran text from Ubayy, insists that in Ubayy's personal codex appeared an additional phrase:

> 'and, in consideration of what you enjoy from these women *for a stipulated period of time*, give them the obligatory payment'.

That is another instance of 'applied exegesis'. ʿAbdallāh is shown correcting other men's recitation of this passage, insisting that they insert the additional phrase. One man protested that that was not how he had been trained to recite the passage. 'Nevertheless,' swears ʿAbdallāh, 'by God! that is how it was revealed.'

Some who claim to have seen the Ubayy codex swear that it contained the expression 'for a stipulated period'.[240] Possibly a superficial reading of Q 4.24 might suggest to some the idea of temporary marriage, but it is doubtful that it can give that sense to most unless they had heard that term and knew how it was being defined. Once the discussions on the extensive legal consequences that flow from marriage were under way, that was an interpretation that could be sustained only by the interpolation that was now being attributed to a Companion. The primitive exegesis of the verse that first gave rise to the notion of 'temporary marriage' is detectable in an exchange reported between ʿAmmār and ʿAbdallāh.

> ʿAmmār had asked him, 'What exactly is *mutʿa*? Is it some form of valid Muslim marriage, or is it a kind of illicit sexual behaviour?' Ibn ʿAbbās had replied, 'It is neither. It is simply *mutʿa as God calls it*.'[241]

The legal consequences of valid Islamic marriage are many. The pertinent civil contract must contain no expression implying intent to form only a temporary alliance. The dowry must be negotiated, agreed and accepted. The contract may be dissolved in only one of two ways: by the death of one of the partners, or legally, that is, by divorce. Both parties enjoy reciprocal inheritance rights, as do the offspring, who are assigned to the husband as his heirs. Dissolution of the marriage entails on the female a 'waiting-period' whose length varies with the cause of the dissolution and which must be observed by the female before she may contemplate a valid remarriage.

Persisting with his enquiries,

> ʿAmmār asked, 'What then, is the 'waiting-period' for the *mutʿa* female?' to which ʿAbdallāh returned the purely arbitrary reply that it is one menstrual cycle.[242]

That bears no relation to any of the known 'waiting-periods'. Pressed on whether the *mutʿa*-partners enjoyed mutual rights of inheritance, ʿAbdallāh declared that they did not.[243] That does not conform with the Islamic marriage law either. Examining the conditions attaching to the *mutʿa* arrangement and finding none of the basic features of Islamic marriage present, the Sunnī scholars unanimously determined that this was no form of valid marriage. In addition to the several

Quran verses regulating the conditions of marriage, two further contexts listing the attributes of the true believer whose life is pleasing to God, both Q 23.7 and Q 70.31, exclude *mutʿa*:

> 'those who restrict their sexual activity to their wives or the slaves they possess. Any who seeks to go beyond that transgresses.'

Lacking the qualifications of 'wife' and untrammelled by the strict conditions imposed by matrimony, while lacking the attribute of the object of full legal ownership, the female *mutʿa*-partner falls beyond what is legally permitted. In the Sunnī view, she could never be a legitimate partner. Fierce verbal battles have raged over this important social question throughout all periods, and, in our own day, it continues to divide Sunnī from Twelver Shīʿa theory and practice. The Shīʿa claim the authority of the Prophet, who is said, as we have seen, to have approved the practice. In addition, they claim the authority of ʿAlī, ibn ʿAbbās and ʿImrān b. Ḥuṣayn. They do not recognise the prohibition said to have been pronounced not by the Prophet but only by ʿUmar, who, for the Shīʿa, had no legal right to arrogate to himself the authority to ban anything that the Prophet had condoned.[244]

> The Companion Abū Dharr declared, '*Mutʿa* during the pilgrimage was restricted exclusively to the contemporaries of the Prophet.'[245]

A second Companion,

> Saʿd, questioned about *mutʿa*, replied, 'We practised *mutʿa* when this fellow [identified as Muʿāwiya]' was still a heathen, living in Makka'.[246]

A series of *ḥadīth*s, reported as from ʿImrān by one man, Muṭarrif, shows an interesting development in the wording:

1. 'We *tamattaʿ* in the Prophet's company. The Quran did not reveal anything [to the contrary], whatever a man may say.'
2. 'The Prophet did it and we did it.'
3. 'The Prophet combined a pilgrimage with an *ʿumra* – whatever personal opinion a man may express.'

The 'man' is identified in one version as ʿUmar.[247]

Also reported from ʿImrān, but on the authority of Abū Rajāʾ:

4. 'The *mutʿa* verse was revealed in the Book of God – that is, *mutʿa* of the *ḥajj* – the Prophet recommended that we do it. No Quran verse ever subsequently abrogated the verse on the *mutʿa* of the *ḥajj* – whatever personal opinion a man may have.[248]

Both Salama and Jābir claim that the Prophet permitted *mutʿa*, glossed in one version as 'the *mutʿa* of women'.[249]

'Aṭā' tells us that

when Jābir arrived in Makka for the *'umra*, people took the opportunity to question him on various things including *mut'a*. 'Yes, indeed, 'he said, 'we did that in the Prophet's time and in the reigns of Abū Bakr and 'Umar.'[250]

Sabra b. Ma'bad, who accompanied the Prophet in AH 8 at the Conquest of Makka, took advantage of the Prophet's permission to engage in *mut'a*. Before they left Makka, however, the Prophet had prohibited the practice.[251]

Abū Mūsā joined the Prophet on the farewell pilgrimage in AH 10. Muḥammad asked which rite he proposed to perform. 'That which the Prophet proposes', he replied. 'Good.' said the Prophet, 'perform the circuit of the Ka'ba and of Ṣafā and Marwa, then feel free of what is prohibited to the pilgrim.' He did so, then repaired to a woman of his clan who cleaned his head. Later, he proclaimed the solemn intent to perform the *ḥajj*. Abū Mūsā continued to teach this to the people until the time of 'Umar, when a friend warned him that he was evidently unaware of the change 'Umar had introduced in the rite. On 'Umar's arrival, Abū Mūsā mentioned this to him and 'Umar explained, 'We adhere to the Book of God which commands us "to complete the *ḥajj* and the *'umra*" and we adhere to the *sunna* of the Prophet who did not abandon any prohibitions "until his sacrificial offering had reached the place where it was to be consecrated"'.[252]

Version 2 makes clear that

the Prophet had advised Abū Mūsā on how he should act only after first having ascertained that he had brought no sacrificial offering with him.[253]

Version 3:

Abū Mūsā used to instruct the Muslims that *mut'a* was valid. Here, 'Umar declares, 'I know perfectly well that the Prophet and his Companions did it, but I disapprove of their disporting themselves in the shade and then going out to the pilgrimage with their heads dripping'.[254]

In a parallel to the Abū Mūsā report,

the Prophet mentions that 'Alī's wife is present, before asking him which rite he proposes to perform.[255]

According to Jābir, the Companions had solemnly proclaimed the intent to perform the *ḥajj*. When the Prophet arrived, he told them to abandon the prohibitions and to *enjoy the women*. That was not a peremptory command, merely permission to do so. The Muslims protested at the thought of having relations with women so near the time when they would depart for ʿArafa, arriving there with penises dripping. Addressing the throng, the Prophet said, 'You know that of all of you, I fear God the most. I am the most truthful and the most faithful. I too, should have laid aside the prohibitions, were it not for this sacrificial offering I have brought. Had I my time over again, I would not have brought it.' At this, the men did as they had been ordered.[256]

The Prophet told them to turn what they had intended into *mutʿa*. As for himself, he was free to relax from no prohibition 'until his sacrificial offering had reached the place where it was to be consecrated.'

Informed that ʿAbdallāh b. ʿAbbās recommended *mutʿa*, whereas ʿAbdallāh b. al-Zubayr prohibited it, Jābir exclaimed, 'I have the very *ḥadīth*! We *tamattaʿ* in the Prophet's entourage. When ʿUmar became caliph, he said, "God allowed what He pleased to His Prophet for His own reasons. The Quran has now been revealed, so 'Complete the *ʿumra* and the *ḥajj* to God', as God commands. See to it that when you marry women, you intend permanency, for no man who marries a woman 'for a stipulated period' will be brought before me but I will stone him."'[257]

Informed that ʿAbdallāh b. ʿAbbās and ʿAbdallāh b. al-Zubayr disagreed about *the two mutʿa*s, Jābir said, 'We did *both* with the Prophet. Later, when ʿUmar prohibited *both*, we desisted.'[258]

Abū Dharr insisted that *the two mutʿa*s were restricted solely to the Companions: the *mutʿa* of women and the *mutʿa* of the *ḥajj*.[259]

Whereas ʿUthmān prohibited *mutʿa*, ʿAlī recommended it. ʿUthmān spoke to ʿAlī, who replied, 'You know perfectly well that we *tamattaʿ* with the Prophet'. ʿUthmān conceded that that was true, 'but we feared that we might be attacked'.[260]

Versions speak of ʿUthmān's banning *mutʿa* – or the *ʿumra*.

ʿAlī asked him what he thought he was doing banning something that the Prophet had done. ʿAlī went out and proclaimed his most solemn intent to perform *ḥajj* and *ʿumra* jointly.[261]

Hearing that ibn ʿAbbās was lenient on the topic of *mutʿa*. ʿAlī warned him to be careful. The Prophet had prohibited *mutʿa* with women during the Khaybar expedition [AH 7].[262]

ʿAbdallāh b. al-Zubayr inveighed against those who recommended

> *mutʿa*. Summoning a particular man, ʿAbdallāh raged at him, 'You're a coarse, ignorant fellow!' The man insisted that *mutʿa* had been practised in the days of 'the leader of the saints'. 'Very well,' said ʿAbdallāh, 'try it, and by God! if you do, I'll stone you.'[263]

The reader of these discussions will not doubt that what they represent is the debris of arguments between persons who do not stand in the line of unbroken continuity of transmission of the views of the Companions of the Prophet, let alone the acts and instructions of the prophet himself. The confusions and the contradictions that we have just witnessed speak rather, with a very strong voice, of a breach in that alleged continuity. We have experienced the floundering of men who no longer knew the circumstances in which some of the revelations had reached the Prophet and consequently no longer understood the import of certain of the Quran's regulations. For what we have here is evidence of a collision between the interpretations of two quite separate and independent Quran contexts. Q 4.24 deals with Islamic marriage. Q 2.196 deals with an aspect of the journey to Makka to perform one or other of the two visitations, the *ʿumra* and the *ḥajj*. The latter verse reads:

> Complete the *ḥajj* and the *ʿumra* to God. If you are obstructed, then such sacrificial offering as you can afford. But do not shave your heads until the offering shall have reached its place of consecration. He who chances to be ill, or suffering some disorder of the head – the ransom of fasting, or charitable giving, or further rites. Then, when you feel safe, whoever *tamattaʿ* the *ʿumra* until the *ḥajj*, such sacrificial offering as you can afford. He who cannot afford that, a fast of three days during the *ḥajj* and seven on returning, making a total of ten days. This is for those whose households are not present in the sacred mosque.

The verse caused the greatest imaginable difficulties for the commentators. The one occasion spoken of in the biographical tradition when Muḥammad and his followers suffered obstruction on their way to the sacred mosque was that of the abortive *ʿumra* of AH 6–7, when they were stopped by the Makkans at a place near Makka called Ḥudaybiya. There followed prolonged negotiations, culminating in the treaty of Ḥudaybiya among whose provisions was the offer by the Makkans to permit the Muslims to perform an *ʿumra* the following year. There is said to be a reference to this event in Q 48.24ff., where, however, the word for 'obstruction' is the more usual Quranic *ṣadd*, as opposed to Q 2.196's *iḥṣār*. Q 48 does further mention that the sacrificial offering was prevented from reaching the place of its consecration. God had prevented fighting on that occasion in the valley of

Makka, but the tradition is divided on the question of whether Muḥammad sacrificed his offering at the spot where he had been checked, or whether he had been able to arrange to forward it in the care of others. We have already heard that this uncompleted visitation had been provoked by a dream. The Quran insists that the dream was true and that the Muslims would, God willing, enter the sacred mosque in perfect safety, fearing none, some with shaven heads and some with trimmed locks.

> In the year in which al-Ḥajjāj arrived in the Ḥijāz to do battle with ʿAbdallāh b. al-Zubayr, the counter-caliph, two sons of ʿAbdallāh b. ʿUmar attempted to convince their father that it would not harm him to forgo *ḥajj* that year, for they feared that he would find his path obstructed. ʿAbdallāh, however, proved obdurate. 'If the way is obstructed, then I shall do what the Prophet did when I was with him and the unbelievers of Makka obstructed him. I call you to witness my solemn declaration of intent to perform the *ʿumra*.' That he did at dhu ʾl-Ḥulayfa, adding, 'If I get there, I'll complete my *ʿumra*, but if I'm obstructed, I'll do as the Prophet did when I accompanied him – "Indeed, there is for you in God's Messenger a fine model"' [Q 33.21]. Later, ʿAbdallāh halted, declaring, 'But the two are one thing. If my *ʿumra* is obstructed, so too will my *ḥajj* be obstructed, so I call you to witness my solemn declaration of intent to perform a *ḥajj* together with an *ʿumra*.'[264]

Q 2.196 states: '1. the Muslim must complete *ʿumra* and *ḥajj* to God; 2. if some [unspecified] obstruction is met, a sacrificial offering must be made; 3. when safety returns, the *tamattuʿ* of the *ʿumra* into/until the *ḥajj* will also involve a sacrificial offering'.

Niyya

Every ritual act in Islam, *wuḍūʾ*, prayer, fast, *ʿumra* or *ḥajj* requires for its validity that the worshipper formally declare before the act his solemn intent to perform it, *niyya*. This declaration once pronounced, the worshipper is bound by solemn contract to complete the act in its approved form and, until the act is completed, is under a series of bans known by the general title of consecration, *iḥrām*, from which he is released only on the formally correct completion of the act. The title of the release, *iḥlāl*, is distinguished from the preliminary solemn declaration which, in the case of an *ʿumra* or a *ḥajj* is known as *ihlāl*. The *ḥajj* proper may be performed only during the first ten days of the last month of the year; the *ʿumra*, which is a much shorter form of the visitation of the holy house, the Kaʿba at Makka, and all of whose rites fall within the boundaries of Makka itself, may be performed at any time of the year, although whether it might be performed during the period set aside for the *ḥajj* was a most warmly debated topic, as may be judged from the wording of a declaration reported from 'Imrān:

> 'Know that the Prophet permitted certain of his womenfolk to perform an *'umra* during the ten days [of the *ḥajj*]. No Quran verse was subsequently revealed to abolish that practice, nor did the Prophet prohibit it until he passed away – whatever some man may say to the contrary.'[265]

Iḥrām

Both *ḥajj* and *'umra* are governed by strict dress regulations and particularly governed by a total ban on any sexual relations, dressing or cutting the hair, paring the nails and the shedding of blood, the bearing of arms and other taboos.

According to Mālik, he whose solemn declaration of intent was for the *ḥajj* may not, thereafter, add to his *ihlāl* the intent to perform an *'umra* in addition.[266] He whose solemn declaration had been to perform the *'umra* may, however, but before arriving at the Ka'ba, add the intent to perform the *ḥajj* in addition.[267]

A discussion of Q 2.196, on the occasion of Mu'āwiya's *ḥajj*, shows the extent of Companion disagreement. The expression:

> 'the *tamattu'* of the *'umra* until the *ḥajj*' having been mentioned, one Companion stated that that was never done, except by those who are thoroughly ignorant of God's regulations. When Sa'd strenuously countered this, Ḍaḥḥāk pointed out that, in any event, 'Umar had prohibited that. Sa'd now insisted that the Prophet had done it and the Companions who had accompanied him had imitated him and done so also.[268]
>
> According to ibn 'Umar, *tamattu'* refers to the performance of an *'umra* in months ten, eleven and, if in month twelve, performing the *'umra* before the *ḥajj* proper, then staying on in Makka until the *ḥajj* ceremonies commence. Should one then participate in that year's *ḥajj*, a sacrificial offering must be made. [Here, there is no mention of any obstruction]. Mālik emphasises that *tamattu'* and the penalty attaching to it apply solely to those whose permanent abode is elsewhere than in Makka itself, since God specifically said, 'that is for those whose household is not present in the sacred mosque.'[269]

He who is obstructed by enemy action and cannot reach the Ka'ba abandons all taboos, sacrifices his offering and shaves his head at the point where he was halted. He is not required to substitute a later pilgrimage for this aborted one.

> The Prophet had done precisely that at Ḥudaybiya, not having been able to make the circuit of the Kaʿba and before his sacrificial offering had reached the place where it would have been slaughtered.[270]

Muḥammad's *ihlāl* had, on that occasion, been for an *ʿumra* and, in terms of Q 2.196, *tamattuʿ* occurs *after* removal of any obstruction. For Mālik, obstruction refers solely to enemy action.

> A Basran, making his way to Makka, had an accident and suffered a broken thigh. Messengers were sent to Makka to make enquiries. ʿAbdallāh b. ʿAbbās and ʿAbdallāh b. ʿUmar were consulted, among others, and none permitted the man to abandon *iḥrām*. He was detained at the scene of the accident for seven months before he could release himself from *iḥrām* when he was fit enough to proceed and complete an *ʿumra*.[271]

> A second person was unseated by his mount. Making enquiries of ʿAbdallāh b. ʿUmar, ʿAbdallāh b. al-Zubayr and Marwān b. al-Ḥakam, he was informed that any indispensable medication might be applied, but he would be required to furnish one of the three penalties listed in Q 2.196. When sufficiently recovered, the performance of an *ʿumra* would release him from *iḥrām* for the time being, but he would be required to return the following year to purge the *ihlāl* of the *ḥajj* by the completion of the pilgrimage. For the present, the release from *iḥrām* required that he provide a sacrificial offering.

ʿUmar had delivered similar judgment in cases when, miscounting the days, people arrived late for the *ḥajj* ceremonies.[272]

> ʿAbdallāh b. ʿUmar stated that he would rather perform the *ʿumra* before the *ḥajj* and have to provide a sacrificial offering than perform the *ʿumra* after the *ḥajj* in the twelfth month.[273]

> He also reports his father's saying, 'Keep your *ʿumra* separate from your *ḥajj*. To perform the *ʿumra* in any except the pilgrimage months makes both your *ʿumra* and your *ḥajj* complete.'[274]

ʿAbdallāh explains that 'the pilgrimage months' are months ten, eleven and twelve.[275] That the 'pilgrimage season' is one of months, rather than one of the first ten days of the last month of the year, may well reflect God's words: 'The *ḥajj* is well-known months'. Being plural, that would suggest at least three.

> Asked if the Prophet had performed the *ʿumra* before the *ḥajj*, the Madīnan scholar Saʿīd said he had. ʿUrwa clarifies this: the Prophet performed three *ʿumras*: once in the tenth month, and twice in the twelfth month.[276]

That has nothing to do with the questions discussed by ʿUmar and the others who were concerned with the effects of the performance of an *ʿumra* and a *ḥajj* in one and the same visit.

In the foregoing series of *ḥadīth*s on the *mutʿa*, the term had attracted a range of definitions. It was said to mean:

> 1. temporary marriage; 2. the combination of an *ʿumra* with a *ḥajj*; 3. *tamattuʿ*; 4. the abandonment of all the taboos attaching to the *ḥajj*, on completing an *ʿumra*; 5. the completion of an *ʿumra* and a *ḥajj* in the course of a single visit to Makka; 6. the enjoyment of women during the *ḥajj*; 7. the alteration of a solemn declaration to perform a *ḥajj* and the substitution of an *ʿumra* instead; 8. the performance of an *ʿumra* 'during the first ten days', that is, during the period peculiar to the *ḥajj* alone.

We touched above on the strict dress regulations attaching to the pilgrimage.

> Asked about this, the Prophet replied, 'Wear no shirt, nor turban, nor trousers, nor burnus, nor boots – unless one of you has no sandals. He may then take boots and cut them below ankle-height. Wear no garment that has come into contact with saffron or turmeric.'[277]

An alternative form of this wording was in circulation: 'boots are for those who cannot afford sandals; trousers for those who have no waist-wrapper'. When asked about this version, Mālik declared he had never heard it. The Prophet had prohibited the wearing of trousers.[278]

THE USE OF DYESTUFFS

> ʿUmar saw Ṭalḥa in a dyed vest when in *iḥrām* and asked him to explain that, 'It's just clay-stained', he said. 'Listen,' said ʿUmar, 'you men are leaders whom the people imitate. If some of the unlearned see this, they'll say: "Ṭalḥa used to wear dyed garments when in *iḥrām*", so see that you don't wear anything coloured in this way.'[279]

> Asked whether he disapproved of a garment that exuded perfume, Mālik replied that that was indifferent, so long as, in the case of *iḥrām*, there was no hint of any yellow colour.[280]

> Yaʿlā had long cherished the wish to see revelation descend. One day, a man, wearing a vest dyed with some yellowish colouring, approached the Prophet and asked him about the *ʿumra* rites. Revelation came down and the Prophet had to be covered in an overgarment. Raising the corner of the garment, ʿUmar beckoned to Yaʿlā. Looking inside, he saw the Prophet's face had gone red and he was snuffling like a young camel. The revelation ascended and the Prophet, recovering, said, 'Wash off all trace of

yellow, put off the vest and do in the *ʿumra* precisely what you do in the *ḥajj*'.[281]

Instead of 'yellowish', variants have 'exuding perfume'.[282]

Sniffing, ʿUmar detected the smell of perfume. 'Where's this odour coming from?' he demanded. Muʿāwiya said his sister had perfumed him before he set out. 'Go back this minute,' thundered ʿUmar, 'and wash all that stuff off.'[283]

Mālik thought there was no harm in a man's greasing his hair, if the preparation contained no perfume, but he admitted that his older authorities were divided on this question.[284]

ʿUmar detected an odour of perfume from one man's head. The man said he had smeared it, but had no intention of cutting his hair until he had completed the *ḥajj*. ʿUmar made him use the water at the base of a palm tree to wash it off.[285]

Ibn ʿUmar would oil his hair when setting out on pilgrimage. But the oil he used was quite odourless.[286]

On the contrary,

ʿĀ'isha insisted that she used to smear the Prophet's person with perfume before he assumed his *iḥrām*. She repeated the process towards the end of the *ḥajj*, to prepare him for his *iḥlāl*, before his final visit to the Kaʿba.[287]

ʿUmar is reported to have declared that the final act of the pilgrimage and the shaving of the head frees the pilgrim from all restrictions *except* those in respect of women and perfume.[288]

Sālim, grandson of ʿUmar, and cited by Mālik for the contrary proposition, reporting, sometimes on his father's authority, sometimes on his own authority, is quoted as saying, 'But the practice of the Prophet has more claim to be followed'.

ʿĀ'isha's claim is not contradicted by the Prophet's reply to the man in the dyed vest. What he objected to was not the odour of perfume, but traces of the yellow dyestuff. Both that man and the Prophet had applied the perfume before assuming the *iḥrām*. That the odour persisted after the adoption of *iḥrām* is irrelevant.[289]

The above Sālim report had appeared between Mālik and Shāfiʿī.

MARRIAGE DURING THE PILGRIMAGE

A man invited Abān, who was presiding over the *ḥajj*, to join him in celebrating the marriage of his son to a certain lady. Abān disapproved, informing the man that his father, the caliph ʿUthmān, had told him that the Prophet had said, 'The pilgrim

> may neither wed, nor arrange any marriage, nor ask for any woman's hand in marriage'.
>
> ʿUmar dissolved a marriage contracted by a pilgrim. ʿUmar's son taught that no man might wed, nor ask for a woman in marriage for himself or for another, if in *iḥrām*.
>
> The three ancient authorities at Madīna, Saʿīd, Sālim and Sulaymān, when consulted, all said, 'In *iḥrām*, none may wed, nor arrange another's marriage'.[290]

The greatest confusion attends the circumstances in which the Prophet married his last wife, Maymūna. She was sister-in-law to his uncle, ʿAbbās, who is said to have arranged the union in the course of 'the fulfilled *ʿumra*'. The claims that both groom and bride were in *iḥrām*, and that neither of them was, show such perfect balance that it is impossible to decide between them.

> The prophet is said to have sent two messengers to ʿAbbās. Their camels going astray, they were delayed and were, in fact overtaken by the Prophet on his way to Makka. They therefore accompanied him and, on reaching Makka, he sent them on their errand. The Prophet then asked ʿAbbās for her hand in marriage and ʿAbbās concluded the contract.[291]

One pole of the discussion is represented by reports handed down by one of the three ancient Madīnan authorities mentioned above, Sulaymān b. Yasār. He was the freedman of Maymūna, and

> he reports from one of the two men whom the Prophet is said to have sent from Madīna, Abū Rāfiʿ, the Prophet's freedman, that he and another wed Muḥammad to Maymuna before he had even left Madīna, i.e. before he had assumed the *iḥrām*.[292]

A second of the old Madīnan authorities,

> Saʿīd, when informed that ʿIḳrima, the freedman and pupil of ʿAbdallāh b. ʿAbbās, reported that the Prophet had been *muḥrim* when he married Maymūna, replied, 'Go back and insult that fellow. The Prophet arrived in *iḥrām* but married her only after his *iḥlāl*.[293]
>
> Maymūn b. Mihrān was sitting with the great Makkan scholar, ʿAṭā', when a man approached and asked, 'May the *muḥrim* wed?' ʿAṭā' replied, 'Since the day He instituted marriage, God has not declared it unlawful'. Maymūn said, '"Umar b. ʿAbdul ʿAzīz wrote to me when I was Governor of the Jazīra, telling me to send for Yazīd b. al-Aṣamm and ask him whether the Prophet had been *ḥalāl* or *ḥarām* the day he married Maymūna. Yazīd said, "He was *ḥalāl*" – now Maymūna was Yazīd's aunt.' ʿAṭā', however, said, 'We would accept only Maymūna's word on that.

Now, we have heard that the Prophet was *muḥrim* when he married her.'[294]

Yazīd b. al-Aṣamm insists that Muḥammad was *ḥalāl* when he wed Maymūna and he was *ḥalāl* when he consummated the marriage.[295]

The second pole of the discussion is 'Aṭā''s report that 'ibn 'Abbās said that Muḥammad had been *muḥrim* when he wed her'.[296] The complication is that Maymūna was also ibn 'Abbās's aunt. Despite one curious *ḥadīth* in which 'Yazīd b. al-Aṣamm reports from ibn 'Abbās that he had said that the Prophet had wed Maymūna when he was *ḥalāl*, ibn 'Abbās is the chief authority for the opposite view that he had been *muḥrim* when he married.[297] That view was then, as we see, taken up by his pupils in Makka.

It was also disseminated by some who had heard him in Iraq.

Sufyān b. 'Uyayna mentioned the ibn 'Abbās *ḥadīth* to Zuhrī, who replied, 'But Yazīd b. al-Aṣamm told me that he was *ḥalāl* when he married her'.[298]

Yazīd b. al-Aṣamm told another man, 'Maymūna told me herself that the Prophet was *ḥalāl* when he married her – she was my aunt and ibn 'Abbās's aunt'.[299]

The Makkan scholar 'Amr ask Zuhrī, 'Are you putting Yazīd on a par with ibn 'Abbās?'[300]

For Shāfi'ī, nephew cancels out nephew, leaving Sulaymān,

Maymūna's freedman who would be well informed on her affairs, and 'Uthmān who was certainly well informed on Muḥammad's, having been converted at a very early date, and thus accompanied the Prophet for many more years than most Muslims. 'Uthmān's reference to the declaration of the Prophet was immediate and direct and is the strongest source of information that could be wished for.[301]

It is, however, Mālik's Iraqi pupil, Muḥammad, who brings out clearly that this is a matter of regional disagreement.[302]

There is disagreement on this topic. The Madīnans consider the marriage of the *muḥrim* null and void. The Makkans and the Iraqis recognise the marriage as valid. 'Abdallāh b. 'Abbās reported that the Prophet was *muḥrim* when he wed Maymūna, and we know of no-one more likely to be informed on the Prophet's marriage to Maymūna than her own nephew. We see nothing amiss in the *muḥrim*'s marrying, although he must neither kiss nor consummate until he is *ḥalāl*. That was also the view of Abū Ḥanīfa and the great number of our *fuqahā*'.

Although Muḥammad disapproved of the use of perfume by one intending to assume the *iḥrām*, unless he immediately washed it off, he reports that Abū Ḥanīfa had seen nothing amiss in its use. Iraqi opinion had shifted within one generation.[303]

Had the Successors been in direct contact with the generation of the Companions and so, through them, with the Prophet himself, as is both the presupposition and indeed, expressed claim of those who cultivated the *Ḥadīth* so energetically, one would not expect this degree of uncertainty, ignorance and disagreement on cardinal chapters of the law, the pilgrimage and the marriage regulations, both said to have been definitively regulated by the Prophet in his day. To Shaybānī we owe the information that the two parties to this dispute were, on the one hand, the Makkan and Iraqi schools, and on the other hand the school of Madīna. Characteristic is the role played by ibn ʿAbbās in the documentation of the Makkan view. Somewhat surprising is the non-appearance of ibn Masʿūd, the normal representative of the Kufan view. The question at issue may well not have arisen until Umayyad times, when locally fixed attitudes were seen to be at variance and the search for documentation first undertaken. That the result was stalemate, neither side succeeding in convincing the other, meant that it would prove impossible to achieve a Muslim consensus on the question. The schools had no alternative but to agree to continue to disagree, consoling themselves with the reminder that the Prophet himself had said: 'Differences among my people are a divine mercy';[304] where final agreement proved impossible, a resigned recognition of each locality's right to maintain its traditional attitude came to prevail. Such conflict of *ḥadīth* with *ḥadīth* naturally raises the question of the source of both sets of documentation. It does suggest that one function of the *ḥadīth* was the documentation of locally achieved consensus.

THE PENALTY FOR ADULTERY

Not merely Iraqis and Ḥijāzīs, but all Sunnīs and Shīʿīs achieved unanimity on a major question in the penal law. It was the opposition of a minority that provoked, in response, the efforts of the scholars of all regions to locate the source of their agreement that the penalty for adultery was death by stoning. The question involved matters of much greater import than conflict of *ḥadīth* and *ḥadīth*. It was a matter of the apparent conflict of *ḥadīth* with Quran. The results of the scholarly effort reinforced, if it did not create, differing attitudes among the schools on how to proceed in the event of such an embarrassing problem as had been forced into the open by this discussion. What is one to say when *ḥadīth*s traced from the Prophet contradict the Book of God which has reached us only through the Prophet?

The oldest surviving attempt to locate the source of this death penalty is that undertaken by Mālik, whose analysis identifies three separate sources suggested by scholars active in earlier generations. Mālik had heard that the historical source of the penalty had been 'the Book of God'. The Quran recognises a series of divine revelations or books of God. The pre-Tora, Tora and post-Tora prophets had all been granted written revelations: Abraham, Moses, Christ and Muḥammad.[305] Certain Quran verses mention the distinction between the books compiled by the rabbis and the divinely guaranteed Tora.[306] Other verses speak of their suppression of the divine word, such as the previous revelations foretelling the coming of Muḥammad;[307] yet other verses condemn the distortion of 'the word of God'.[308]

Most early commentators teach that whenever Muḥammad approached the rabbis for information, they gleefully misinformed him, from jealousy at his having been selected for the office of Prophet. Many versions circulate of a story that, when a Jewish couple were discovered to have committed adultery, the rabbis preferred to send them to Muḥammad for judgment, hoping that he would be ignorant of their law, or disposed to impose a more lenient penalty. Warned either directly by Heaven, or indirectly through his suspicion of their motives, Muḥammad closely questioned the Jewish party, at length demanding that the scrolls be brought out from the synagogue to reassure himself of the truth. Jewish hypocrisy is emphasised in these stories. Either, when questioned, the rabbis informed Muḥammad that the penalty in their law was flogging, or, once the scrolls were brought out, the rabbi lector leaned his hand on the page as he recited the sacred texts above and below his hand. Only when a Jewish convert to Islam forced the man to remove his hand was the wording of the stoning-verse of the Tora visible for all to see. Muḥammad ordered that the penalty be carried out. 'Abdallāh b. 'Umar avers that he attended their execution.[309]

When, in a later compilation, one scholar asked another whether Muḥammad had ever verifiably imposed the stoning penalty, the reply could be given with confidence. He had indeed done so.[310]

The second section of Mālik's study consists of *ḥadīth*s that illustrate the claim that Muḥammad had equally verifiably applied the stoning penalty to Muslim offenders, male as well as female, when his demand for four witnesses was satisfied, or, by analogy, an offender confessed four times. The contents of the several *ḥadīth*s are summarised:

> ibn 'Abbās heard 'Umar say: 'The stoning penalty is a just claim made in the Book of God against any male or female who, being married [*muḥṣan*], engages in extra marital sexual activity, when

evidence is laid, pregnancy results, or a confession is volunteered'.[311]

The four witnesses, or their equivalent, the fourfold self-condemnation, is reminiscent of Q 4.15 which, however, concerns only females guilty of an 'abomination', *fāḥisha*. If four bear witness against her, the woman is to be locked up for life 'or until God appoint a way'. The four witnesses and the fourfold accusation motifs recur at Q 24:4–6, on slander.

Among the *ḥadīth*s in Mālik's second section is a report in which pains are taken to stress that, invited in one case to adjudicate on the basis of *the Book of God*, the Prophet formally undertakes to render judgment on the basis of *the Book of God*. Here, offenders were of mixed status. Muḥammad stoned the married party; he flogged the unmarried male and banished him (or ostracised him?) for twelve months. The man received 100 lashes – a motif that occurs at Q 24.2.[312]

It is Mālik's third section which is the most illuminating.

> In the course of a public address to the believers of Madīna, 'Umar insists that the duties have been established and the obligations put in place. Men had been left in perfect clarity. Should they thereafter stray from the path, it would be their own doing. They must not neglect the stoning-'verse', which would be the result of someone's saying, 'But we don't find two penalties in the Book of God'. 'Umar insists that the Prophet had stoned and the caliphs after him had stoned. Only the fear that he might be accused of 'adding to the Book of God' prevented him from then and there writing into the text: 'the mature male and female, stone them to death'. 'We certainly recited this verse in the ritual prayers.'[313]

Only what was verifiably revealed to Muḥammad may be recited in the ritual prayers or recorded in the sacred texts.

That Mālik may have heard, although he does not record a relevant *ḥadīth*, is suggested by his glossing 'Umar's words, *shaykh wa shaykha*, as *thayyib wa thayyiba*.[314] The latter have the meaning 'non-virgin', that is, currently or at least previously, married. The expression 'We don't find two penalties in the Book of God' doubtless refers to the penalty which is present in Q 24.2: 'the female and male fornicators, flog each of them 100 strokes of the lash'.

When the Prophet undertook to judge on the basis of *the Book of God*, he flogged the unmarried male. Mālik drives his search for the source of the stoning penalty no further. His pupil, Shāfi'ī, took up what Mālik had initiated. For him, the fact that the *ḥadīth*s, especially those traced from the Prophet, must be followed, is a belief founded on the interpretation of all the verses in the Quran in which Muḥammad's contemporaries had been commanded to obey God and His Prophet. Those who disobey the Prophet disobey God; those who obey Muḥammad obey God.[315] All are bluntly advised that they will not be true believers until they appoint Muḥammad to adjudicate on all matters.[316] They are required to 'take what the Prophet gives you and desist from what he denies you'.[317] All questions must be submitted to God and His Prophet. In the post-Prophetic age, such verses proved a potent weapon in response to any who raised against any *ḥadīth* the protest: 'But we don't find that in the Book of God'. God threatens with Hellfire any who stubbornly refuse to hear what Muḥammad commanded or fail to do precisely as he says. Paradise is promised to all who subordinate their will to that of Muḥammad and hasten without hesitation to do his bidding. The warning and the promise verses were resurrected and pointed at any who dared set Quran against *Ḥadīth*. The divine command is directed not solely to the Prophet's contemporaries, but is for all ages and falls upon all who hear it. Nor would God lay a command upon men without providing the means by which they might fulfil it. God has made it possible for all who are distant from Muḥammad to acquaint themselves with the will of Muḥammad and knowledge of his commands and prohibitions. Not to have met Muḥammad, or seen him, or heard him is no excuse for failing to adhere unquestioningly to his instruction. All have access to the knowledge of God's will and that of His inspired Prophet. The function of the *Ḥadīth* is not to provide a distant echo of the Prophet's voice. It is the means created by a solicitous Lord to preserve the Prophet in men's midst, despite his physical separation from them in death. The divine command to hear and obey Muḥammad extends to his *Ḥadīth* in which the Prophet continues to command and prohibit. Whoever is commanded to obey the Prophet is commanded to obey the *Ḥadīth* of the Prophet, for only so does the eternal command make sense. To accept the *Ḥadīth* as from Muḥammad is to accept it from God.[318]

We saw that in the mid-second century the concept of *sunna* was still that of the continuous practice of the Muslims that had come down from the past. In the work of Shāfiʿī, this concept was irreversibly modified. His discursive analyses of the current state of the Law, more especially of the bases on which it had been erected, the fabric of which must be constantly maintained, were conducted in the entirely novel light of regarding Islam as a divine revelation, not solely in its origin but in its historical continuation. For Shāfiʿī, Islam was an abiding, a continuing revelation and its sources were two: the Book of God and the *sunna* of the Prophet of God to whom alone God had granted the prerogative to interpret/elucidate His Book. To obey

Muḥammad is to obey God; to disobey him is to disobey God, or, as Shāfiʿī words it, 'Muḥammad's rulings are God's rulings'.[319] The path to obeying Muḥammad is the path to obeying God, that is, acceptance of and adherence to the *sunna* of the Prophet alone. To guarantee purity of belief and practice, it is essential to identify for every question, and especially for every disputed question, the uniquely authoritative ruling established by God and His Prophet. Determined that His holy will would be unambiguous to all men, God had never permitted His Prophet to diverge from the instruction He had selected him to deliver. Having been called to high office and not having achieved prophethood by any effort on his part, Muḥammad had been perfectly aware that he had no liberty to vary the message which he had been sent to deliver. When the Makkans, who neither aspired to nor feared an afterlife, complained to Muḥammad about the message and advised him to change it or bring another, God told him to reply:

> 'It's not for me to alter it on my own initiative. I merely follow what is implanted in my mind. If I disobeyed my Lord, I'd dread the punishment of a most terrible day.' [Q 10.15].

In the Q 53 passage, construed by some as reporting an actual encounter with the Creator, Muḥammad was commanded to recite:

> 'Your compatriot has not erred, nor gone astray. He does not speak as he desires. It is but divine inspiration that is implanted in his mind. One of great powers has taught him. One of might who ascended. He was on the highest point of the horizon. He then descended and drew near until only two bows' length distant, or even nearer. He revealed to his creature what he revealed.'

Citing these two passages, together with the numerous contexts in which the Quran identifies the will of Muḥammad with the will of God, Shāfiʿī seeks to convince that the extra-Quranic utterances of Muḥammad are, like the Quran, of divine origin. There are two revelations, that which may be recited in the daily ritual prayers, and that which may not be recited in the prayers since, although, like the other, the content is revealed, the wording had been left to Muḥammad's discretion. This second revelation is the revelation of the *Ḥadīth* of the Prophet.[320]

This conviction enabled Shāfiʿī to make sense of the apparent confusion in the development of the attitudes of the Muslims on every significant question. Had Islamic Law, for instance, been based exclusively on Quran texts, the Muslims would have amputated a limb in every single instance of theft. They would have inflicted 100 lashes in every single instance of sexual irregularity.[321] That they do not may not be taken as grounds for alleging that the Prophet's instructions departed from those of the Quran. A Prophet ruling could never conceivably conflict with the Book of God.

Q 24.2 appears to impose 100 lashes on every fornicator.[322] But Q 4.25 imposes on slave-fornicators one half of the penalty.[323] There is therefore a category of fornicator to whom Q 24.2 does not apply. A whole category has been excluded from the provisions of the Q 24 verse.[324] The *ḥadīth*s show that, in stoning married offenders, the Prophet did not flog them in addition.[325] Taken together, Quran and *Ḥadīth* show that Q 24.2 applies solely to unmarried, free Muslims. If the free, married Muslim had been intended initially to be included in the provisions of Q 24, the *Ḥadīth* has shown that they form a second excluded category. On the other hand, married persons are different from unmarried persons, so they probably were never intended to be included in the Q 24 provision. No slave is ever stoned – indeed, there is no definable half for stoning. Slaves are flogged fifty lashes. Q 4.25 said that their penalty was to be half of the penalty: 100 lashes are imposed only on free Muslims. The *Ḥadīth* records its imposition on the unmarried partner. Thus, Q 24.2 applies exclusively to the free, unmarried fornicator.[326]

The stoning penalty entered the Islamic penal code by inadvertence. The focus of Mālik's *ḥadīth* about the Jews who applied to Muḥammad for judgment was not, in fact, the stoning penalty as such. Any clauṣe of the law could have been used to illustrate the main theme of the story: the unreliability of the rabbis and their constant readiness to misinform Muḥammad whenever he applied to them for information on a religious or a legal question. The story inevitably reminds one of that in John, 8: 1–11, with which it shares the common propaganda theme of showing the new Prophet scoring points over the representatives of the older code. Mālik's text shows the literary provenance of his story. His wording, 'The Jews came to Muḥammad for judgment', is the exegetical-cum-biographical reflex of Q 5.42: 'and if they come to you, either judge between them or ignore them ...'. There follow instructions on the source in which the judgment should be sought: 'the Tora in which is guidance and light and on whose basis the prophets who professed Islam judge the Jews ...'.

Mālik, whose opening words suggest the nature of his report, makes no direct reference to the details of the Q 5 passage. His pupil, Shāfiʿī, on the other hand, who was much exercised by this question of stoning, cites the Q 5 passage extensively to develop at much greater length the theme of the unreliability of Jewish scholars, the fate of the divine revelations at the hands of the rabbis and their unacceptability as witnesses in Islamic courts. One will find here the classic statement of the allegation that the Jews had not merely concealed but actually distorted and even altered the wording of the sacred texts entrusted to their care.[327] It is a matter of total indifference to Shāfiʿī that there is a stoning-verse in the Tora. That is quite irrelevant, since Muḥammad had consistently rendered judgment solely on the basis of what had been revealed *to him* in the latest divine revelation in which was no trace of any extraneous matter. Muḥammad stoned adulterers since that is what had been revealed *to him*, and in stoning the Jews he had merely applied to them the penalty instituted in Islam which he had *already* applied to Muslim offenders.[328] Shāfiʿī expended much time and ingenuity in seeking to restore the position that had been disturbed by those who complained that they could not find two penalties in the Book of God. Reviewing the history of the evolution within Islam of the penalties established in Islam, he worked out a clear chronology. His starting point is Q 4.15.

> Women accused of 'abomination' are to be locked up for life on the evidence of four Muslim witnesses ... until God appoints a way.

Mālik had not cited the following *ḥadīth*, yet it proved to be the very cornerstone of Shāfiʿī's apparatus.

> ʿUbāda reported that the Prophet one day said, 'Take it from me, take it from me! God has now appointed the way for the *women*: the unmarried with the unmarried, 100 lashes and twelve months' banishment; the married with the married, 100 lashes and death by stoning.'[329]

This *ḥadīth* circulated in numerous versions, several of which underline that this wording had been *revealed* to the Prophet.[330] The artificiality of this wording is transparent. Apart from its appropriation of the Q 59.7 wording – a favourite Shāfiʿī proof of the religious obligation to adhere to the *Ḥadīth* of the Prophet – the use to which this *ḥadīth* is put by Shāfiʿī is obvious. It existed to bridge the gap between Q 4.15, Q 24.2 and the stoning penalty of the law. ʿUbāda, he says, as is clear from the expression 'Now God has appointed the way for the women', reports on the first *revelation* to reach Muḥammad after Q 4.15. The fresh revelation abrogated Q 4.15's locking up for life. The next revelation to come down, Q 24.2, 'endorsed' the flogging element in the two dual penalties contained in the ʿUbāda report. Q 4.25 imposed on slaves half the penalty – that is, half the Q 24.2 penalty, since slaves are flogged fifty strokes. For the *thayyib*, or married offender, ʿUbāda's report shows that the penalty had once been *both* flogging and death by stoning. Reports show the Prophet stoning married offenders *without* flogging them. This indicates that, in respect of those who are stoned, the additional flogging element has been dispensed with entirely.[331] The entire series of reports shows for

Shāfiʿī only conflict of *ḥadīth*s. The stoning *ḥadīth*s abrogated the stoning-with-flogging *ḥadīth*s.[332]

Those who had rejected the stoning penalty on the grounds that they could not find two penalties in the Book of God would have approved of a *ḥadīth* which has the Prophet say:

> 'Compare what purports to come from me with the Book of God. What agrees with it, I have said; what disagrees with it, I have not said.'[333]

The report claims that, as the Prophet would never have said or done anything not in conformity with the Quran, the Quran is the criterion by which reports as to the Prophet's acts or words are to be judged. That claim was, however, as we have just seen, in the case of the Islamic penalties for adultery, judged to be highly subversive. It threatened a structure of laws that had developed in the period since the Prophet and had been inherited by the generations before Mālik and Shāfiʿī, the very men engaged in working out a theory of sources and, in the case of the latter, a theory of the *Ḥadīth* that would document and preserve that heritage. Shāfiʿī knew and cited the *ḥadīth*, only to dismiss it on the grounds of inadequate attestation. It had not, he says, been transmitted by any person recognised by the *Ḥadīth* specialists as reliable. Its curt dismissal was inevitable. The role of the *Ḥadīth* scholars was one of defending and justifying the practices which they upheld in the belief that they were part of the Tradition. They could not approve of any document which challenged the very basis of the same practices. Shāfiʿī and his fellow *Ḥadīth* specialists preferred a second *ḥadīth*:

> The Prophet said, 'Let me not find any of you who says, when a command or a prohibition that I have uttered comes to him, "I don't know. We shall follow what we find in the Book of God."'[334]

Shāfiʿī alleges that vis-à-vis the Holy Quran, reports from the Prophet fall into three categories, on two of which there is agreement among the scholars.

1. where there is a text in the Quran and the relevant *ḥadīth* from the Prophet conforms precisely with that text.
2. where the text in the Quran is couched in general terms and the *ḥadīth* illustrates the precise meaning that was intended.
3. where there is a *ḥadīth* on a topic on which the Quran is silent.

It is the third class of *ḥadīth* that occasioned contention.[335] Some scholars insisted that Muḥammad had never instituted any ruling on any matter unless it was referred to, at least in principle, in the Quran. For example, the Quran insists on the obligation to pray. It was the Prophet who showed how many prayers were required, and when, and the precise manner in which they were to be performed. Similarly, he showed precisely how commercial transactions were to be validly conducted and all other such legal matters. Others say that all his enactments were guaranteed by the fact of his sacred office. Some held that God had imposed on all men the religious obligation to adhere to all Muḥammad's commands and prohibitions, having determined from all eternity to direct Muḥammad to what is pleasing to Himself in whatever he instituted on topics not mentioned in the Quran. Finally, it was said that all of Muḥammad's activities were directly revealed. The *Ḥadīth* of the Prophet supplements the Quran, elucidating on God's behalf what God intended by His regulations. Furthermore, the *Ḥadīth* is complete.

> The prophet stated, 'I have omitted to command nothing that God commanded, and have omitted to prohibit nothing that God prohibited'.[336]

In Shāfiʿī's view, God had appointed Muḥammad both to deliver and to interpret the minutest details of the revelation, and both functions are covered in the peremptory divine command that men obey the Prophet of God in all things.

The reports that Muḥammad had ever stoned anyone had determined the development of that aspect of the law. That they had come into circulation at a very early date tends to be indicated by the impressive unanimity on the topic, not only among all the Sunnī scholars in all centres throughout the Empire, but also between the Sunnīs and the Shīʿīs. The attempt by a minority to question the validity of the ruling serves to underline this unanimity which contrasts with their differences and disputes on a host of other questions, great and small. That the scholars of the second century no longer understood how that regulation had originated is clear from Mālik's efforts to locate its source. His three attempts to trace it had in common the belief that it had originated in 'the Book of God', which he then defined further as the Tora, or the Prophet's legal practice, or the Quran. The efforts of Shāfiʿī to meet the challenge thrown down by those who rejected stoning on the grounds that they could not find two penalties in the Book of God, that is, in the written texts of the Quran in circulation, merely served to heighten the tension between the Quran and the *Ḥadīth*, although they showed Shāfiʿī's position and that of the *Ḥadīth* scholars in general. It is the *Ḥadīth* that exerts priority over the Quran, and not the other way round. The protest of those who complained that they could not find two penalties in the Book of God came after scholars had agreed on the stoning penalty, and so too late to affect the issue. Seen as acting in defence of the legal proposition, Shāfiʿī's argumentation and the *ḥadīth*s which he deployed to retain and justify the stoning penalty may be called technical. That is, the *ḥadīth*s were not aimed at ascertaining the prophet's attitude, but, using what is alleged to have been his attitude, as displayed in the reports which Shāfiʿī's generation had inherited, the *ḥadīth*s aim rather to entrench the legal ruling and provide a mechanism for linking it with the prophet in such a way as to obviate objections to it.

Other instances of *ḥadīth*s serving a technical need would, for example, include the report to the effect that, leading the ritual prayer on one occasion, the Prophet is said to have omitted a verse in his Quran recitation. On completing the prayer, Muḥammad asked Ubayy why he had not prompted him.

> 'I thought perhaps the passage had been withdrawn', replied Ubayy. 'No,' said the Prophet, 'it wasn't withdrawn; I just forget it at that moment.'[337]

The technicalities of this exchange are, first, the allegation that a clear distinction should be drawn between Muḥammad's reported forgetting an item of revelation and a divine decision to withdraw a portion of revelation.

In the very long-drawn-out debates among the scholars on abrogation, considerable attention was given to the Quran passages alleged to refer to various aspects of the procedure. In Q 87.6–7, God assured His Prophet that

> He would instruct him in the Quran and that he would never forget – except what God willed.

When God wished Muḥammad to forget, Muḥammad would assuredly forget. But, could Muḥammad forget where God did not will it? Some had gone so far as to deny that Muḥammad had ever forgotten any item of revelation – unless it had been withdrawn. That may have represented not merely a technical argument, that is, on the methods by which abrogation could be effected, but a reading of the relevant verse in which both terms occurred side by side: Q 2.106: 'Whatever *āya* We *naskh* or you forget', which took the second verb to be a gloss on the first, the rather difficult term *naskh*.[338]

In the circles which cultivated the *Ḥadīth* and would insist that the goal of the pious Muslim should be to discover what the Prophet had done in various situations, and then model one's own conduct on his prophetic example, to be sure of acting correctly, a question that arose and had to be faced was: what action ought a Muslim to take in the event that he miscounted the elements of the ritual prayer? From reports, it was discovered that the Prophet had suffered such a mishap more than once. He had on one occasion performed too few, and on another too many *rakʿa*s. The congregation, pointing this out to him, in order to make certain that the ritual had been neither shortened nor lengthened, received the reply: 'I am human. I forget as you forget, and when I forget, please remind me.'[339] A version has: 'I forget – or am made to forget – in order that I may establish a practice',[340] that is, the practice of the two prostrations to be performed in the event of miscounting the constituent elements of the prayer. The above Ubayy *ḥadīth* similarly established, second, the distinction between Muḥammad's prophetic and his human memory.

Much debated was the difficult term which the scholars employed to signify abrogation, namely *naskh*. The word occurs twice in the Quran and, in the prolonged debates that raged over the etymology and meaning of the term, the scholars, both exegetes and legal theorists, tended on the whole to favour the opinion that it means 'to replace'. Abrogation, however, as discussed by the Muslims, is a complex, multi-faceted phenomenon certain aspects of which cannot be clearly grasped on the basis of restricting the meaning of *naskh* to 'replacement' alone. It could even be argued that in the key reference to abrogation, Q 2.106, 'Whatever *āya* We *naskh* or cause you to forget', it would not be certain that the word meant 'to replace' without the apodosis: 'We shall bring one better than it, or similar'. That one *āya* replaces another owes rather more to Q 16.101: 'and when We substitute one *āya* for another, they say: "You're just making this up"' than to Q 2.106, or, at any rate, to its protasis, 'When We *naskh*".

5

The Theological Dimension of the Ḥadīth

The Quran was not designed as a handbook of systematic theology. Intended to persuade, it emphasises now the limitless powers of the Almighty, now the freedom of the individual to choose the path to salvation or that to damnation.

Otherwise intelligent listeners who ignored or scoffed at the Prophet's urgent warnings may be portrayed as denied by deliberate divine action of the power to see and hear. The heedless had been rendered incapable of belief and so of benefiting from the divine communications. Muḥammad cannot make the deaf hear, nor the blind see. He cannot guide those whom he chooses. Only those whom God pleases will have their breasts expanded to receive the message.

> Those who reject belief, it is all the same whether you warn them or not, they will not believe. God has sealed their minds and their ears and over their eyes there is a covering. (Q 2.6–7)

Yet, there appears to be some choice for which the listeners must bear some responsibility; but even that is removed.

> This is but a reminder. Whoever chooses may take the path to God. But they cannot wish to do so, unless God wishes. (Q 73.19)

> It is but a reminder to all beings, To those of you who wish to go straight. But you will not wish so, unless God, the Lord of all beings, wish it. (Q 76.29–30)

> We have sent into every people a prophet [instructing them]: 'Worship God alone and avoid rebelliousness'; there were those whom God guided, and there were those who deserved error. (Q 16.36)

> Consider those who have made their desires their god, whom God has knowingly misled, and sealed their hearing, their mind, and covered their eyes. Who, apart from God, can guide such? (Q 45.23)

> We have sent no messenger, but with his people's language, so that he can make clear to them. But God misleads whom He pleases and guides whom He pleases. He is the Almighty, the Judicious. (Q. 14.4)

> Even if you are eager to guide them, God does not guide those whom He has misled. (Q. 16.37)

> You cannot guide whom you choose. God guides whom He chooses. (Q. 28.56)

But the Quran also urges to action and promises ample reward.

> We shall certainly repay those who have been patient according to their best acts. Whoever does good, whether male or female, being a believer, We shall bring to a pleasant rebirth and will certainly reward them for the best that they have done. (Q 16.96–7)

> Whoso does good does so to the benefit of his soul; whoso does evil does so to his own soul's hurt. Your Lord is not unjust to those He has created. (Q 41.46)

> God promises those who believe and do good works that they will find forgiveness and a mighty reward. Those who reject and belie Our message will be the inmates of Hell. (Q 5.9–10)

> Whoever earns [the reward of] evil and is consumed by his sins, those will be the inmates of Hell, there to abide. Those who believe and do good works, those will be the inmates of Heaven, there to abide. (Q 2.81–2)

The Quran urges to action. It requires men to worship, to contribute generously to charitable causes; it incites them to involve themselves in 'the cause of God' with their wealth and their lives. It requires truthfulness, faithfulness to one's trusts, generosity, courage and effort. It exhorts men to strive for the great prize awaiting those who believe and engage in the right conduct based on sincere motives. It condemns all untruth, meanness of spirit, cowardice, hypocrisy and empty public display of piety.

Emphasising the absolute dependence of the creature upon the limitless powers of the Creator while at the same time belittling the value of human action, the *Ḥadīth* erected a theology heavily weighted in the direction of bleak predestinarianism.

> Describing the development of the foetus in the womb, the Prophet is reported as announcing: 'The angel sent to breathe the spirit of life into the new creature is given orders to record four things: its provision, its lifespan, its acts, and whether it is destined for Heaven or Hell. Any one of you may perform the deeds of those destined for paradise until only an arm's length separates him from death. Overtaken by his record, he will then perform acts such as are performed by those destined for Hell and so will enter the fire. Another of you may perform the deeds of those destined for Hell, until only an arm's length separates him from death, when he is overtaken by the written record and

> performs the acts of those destined for Heaven, and so enters paradise.'[341]

There are signs that questions were asked about the need to earn one's reward in the Hereafter by acts deserving of a place in either Heaven or Hell,[342] or even about the justice of this notion of predestination,[343] but enquirers were overawed by reference to the authority of the Prophet.

> While attending a funeral, the Prophet bent and wrote something with a stick he was carrying. He then said to the company, 'There is no living soul whose place in Heaven or Hell God has not already decreed'. One of those present said, 'Should we not then await the outcome of the written record and abandon acts?' to which the Prophet replied, 'He who has been recorded as destined for Heaven will be directed to the acts of those destined for Heaven and he who is destined for Hell will be directed to the acts of those destined for Hell. The path of each will be smoothed.' He then recited, 'He who gives and acts circumspectly and believes in the good word, him We shall assist to what is easy; he who was niggardly and felt self-sufficient, and denied the good word, him We shall guide to what is difficult.'[344]

MOSES CONFRONTS ADAM

> Moses said, 'Adam, you are he whom God created with His own hand and breathed into you of His spirit and caused the angels to bow before you and made you dwell in the garden. Then, by your sin, you caused men to be put out of the garden and driven down to earth.' Adam said, 'Moses, you are he whom God selected for His communication and to whom He granted the privilege of direct converse. He gave you the tablets containing an exposition of all things. How long before I was created did God write the Tora?' Moses said, 'Forty years before'. Adam asked him, 'Do you find in it: Adam disobeyed his Lord and went astray?' Moses said, 'Yes'. 'Do you then criticise me', asked Adam, 'for doing something that God decreed that I should do, forty years before He even created me?' The Prophet said, 'Adam had the better of him'.[345]

As to the value of deeds, there is confusion in the *Ḥadīth*.

> Asked which work was most pleasing to God, the Prophet said, 'That which is persisted in, although slight. Undertake what you can manage.'[346]

> 'Walk righteously, sacrifice and be of good cheer,' he said, 'but none will enter Heaven on account of his deeds.' 'Not even you?'

> he was asked. 'Not even I,' he replied, 'unless God smother me in forgiveness and mercy.'[347]

Faith, however, justifies:

> The Prophet said, 'There has just come to me a messenger from God to inform me to be of good cheer, for whichever of my people died without associating any partner with God will enter Heaven. I asked him, "Even if he commits adultery, or even if he steals?" and he said, "Even so".'[348]
>
> ʿAbdallāh b. Masʿūd alleges that the Prophet said one thing but he said something else. 'The Prophet said, "He who dies praying to any partner besides God will enter Hell", but I say, "He who dies, not calling upon any partner besides God, will enter Heaven."'[349]
>
> The Prophet asked Muʿādh, 'Do you know what God can claim from men? That they worship Him and Him alone. Do you know what they can claim from Him? If they do that, that He will not punish them.'[350]
>
> When God created the universe, He wrote in His Book, so binding Himself, 'My mercy will overcome My wrath'. He has kept that Book by Him on the throne.[351]

But the principal hope of the believer resides in the intercession of the Prophet.

> God will assemble the believers on the Day of Judgment. They will say, 'If only we could find an advocate to plead our cause and relieve us of this predicament'. They will apply to Adam, 'Do you not see the people? God created you with His own hand; He made the angels bow before you and taught you the names of all things. Intercede for us with the Lord.' He will reply, 'I'm not the one'. He will mention his sin. 'Go to Noah, the first prophet God sent to men. He will advise.' They will appeal to Noah, who will say, 'I'm not the one', and mention his sin. 'Go to Abraham, confidant of the Merciful.' They will appeal to Abraham. He will mention his sins and say, 'I'm not the one. Go to Moses, the person to whom God gave the Tora and to whom he spoke directly.' They will appeal to Moses. He will say, 'I'm not the one'. Mentioning the sin he committed, he will advise them to try Christ, God's creature and prophet, His word and His spirit. Christ will say, 'I'm not the one. Ask Muḥammad, the man whom God forgave all his sins, early and late.' They will then come to me and I shall go and ask God for permission to enter and will be ushered into His presence. On seeing Him, I shall fall

down in obeisance where He will leave me as long as He pleases. Then I shall be told to rise. I shall be told, "Speak, and you will be heard; ask, and you will be given; beg permission to intercede, and it will be granted." I shall then praise the Lord with words He will teach me. I shall intercede, but a limit will be placed on the numbers for whom I may plead. He will grant them entry into Heaven. I shall return and repeat this twice, then I shall say, "Lord, there remain in the Fire only those detained by the Quran who will stay there for evermore". Thus, there will emerge from Hell those who said, "There is no God but God alone", in whose hearts there is a barley grain's weight of good, and after them, those whose hearts contain a wheat grain's weight of good, and finally, those whose hearts contain a maize grain's measure of good.'[352]

When God has finished with the Last Judgment, and wishes to extract from Hellfire some people out of mere mercy, He will order the angels to remove those who did not associate any partners with Him, but who had uttered, 'There is no god but God alone'. They will be recognised from the marks made on their limbs by the performance of the ritual prayers. Every part of the human body will be consumed in the Fire except the traces of praying, for God has prohibited Hell from eating those parts. They will be brought out burned to a cinder and the water of life will be poured over them. They will then sprout as the seed borne along in the torrent of the flood sprouts. God will then complete the Judgment.[353]

In Heaven, the people who were released from Hell for having said the profession of faith will be known as *jahannamīs*.[354]

THE BEATIFIC VISION

The people asked the Prophet whether they would see God at the Last Judgment. He asked them, 'Do you doubt the moon on the nights when it is full and there is no cloud? Do you doubt the sun by day, when there is no cloud? You will certainly see God on the Day of Resurrection.'[355]

Although God is very jealous, which is why He prohibited all abominations, none is fonder of praise than He.

He says, 'I am as My creature imagines Me. I am with him when he thinks of Me. If he thinks of Me inwardly, I think of him inwardly; if he mentions Me in company, I mention him in a superior company. If a man approaches Me a span, I shall approach him an ell; if he approaches Me an ell, I shall approach him a

> fathom. If he comes to Me walking, I shall go to him at a swift pace.'[356]

But bleak predestinarianism and simple optimism that salvation awaited every believer was mitigated by a body of *Ḥadīth* that imparted clearly-defined ethical principles.

MIRACLES

One area where a gap opens between the Quran, a contemporary document, and the supposed biographical record of the *Ḥadīth* is the reports on the Prophet's miracles. The Quran several times had to respond to the demand that Muḥammad perform miracles to confirm his claims to be a prophet sent from God.

> They said, 'Why has no miracle come from his Lord?' Say, 'God is capable of sending down miracles, but most of them do not know'. (Q 6.37)
>
> They swear their most solemn oaths that if there came to them a miracle, they would accept it. Say, 'Miracles are God's business'. How do you know, if they came, whether they would believe? (Q 6.109)
>
> They say, 'We will not believe until we are shown the like of what the prophets of old were sent with'. But God knows where He places His commission. (Q 6.124)
>
> When no miracle was forthcoming, they said, 'Why did you not obtain one?' Say, 'I merely follow what is implanted in me from my Lord'. (Q 7.203)
>
> Those who refuse to believe say, 'Why has no miracle come to him from his Lord?' You are merely a warner; every people has a guide (Q 13.7). [To the same question,]
>
> Say, 'God misleads whom He chooses and guides those who repent'. (Q 13.27)
>
> You find their aversion hard to bear. If you could find a way to burrow into the earth, or a ladder up to the sky to bring them a miracle ... (Q 6.35)
>
> If only We sent down to you a book written on parchment and they could feel it with their hands, those who refuse to believe would say, 'Obviously a magician's ruse'. (Q 6.7)
>
> It is not for any prophet to bring a miracle, other than by God's permission. (Q 13.38; 40.78)

You are just another human like ourselves. Bring us a sign if you are speaking the truth. (Q 26.154)

Anas reports: 'One of the Prophet's expeditions found us, when the time came for prayer, without water for the ritual ablution. The Prophet was brought a small dish with some water in it and he ordered the troops to perform their ablution from the dish. I could see water gushing up from under his fingers until the entire force had performed their ablution. They totalled some seventy men'.[357]

Jābir reports that, on the occasion of the Ḥudaybiya *'umra*, the people were afflicted with thirst. From a waterskin in front of him, the Prophet performed his ablution. Suddenly, the entire force rushed at him. 'What's wrong?' he asked. The men said, 'We've no water to drink or to perform the ablution with'. There was a well at Ḥudaybiya, but the army had already exhausted its water. The Prophet sat on the edge of the well, prayed and rinsed out his mouth, then spat into the well. We were able to draw water until each had his fill and we watered all the mounts. We were about 1,400 men.[358]

Anas recalls Abū Ṭalḥa remarking to his wife that the weakness of the prophet's voice was a sign of extreme hunger. He asked if she had anything in the house. 'She brought some bits of coarse bread and wrapped them in her scarf and put it into my hand, attached to the wrist and sent me off to the Prophet. I found him in the mosque among the people. He asked if Abū Ṭalḥa had sent me, and if I had brought anything to eat. When I said that that was the case, he invited those with him to accompany him. I went back fast and told Abū Ṭalḥa they were coming. Abū Ṭalḥa said to his wife, "The Prophet's coming, and we haven't enough for all of them". She said, "God and His Prophet know best". Abū Ṭalḥa went to meet them. The Prophet said, "Umm Sulaym, bring out what you have". She set out that bread which the Prophet ordered to be broken and Umm Sulaym pressed some clarified butter out of a skin to flavour it. The Prophet then said, "Call ten men". They all ate their fill. When they left, he said, "Call ten more". They all ate their fill, then the next ten, and the next. In all, they were between seventy and eighty persons.'[359]

'Abdallāh said, 'We used to consider miracles a blessing, but nowadays, you people think they are sent to frighten us'. He then recounted another story about the production of water on one of their expeditions.[360]

Jābir's father died in battle, leaving mountainous debts. Jābir had only very few palm trees the crop of which for several years would never match the crippling debt. He sought the Prophet's intercession with his creditors. The Prophet walked around the drying-floor, praying, then withdrew. He then said, 'Share them out'. He paid everyone in full and the quantity that remained equalled what had been distributed.[361]

The food at one dinner that Abū Bakr, at the Prophet's behest, had provided for three of the poorest in Madīna, increased the more they ate and was, after the meal, much more than it had been at the outset, perhaps three times more. The food was sent to the Prophet who, next day, fed a dozen delegations.[362]

An Arab interrupted the Prophet's Friday sermon once. 'The cattle are perishing and the sheep are dying from this drought. Pray to God for rain.' He stretched out his hand and invoked God. The sky was as clear as glass. Suddenly a wind got up bringing clouds and the heavens opened. We left the mosque, wading through water. It continued to rain for an entire week. The next Friday, a man rose and said, 'The houses have collapsed, pray to God to call off this rain'. Smiling, the Prophet said, 'Around us, but not on top of us'. Suddenly the clouds parted, forming a circlet around Madīna.[363]

ʿAbdallāh ibn ʿUmar reminds us that the Prophet's first mosque had been a fairly primitive structure held up by palm trunks, with its roof beams of palm trunks, the roof itself of palm fronds. Some years later, the Prophet used a pulpit that had been built and presented to him. The palm trunk against which he had been used to lean when preaching was heard to groan at now being neglected. The Prophet went over to it and stroked it to reassure it. Jābir reports that its noise was like the whining of a small child. It used to bawl and weep at the sermon. It could make a noise like a tax-collector.[364]

Jābir relates that, on one of his expeditions, the Prophet halted to relieve himself. There was, however, no shade and nothing to screen him. There were two trees at the edge of the *wādī*, and the Prophet went over to one of them. Taking hold of a branch, he said, 'Come along, with God's permission'. It followed him like a camel with a bit in its nose. He then went to the other tree and did exactly the same. Bringing them together, he said, 'Now, intertwine, with God's permission', and they did just that. Later, I saw the two trees standing in their original position.[365]

> ʿAbdallāh reports that, in the time of the Prophet, the moon split in two. The Prophet said, 'Now, bear witness'. One half went to this side of the hill, the other to the other side.
>
> Anas relates this event to the insistence of the Makkans that Muḥammad produce a miracle. Twice he showed them the moon in two pieces. The same is reported by ʿAbdallāh b. ʿAbbās.[366]

This reminds one of the opening of Q 54:

> The last hour has drawn near and the moon split. If they see any sign, they turn away, saying, 'Continuing magic!'

These stories notwithstanding,

> the Prophet is reported as saying, 'There was no prophet who was not granted the like of which would induce men to believe in him. What I have been granted is revelation which God has imparted to me, and I trust I shall have the greatest congregation on the Last Day.'[367]

ASSORTED ETHICAL STATEMENTS

A brief general statement of Islamic virtues is summarised in the words used by Khadīja when Muḥammad was dejected at not knowing whether his informant was angelic or demonic.

> 'Now, take it as a good omen. God would never disgrace you who honour family ties, speak the truth, share the burdens of others and earn for those without. You are solicitous of your guest and help when difficulties stand before people's rights.'[368]

Precisely the same words are addressed to Abū Bakr by the Arab chieftain to whom he had applied for protection against the treatment he was receiving from his fellow-tribesmen.[369] When asked which is the most meritorious act, the Prophet would reply, 'Filial piety'.[370] The most heinous sin he thought was filial impiety.[371] A man should strive first for his parents and only then for the cause.[372] He should avoid insulting another man's parents, for he might reply in kind.[373]

> A friend commented on seeing Abū Dharr and his slave wearing identical clothes. He explained: 'There had been words between me and a man whose mother was non-Arab and I said something about her. The man complained to the Prophet who asked, "Did you insult so-and-so?" I said I had. "Did you insult his mother, too?" I said I had. He then said, "You're a man who still retains traces of paganism". I said, "At my age?" He said, "Yes. They are your brothers whom God has given into your keeping. You should feed them of what you eat, and clothe them of what you wear and see that you do not overburden them with work that is beyond them, but, if you have to, then give them a hand."'[374]

God has forbidden disobedience to one's mother; refusing help when asked, yet going and asking others; gossip; asking too many questions; squandering one's wealth and wasting good property.[375]

Lying was especially condemned, and not only when under oath.[376]

The sure marks of the hypocrite are three: when he speaks, he lies; when he makes a promise, he does not keep it; and, if entrusted with something, he betrays one's trust.[377]

There are only three excuses for 'white lies': to mislead an enemy in time of war; to reconcile two friends who are quarrelling; and to keep the peace between husband and wife.[378]

The Prophet was especially fond of children. He was often seen carrying them – even in the ritual prayer.[379] He could be led around Madīna by the hand by a little girl wherever she chose to go,[380] and was frequently to be seen kissing his grandchildren.

A man who had ten children said to him once, 'I've never kissed any of them'. Taken aback, the prophet said, 'He who does not treat others gently cannot expect to be treated gently himself, when the time comes'.[381]

God has divided His mercy into 100 portions, retaining ninety-nine and spreading the other one among all His creatures. That is why a mare will tread gently to avoid stepping on her foal.[382]

To work to ease the burden of the widow or the orphan is at least the equivalent of fighting in 'the cause of God'.[383]

The Prophet rebuked one man for overdoing the praying and the fasting. 'Your wife is entitled to some of you as well.'[384]

Others showed the same fanaticism and tended to overvalue celibacy.

But the Prophet said, 'I am the most God-fearing man, but I fast and I also break the fast; I pray, but I also sleep by night, and I marry women. Any man who does not care for my conduct has no tie of relation with me.'[385]

There had been a domestic quarrel and the wife refused to share the husband's bed that night. The prophet thought that she was probably cursed by the angels all night long.[386]

Muḥammad frequently told the story of the traveller afflicted by thirst.

Coming to a well, he noticed that there was no rope and no bucket. So he climbed down the well and slaked his thirst. When he climbed up again, he saw a dog lying, panting with protruding tongue and thought, 'There has afflicted this poor soul what

> afflicted me', so he climbed down the well again, filled his boot and clambered back out, to revive the dog with a cool, refreshing draught.

Sometimes the hero of the story is a prostitute.

> His hearers express their astonishment, not at this, but that anybody should go to such trouble for a dog. 'An act of kindness to any living soul will be rewarded', said Muḥammad.[387]

'Believers', he used to say, 'are members one of another.[388]

> God looks askance on two Muslims who quarrel and stop speaking to one another, until they make up.'[389]
>
> 'He is no believer whose neighbour does not feel safe from his fist, or from his tongue.'[390]
>
> 'He who really believes in God and the Last Day, does not harm his neighbour. He honours his guest. If he cannot help another, then he says a kind word. If he cannot say a good word, then he holds his tongue.'[391]
>
> ʿĀ'isha said, 'Gabriel kept on at the Prophet about a man's neighbour so much that we began to think he was going to allot him an inheritance share'.[392]

Listing a number of commands the Prophet had issued, Barā' mentioned:

1. visiting the sick;
2. attending funerals;
3. blessing those that sneeze;
4. keeping one's oaths;
5. aiding the oppressed;
6. exchanging greetings and spreading the peace;
7. accepting invitations.[393]

The Prophet himself visited a Jewish slave who was ill.

Although the reward for death in battle is the martyr's privilege of direct entry into Heaven, and despite his own figurative comment that he would love to be killed in battle, then returned to earth to be killed in battle again, several times over,

> the Prophet said it was wrong for any Muslim to long for death. However ill one was, one must be patient and pray, 'Lord God, spare me as long as life is better for me, but take me to You if that is better for me'.[394]
>
> When she consulted him as she did not know the answer, the Prophet assured his sister-in-law that it was in order for her unbelieving mother to visit her. She might also, with no qualms, give presents to her mother when she came.[395]

> 'The strong', said Muḥammad, 'is not he who overcomes others. The strong is he who overcomes himself. A man must learn to control his anger.'[396]

The Muslim must always cultivate the habit of patience.

> When accused of unfairness in the distribution of the booty, the Prophet merely said, 'Moses had to put up with worse than that'.[397]
>
> The proud cannot hope to be received into Heaven. That is for the humble, and nothing but good can come of meekness.[398]

Muḥammad's own forbearance was proverbial among his followers.

> ʿAbdallāh reports, 'I can still see him imitating the act of a previous prophet. His people attacked him and drew blood. As he wiped the blood from his face, he said, "Lord, forgive them, for they know not what they do".'[399]

ECHOES

1. Angels came upon Muḥammad sleeping and began to describe him: He is like a man who built a house and prepared a banquet. He sent a messenger to call his guests. Those who accepted his invitation came, entered the house and partook of the banquet. Those who did not accept the invitation did not enter the house and did not join the feast.

   The house is Heaven, the host is Muḥammad. Whoever obeys him obeys God; whoever disobeys him disobeys God. Muḥammad is thus the criterion that distinguishes between people.[400]

2. Zuhrī – Sālim – ibn ʿUmar – the Prophet: Your duration, relative to those before you, is as the space between the afternoon prayer [ʿ*aṣr*] and sunset. The Jews were granted the Tora on the basis of which they laboured until noon and then grew weary. Each was given one penny. The Christians were granted the Gospel and laboured on its basis until the afternoon, [ʿ*aṣr*], then grew weary. Each was given one penny. Then we were given the Quran, laboured until the sun set and were given two pennies. The people of the two revelations protested: 'You have given these folk two pennies; you have given us one penny, yet we laboured longer'. God said, 'Have I wronged you in respect of your hire?' They said, 'No'. He said, 'This is my bounty which I give to whom I choose'.[401]

2a. Qutayba b. Saʿīd – Layth – Nāfiʿ – ibn ʿUmar – the Prophet: Your duration, relative to those before you, is as the space between the afternoon prayer and sunset. You are as a man who hired labourers, saying, 'Who will work for me until noon for one penny?' The

Jews worked until noon and received each man one penny. The man said, 'Who will work from noon until the afternoon prayer?' The Christians worked until the afternoon prayer and took each man a penny. The man said, 'Who will work from the afternoon prayer until sunset for two pennies?' You are they who are working from the *ʿaṣr* until sunset for two pennies. You will take double wages. The Jews and Christians were angered. They said, 'We did more work and got less pay'. God said, 'Have I wronged you?' They said, 'No'. He said, 'This is my bounty which I give to whom I choose'.[402]

2b. Abū Kurayb – Abū Usāma – Burayd – Abū Burda – Abū Mūsā – the Prophet said: Muslims, Jews and Christians are like a man who hired labourers to work until nightfall. They worked until noon then said, 'We have no need of your fee'. He then hired others saying, 'Work the rest of the day and I shall give you what I stipulated'. They laboured until the time of the afternoon prayer, then said, 'Take what we have done for nothing'. He then hired some others who worked for the remainder of the day until sunset and gained the fee due to both groups.[403]

2c. Ismāʿīl b. abī Uways – Mālik – ʿAbdallāh b. Dīnār, freedman of ʿAbdallāh b. ʿUmar – ibn ʿUmar said that the Prophet said: 'You, the Jews and the Christians are like a man who hired labourers saying, 'Who will work until noon for one penny?' The Jews worked for one penny. Then you are they who work from the afternoon prayer until sunset for two pennies. The Jews and Christians were angry and said, 'We worked longer and got fewer wages'. He said, 'Have I wronged you in respect of your hire?' They said, 'No'. He said, 'That is my bounty which I give to whom I please'.[404]

2d. Musaddad – Yaḥyā – Sufyān – ʿAbdallāh b. Dīnār – ibn ʿUmar – the Prophet said, 'Your duration, relative to those who preceded you, is as the interval between the afternoon prayer and sunset. You, the Jews and the Christians are like a man who hired labourers, saying, 'Who will work until noon for one penny?' The Jews did. He said, 'Who will work until the afternoon?' The Christians did. Now you are working from afternoon until sunset for two pennies. They said, 'We did more work and got fewer wages'. He said, 'Have I wronged you of your right?' They said, 'No'. He said, 'That is my bounty which I give to whom I please'.[405]

2e. Sulaymān b. Ḥarb – Ḥammād – Ayyūb – Nāfiʿ – ibn ʿUmar – the Prophet said, 'You and the people of the two revealed books are like a man who hired help, saying, 'Who will work for me from morning till noon for one penny?' The Jews did. He said, 'Who will

> work for me from noon until the afternoon prayer, for one penny?' The Christians did. He then said, 'Who will work for me from the afternoon prayer until the sun sets for two pennies?' You are they. Jews and Christians were angry and said, 'What about us? We worked longer and got fewer wages.' He said, 'Did I give you less than stipulated?' They said, 'No'. He said, 'That is my bounty which I give to whom I please'.[406]

These few selected examples will give a flavour of the variations in the texts of those *ḥadīth*s that were handed down 'according to the general sense'. It is characteristic that Shaybānī, producing Mālik's version of this *ḥadīth*, derives from it a legally relevant ruling:

> Since the Prophet treated the space between noon and the *ʿaṣr* prayer as longer than that between the *ʿaṣr* and the sunset prayer, that shows that it is preferable to delay the *ʿaṣr* prayer – as long as the sun remains of a pure white colour and no yellowing has occurred.[407]

Not all prophets are given precisely the same revelations. For example, one verse that was revealed to Moses but not to Muḥammad was the following:

3. Lord, let not the Devil enter our hearts, deliver us from him, for Thine is the kingdom and everlastingness and power and the kingship and the praise and the earth and the heavens for ever and evermore, amen.[408]

6
The Verification of the Ḥadīth

Assailed from all sides by the propaganda of the warring sects and parties, the Muslims were uncomfortably aware that many false *ḥadīth*s were in circulation.

> Muḥammad b Sīrīn [d. 110/728] said, 'This information one is collecting is religion. So consider from whom you accept your religion.'[409]
>
> As ʿAbdallāh b. al-Mubārak is reported as saying, 'The *isnād* is a part of religion. But for it, anyone could say whatever he pleased.'[410]
>
> Ibn Sīrīn also said, 'They used not to bother to ask for the *isnād*. But when civil dissension broke out, they would say, "Name your men", then examine which were people of the *sunna* and accept their reports, and which were people of the new ways and reject their reports.'[411]

The reference is clearly to transmitters of the later times, since it is characteristic that the following is reported, not only from the caliph ʿUmar and the Companion ʿAbdallāh b. Masʿūd, but even from the Prophet himself in identical words:

> It is sufficient to make any man a liar that he transmits all that he hears.[412]

A variant, from as late an expert as Mālik b. Anas, is worded: 'No man who transmits all that he hears is safe'.[413]

> The Prophet is reported as having said, 'There will come in later days men who will transmit what neither you nor your fathers have ever heard. Beware them, lest they mislead you and seduce you.'[414]
>
> Attributed to ʿAbdallāh is the warning: 'Devils can assume human form and spread lies. One man will say, "A person whose face I know, although I do not know his name, told me so-and-so".'[415]
>
> One man came to ʿAbdallāh b. ʿAbbās and began, 'The Prophet said this; the Prophet said that'. Ibn ʿAbbās paid no attention, so the man said, 'I'm telling you from the Prophet and you're paying no attention to my reports'. Ibn ʿAbbās replied, 'There was a time, before lies were being fathered on the Prophet, when we

exchanged *ḥadīth*s from him. But, when people started going in this direction and that, we gave up reporting *ḥadīth*s from him.'[416]

'If we heard anyone say, "The Prophet said", we would be all ears and eyes. But, since the people started going off in this and that direction, we have accepted from men only what we recognised.'[417]

After ʿAlī's death, they invented all manner of things which wrang from one of his associates, 'Damn these people! They have perverted so much religious information.'[418]

Ibn Sīrīn himself states that the bulk of what has been fathered on ʿAlī is untrue.[419] Another man claimed that the only sound information from ʿAlī was that transmitted by the disciples of ʿAbdallāh b. Masʿūd.[420] ʿAbdallāh b. al-Mubārak warned the people to avoid the *ḥadīth*s of those who insulted the pious forebears.[421] Abū ʿAbdul Raḥmān al-Sulamī warned the young to avoid popular preachers, except one man he named.[422] One he especially warned against was known for Kharijite views.[423] Another man to be avoided was one who held extreme views on 'the second coming of ʿAlī'. For that reason alone, *some* of the people abandoned his reports.[424] Others claimed to have heard his reports *before* he had fallen into that appalling heresy. One elderly fellow transmitted reports purporting to come from Companions who had accompanied the Prophet at his first major victory. But he was recognised as having been formerly a beggar by profession who took up the profession of reporting *ḥadīth*s only late in life.[425] Even the great Basran expert, Ḥasan, had heard no *ḥadīth*s from anyone who had fought in that battle, while the acknowledged Madīnan expert, Saʿīd b. al-Musayyab, had perhaps only one.[426]

Ḥasan reported from several Companions, as from the Prophet, that use of the cupping-glass breaches the fast of both the patient and the cupper. This question divided the scholars. Pressed as to whether his *ḥadīth* did come down from the Prophet, Ḥasan at first insisted that it did. Later, he merely said, 'God knows best'.[427]

Close examination of the *isnād*s disclosed that there must be some name omitted between Ḥasan and the Companion who could have reported this from the Prophet. Comparison with other *ḥadīth*s of Ḥasan's on other questions led scholars tentatively to suggest who that missing intermediary might have been. The process leads to presumptive restoration of the missing link. Others, aware of the gap, but not knowing how to fill it, had accepted Ḥasan's report, but as incomplete.[428] Similarly, a report to the effect that ibn ʿAbbās had demanded from the Basrans the alms payment on the termination of the Ramaḍān fast, and his silencing their protests that they had never heard of such a tax by referring them to a statement made by the Prophet, was described as 'a Basran *ḥadīth* of incomplete *isnād*'. Neither Ḥasan, nor his contemporary, ibn Sīrīn, who both relayed this report, had ever met ibn ʿAbbās. In the case of ibn Sīrīn, the defect in the *isnād* was easily remedied. His other reports from ibn ʿAbbās had been acquired from ʿIkrima, the freedman and 'pupil' of ibn ʿAbbās.[429]

Isnād criticism was essentially a statistical study. One amassed all known versions of a report and, comparing their *isnād*s, reached conclusions, as can be illustrated.

> Ibn Isḥāq reports from Saʿīd b. abī Saʿīd from Abū Hurayra from the Prophet.
>
> ʿAbdul Raḥmān reports from Saʿīd, 'I heard Abū Hurayra say, "The Prophet said ..."'.
>
> In no other report has Saʿīd claimed to have heard Abū Hurayra. Ibn Isḥāq and Layth b. Saʿd both report: Saʿīd, from his father, from Abū Hurayra ...

Following consideration of further reports, the conclusion is:

> ʿAbdul Raḥmān's version cannot possibly be correct. He has made an error and one fears that his memory has betrayed him.[430]

Qāsim, *qāḍī* of Kūfa, and grandson of ʿAbdallāh b. Masʿūd, had two reports from ibn ʿUmar, but had never met him.

> Questioned about a version of one of the two reports, now being carried back to the Prophet, an *isnād* expert declared that that extension was an error. The *ḥadīth* did not come down from the Prophet, but only from ibn ʿUmar.[431]

One of the leaders of the Shīʿa was suspected of fabrication. The content of his reports (*matn*) was authentic, but he used to allege that they were statements of the Prophet when they were not. Their attribution was unsound.[432]

The internecine struggles between the Companions generated the notion that one side must have been in the wrong and, by taking arms against those in the right, must have sinned. This is seen as 'insulting the pious forebears'. A Khārijī would say both sides were in the wrong and, in sinning, had ceased to be Muslims. The Shīʿa, accusing ʿAlī's opponents of sinning, said they had ceased to be believers. A middle way was to argue that one side had sinned, although it was no longer clear which. One man who said this was accused of responsibility for circulating the report to the effect that the Prophet had said: 'He who takes up arms against us does not belong to us'.[433]

The *Ḥadīth* party tended to argue: 'If you do not accept a man's theological views, there can be no justification for accepting his *ḥadīth* reports'.[434] But such reports had, in many cases, long been accepted. Unwilling to give them up, some can be seen claiming to have acquired them before the man had fallen into heresy.[435] Similarly, scholars were vigilant for the first signs of fading memory or of senility. Here, too, it was claimed that the reports had been acquired before the onset of the disability. In the case of heretics, it was also argued that only the reports of those known to have been active in the propagation of the heresy need be suspect. A man might be a sectary, even a heretic, yet be aware of the penalties in the Hereafter reserved for liars – especially for lyingly imputing to the Prophet words that he had never uttered. One sometimes hears:

> So-and-so was a Shīʿī extremist, a really evil person, yet, for all that, scrupulously truthful in his *ḥadīth* reports.[436]

Some extolled the Khārijī devotion to truthfulness, claiming that untruths were seldom to be encountered in their reports.[437] Tales of reformed sectaries repenting in later life of their former beliefs and confessing that whenever they had had an idea that promoted those beliefs, they had dressed it up in suitable *ḥadīth* attire, attached to it an acceptable *isnād* and launched it into circulation among the people, must be seen in the perspective of a remark made by the outstanding scholar and leader of the *Ḥadīth* group, Yaḥyā b. Saʿīd: 'One does not see pious persons more prone to lie than when they transmit *hadīth*s.'[438]

The *isnād* experts found it convenient that, in Arabic, the word often translated, as here, 'to lie', in fact means 'to get things wrong'.[439]

> Shuʿba had asked al-Ḥakam, 'Did the Prophet pray over those slain in the battle of Uḥud?' Ḥakam said he had not. Shuʿba warned Abū Da'ūd against a particular scholar who had reported: Ḥakam – Miqsam – ibn ʿAbbās: 'The Prophet prayed over those slain in the battle of Uḥud'.[440]

Shuʿba provided other examples of this man's behaviour.

> One man asked another about a *ḥadīth*. He transmitted it with an *isnād*. On a second occasion, the man asked him about the same *ḥadīth*. He transmitted it, using a different *isnād*. A third time he asked him about the same *ḥadīth* and the man transmitted it with a third *isnād*.[441]

> Two of the *Ḥadīth* experts confronted some man who transmitted from a particular Companion. The man admitted he had never met him, and swore that he now repented. They had to confront him a second time, as he had reverted to his former practice. The man again repented, but news came later that he was still continuing to recite the same reports.[442]

> One *ḥadīth* collector heard of no *ḥadīth* of Hasan's, but he checked it with a specialist on Hasan's *hadīths*. A colleague of his, who had acquired some 1,000 *hadīth*s from that specialist, had the opportunity to check them all with the Prophet, whom he met one night in a dream. The Prophet recognised only five or six as his reports.[443]
>
> The Syrian scholar, Baqiyya, was criticised. 'Accept from him only when he reports from well-known transmitters' was the caution issued by the experts. Of another man, they advised, 'Do not accept what he reports from the well-known or from the unknown'.[444]
>
> Baqiyya had the trying habit of using only patronymics for men better known by their own names, and their own names for men better known by their patronymics or other soubriquets. He was suspected of trying to hide something, so his practice reduced his dependability as a transmitter.

Another man solemnly reported what ʿAbdallāh b. Masʿūd had said to the Muslims at the battle of Ṣiffīn, fought between ʿAlī and Muʿāwiya. He was challenged by some man who said: 'I suppose he was raised from the dead to tell you that?'[445]

THE CLASSIFICATION OF THE *ḤADITHS*

The *ḥadīth*s were classified principally on the basis of the quality of the *isnād*. The transmitter should be *ʿadil*. That is, he should be known for the scrupulous observance of the ordinances of the religion: prayer, fasting, pilgrimage and support of the poor. He must also avoid all intoxicants. He should be sober in manner and manly in his social conduct. He must, therefore, have the reputation of being truthful and honest in all his dealings. He should be known to have applied himself to the study and collection of *Ḥadīth* and be strictly accurate in reproducing precisely what he had personally acquired from those from whom he transmits. He ought, by preference, also to be competent in Arabic, proficient enough to appreciate which types of words or particles affect the meaning and nuance of what he passes on – that is, if he is one of those who transmit *ḥadīth*s according to the sense, as opposed to the strict letter. In the interests of accuracy, verbatim transmission is to be preferred. If he is among those who transmit from a book, his information will be accepted only if he had memorised his *ḥadīth*s precisely as heard and he did not have to rely upon his text.[446] This point is often misunderstood. The *Ḥadīth* group were not opposed to the use of books. But they did insist on two provisions: that people were aware of the pitfalls presented by the Arabic script itself;

and so a man must actually have heard what he transmits from the person from whom he transmits, and transmit only from those he had heard, restricting himself to precisely what he had heard without embellishment and without omission. Transmitters are, of course, being human, exposed to the dangers of error. That is why transmitters are graded. *Ḥadīth*s were normally communicated by expert teachers to groups of aspiring scholars. It was therefore, simple, if laborious, to compare *ḥadīth*s. Verbal coincidence of the texts transmitted by several persons would indicate who were the most reliable (*thiqa*), the most accurate (*thābit, ḍābiṭ*), and who had the greatest powers of memory (*ḥāfiẓ*). The outstanding transmitter is he who combines all these qualities in the highest degree. The reports of the *ʿadil, thiqa, thābit, ḥāfiẓ* occupy the highest rank of acceptability. They are 'sound', *ṣaḥīḥ*. Should any scholar fall below the highest demands in one or more of these capacities, his *ḥadīth*s will be less 'sound'. Should the shortfall be noticeable, and of frequent occurrence, his reports may fall into the second grade, 'fair' (*ḥasan*), but will still be acceptable in the absence of superior accounts; and if, on the same topic, there are a number of parallel reports which are *ṣaḥīḥ*, the *ḥasan* report may be promoted to the grade of *ḥasan ṣaḥīḥ*.[447] The greater part of the *ḥadīth*s which underpin the system of 'lawful' and unlawful' categories applied to all questions by the lawyers are of the *ḥasan* classification.

A man known to make frequent errors in his reports, whether from carelessness on his part, or from fading memory due to age, will find his *ḥadīth*s classified as 'weak' (*ḍaʿīf*), the third grade of quality. Such *ḥadīth*s are still gratefully received, especially by scholars unable to locate reports of higher grade. In this way, the *ḥadīth*s were categorised in terms of their transmitters. Other reports may be regarded as fabricated.[448]

A second grade of classification depended on the quality of the *isnād* itself. Best of all is the '*musnad*', 'supported'. Here, the chain of authorities shows no break between its successive transmitters. Thus, the frequent *isnād* 'Sālim b. ʿAbdallāh b. ʿUmar – ʿAbdallāh b. ʿUmar – ʿUmar' is *musnad*, since it is in the highest degree probable that Sālim heard and reported from his father, and he from his. Similar father-son connections seen to be of infrequent occurrence, in terms of the statistics of *Ḥadīth* texts, may be treated with reserve or ignored entirely, especially if the son, a great *Ḥadīth* expert himself, warns his peers to accept nothing from his own father, who was no specialist.[449] The above *isnād* is not merely 'supported', *musnad*, it is 'connected', *muttaṣil*. The connections claimed are known to have been feasible and often reported. Each time they are claimed, they are likely to be historically factual. Such an *isnād* would preface a statement about, or even uttered by, ʿUmar. That would make it 'stopped' (*mawqūf*): it issues from ʿUmar and does not claim to go any further back. If the *isnād* had continued, "ʿUmar – the Prophet', it would have been of the highest possible grade, *marfūʿ* (raised), that is, 'raised' to the Prophet himself. The *isnād* thus becomes *musnad muttaṣil marfūʿ*.

It commonly happens that a man not known to have been a contemporary of the Prophet, or known not to have been so, transmits information from or about the Prophet. The *isnād* is then said to be 'broken', *maqṭūʿ*, or *munqaṭiʿ* – usage will vary from scholar to scholar. If the gap is of one generation only, a very frequent type of *isnād*, it will be said to be 'unattached' (*mursal*), the act of transmitting it being *irsāl*.[450] Some experts use this term for any single gap at any point in the chain of authorities, but what is here described is the most frequent usage.

Attitudes to the *mursal ḥadīth* varied, although the greatest scholars, especially those engaged in codifying the Law, view it with indulgence, this type of *ḥadīth* being the source of a great quantity of badly-needed material. The degree to which it was relied on was dictated by necessity and governed by due regard to the transmitter's reputation. Considerable reliance was placed at Madīna, for example, on the *mursal* reports of Saʿīd b. al-Musayyab and, at Kūfa, on those of Ibrāhīm. Both died some eighty years after the Prophet; while, at Baṣra, Ḥasan and Muḥammad b. Sīrīn, on whom reliance was also placed, both died 100 years after the Prophet.

A second 'ailment' (*ʿilla*) of the *isnād, tadlīs*, 'fibbing', may be thought of as a kind of 'contrived *irsāl*'. A man disguises or even omits, deliberately in both cases, it was thought, the name of his immediate informant. Motives named include pride or professional jealousy, or fear that to name the source might 'weaken' the report, if the informant were not fully 'reliable'.[451] The transmitter names his informant's source as his own. We saw that the scholars raised no objections to writing the *ḥadīth*s. Indeed, one of the commonest expressions of approval/disapproval of a transmitter is: 'So-and-so's *ḥadīth*s may/may not be written'. The real demand was that the *ḥadīth*s must first be heard and only then transmitted. Thus, included in *tadlīs* are numerous cases of scholars suspected by later experts of passing on their *ḥadīth*s from books written by their predecessors whom in many cases they had never met, nor thought that they needed to meet.[452] That suggests a generation who considered the transmission of what they had acquired by reading to be legitimate, thus, the opposition to the transmission of written *ḥadīth*s was based on another consideration, for example the pitfalls of the Arabic script.

The demand that *ḥadīth*s must be 'heard' before transmission came too late and was already an anachronism, as can be seen from the impressive lists drawn up in the late second and early third centuries of the greatest authorities in their own discipline who were now accused of the misdemeanour of *tadlīs*.[453] It had to be decided that, as *tadlīs* was not lying, it must be tolerated.[454] To have insisted too strenuously on their own canon of 'hearing' would have deprived the *Ḥadīth* group of much vital information and, in the strictest circles, has probably had that effect.

Similar lists were also drawn up of the names of key persons in the history of the *Ḥadīth* who, regrettably, had apparently espoused doctrines which in a later generation would have quite disqualified them.[455] But it was now too late and would have been impossible to reject out of hand the information that had come down from such men. They were therefore declared 'respectable' in relation to *ḥadīth*s which did not involve those doctrines.

It was also observed that many of the names that figured prominently in the transmission of information from the Prophet used in the elaboration of the regional codes of the Law were of persons who, on the Prophet's death, had still been minors.[456] That, too, had to be blinked at, when the main aim of the *Ḥadīth* experts was to link current doctrine and practice with the name of the Prophet by means of continuous chains of authorities.

Of considerably greater moment were accusations brought by enemies of the *Ḥadīth* party that their *ḥadīth*s showed mutual contradiction or, worse, that some of them contradicted rulings established in the Book of God. The general adoption of the theories of abrogation gave a further fillip to the examination of *isnād*s, to determine which *ḥadīth*s had been passed on by men of later and later date of conversion to Islam. Abrogation, as now applied to the *Ḥadīth*, allegedly rested on the analogy of its application in the Quran, some of whose verses were thought to have superseded revelations of earlier date. That, as I have argued elsewhere, was based on dubious interpretations of a few Quran verses and on a number of even more dubious alleged instances of actual abrogation of one verse by another. For example, Q 2.234 is usually adduced as a clear case. It had abrogated Q 2.240. But, as the first verse deals with the 'waiting-period' of the widow, and the second concerns the financial and accommodation rights established in the widow's favour which the Quran requires the husband's other heirs to honour, the two verses clearly do not address a common issue.[457]

It is thus not clear, outside the exegesis, that they are in conflict with one another. Shāfiʿī had been forced to face up to the even more serious challenge that some of the *ḥadīth*s contradicted the Quran. In the case of stoning for adultery, he had attempted and failed to persuade the Muslims that that had merely been an instance of *ḥadīth-ḥadīth* conflict and thus only of the abrogation of one *ḥadīth* by another. The fact remained that nowhere does the Quran mention a stoning penalty. Since present in the Law, it could have come only from the *sunna*. Shāfiʿī, however, had insisted that the *sunna* had never once abrogated the Quran's rulings, since the *sunna* was never in conflict with the Quran, its function being limited to the elucidation of the Quran. As stoning does conflict with flogging, if stoning cannot be a *sunna*, it can only be a Quran regulation. It must represent an instance of the abrogation of one Quran ruling by another Quran ruling. Mālik had reported ʿUmar's insistence that a stoning-'verse' had actually been revealed to Muḥammad as part of the revelation of the Quran.[458] Stoning must, therefore, represent the interesting variety of abrogation where what had been abrogated was not the Quran ruling, but merely the Quran wording. Thus, the response wrung from the scholars by those who had rejected the stoning penalty, since they could not find two penalties in the Book of God, was that there had indeed been two penalties in the Book of God. Both had survived in the Law, but were to be applied to two separate categories of offender. The scholars' dilemma was thus to concede that, on stoning, the *sunna* had abrogated the Quran – which their opponents rejected on principle – or to insist that only the Quran can abrogate the Quran and, on stoning, the Quran text is shown to be incomplete – which their opponents rejected on principle.

What must interest us here is that in the period following Shāfiʿī, although only those who were persuaded by his argument that the *sunna* had never abrogated the Quran need ever agree that the Quran text is incomplete, since those who continued to argue that the *sunna* can abrogate and can be shown to have abrogated the Quran rulings had no such need, nevertheless both views can be seen being simultaneously canvassed by one and the same scholar. In one such case, the scholar was an adherent of the school of Mālik,[459] but in another case, the same attitude was adopted by an adherent of the school of Shāfiʿī.[460] This testifies both to the power of Shāfiʿī's arguments and to the fact that the challenge faced by Mālik and Shāfiʿī had been removed in the meantime.

Pace Goldziher, Shāfiʿī did not believe that any *ḥadīth*, even a well-authenticated *ḥadīth*, could abrogate the Quran.[461] Pace Schacht, Shāfiʿī did believe that the *sunna* of the Prophet was revealed.[462] He spoke of the revelation that may be recited in the prayer and the revelation that may not be recited.

In the following generation, that itself had become a *ḥadīth* from the Prophet.

> 'If the Quran can abrogate the Quran, the *sunna* of the Prophet can abrogate the Quran, since Gabriel brings the *sunna* from God, and one form of revelation can abrogate the other form of revelation. On this, the Prophet said, "I have been granted the Book and along with it its equal", that is, the *sunna*. That is why God said in Q. 59.7: "Whatsoever the Prophet brings you, accept; whatsoever he prohibits, refrain from". God knew that we would accept that which the Prophet delivered as the actual Word of God. But He also knew that He intended to abrogate parts of the Quran by the revelations He would make to Muḥammad and that when that happened, some would hesitate. He therefore commanded us to accept what the Prophet brings that is not in the Quran or that abrogated the Quran.'[463]
>
> 'Yaḥyā b. abī Kathīr expressed this in his dictum: "The *sunna* prevails over the Quran; the Quran does not prevail over the *sunna*".'[464]
>
> 'It is feasible that God reveal a verse in the Quran and subsequently annul its wording, as ʿUmar reports in the case of the stoning-verse and others report on other cases. Such verses appeared in the Quran before it was collected into book-form. That is as feasible as annulling a Quran ruling while preserving its wording in the Quran.'[465]
>
> 'Mālik reported ʿĀ'isha's *ḥadīth*: "There was revealed a Quran verse prohibiting marriage between a male and any female relatives of the nurse who breast-fed him on ten separate occasions. That was subsequently abrogated by a second verse setting the number of occasions at five. The latter verse was still part of the Quran when the Prophet died."[466]
>
> Shāfiʿī acted on the basis of this *ḥadīth* in framing the law on marriage.'[467]

Ibn Qutayba fails to mention that Mālik curtly rejected this *ḥadīth*, or that, when challenged on the possibility that one of his authorities had 'heard' the relevant pronouncement by the Prophet, Shāfiʿī had replied: "ʿAbdallāh b. al-Zubayr certainly "heard" the Prophet and preserved *ḥadīth* materials from him, for, at the time of the Prophet's death, ʿAbdallāh was already nine years old'.[468]

Shāfiʿī was certainly inconsistent in his application of the 'rules' governing abrogation, which, as we have seen, required acceptance of the later of two reported statements of the Prophet. On at least two questions, that of the 'fear-prayer' and that of the marriage of the pilgrim, he had laid great stress on his reliance on the informant of earlier date of conversion, and hence of longer association with the Prophet.[469]

THE APPEARANCE OF THE *ISNĀD*

In view of their attitude to the political and theological issues that stemmed from ancient wars and had since then continued to stir intellectual circles, the *Ḥadīth* experts can be identified as themselves forming yet another party. Scholars have argued about Muḥammad b. Sīrīn's comment that until 'the civil dissension', men had not even bothered to ask each other for *isnād*s, and have sought to identify which civil dissension was meant.[470] Some have suggested that the reference was to the strife that followed the murder of ʿUthmān and especially the ʿAlī-Muʿāwiya split, that is, only a quarter of a century after the Prophet's death. There are, however, very solid reasons for rejecting such an early date. Chief of these is that, from what we know about the state of Islamic literature during the 100 years following the Prophet's death, the *isnād*, as defined by the experts of the late second century, did not yet exist in the first century. It is true that second-century scholars report their predecessors as demanding at the turn of the century that men name their sources. That, however, should be seen rather as their applying their own standards to scholars of earlier time. Indeed, their insisting that a scholar of the repute of Al-Zuhrī, for example, would insist that his informants name their sources, suggests that the demand was something of a novelty.[471] Al-Zuhrī himself would have had difficulties meeting the later standards. The *isnād* had come into use by his day but can be seen when studied to be rudimentary and imprecise. Many of his own *isnād*s are imperfect, and he also makes free use of what would later be called 'the composite *isnād*', which amalgamates information received from several sources. He prefaces lengthy reports with lists of names of men 'some of whom report more than others, but the reports of each corroborate the reports of the others', without the reader being informed of precisely which parts of the reports were transmitted by which man.[472] The same attitude to the *isnād* would be levelled, but as an accusation, against Muḥammad b. Isḥāq, author of the Prophet's biography. Al-Zuhrī died 124/741; ibn Isḥāq in 151/768. Al-Zuhrī has left us none of his own writings, but his celebrated pupil, Mālik, has bequeathed us the oldest surviving Sunnī law book, on the *ḥadīth*s of which the following statistics were later calculated. In one of the two surviving recensions, that of Yaḥyā, there is a total of 1,720 *ḥadīth*s. Of these, 600 are traced back to the Prophet; a further 222 have incomplete *isnād*s; 613 reports go back to Companions, while a further 285 present the views of later scholars. There are sixty-one statements with no *isnād* at all.[473] The second surviving recension, that of Shaybānī, contains 1,179 *ḥadīth*s, 174 from other sources, and 1,005 from Mālik. Of these, 429 are traced to the Prophet, 628 to Companions, 112 to the following generation, the Successors, and ten come from later informants.[474]

Mālik, who died in 179/795, is lauded by later generations as having been one of the greatest pioneers in the close scrutiny of the *isnād*s. He is portrayed, when questioned as to the qualifications and credentials of a list of *ḥadīth* transmitters, as replying: 'If they are reliable, you will find them cited in my writings'.[475] All but four of the sixty-one reports that Mālik produces with no *isnād* will be found in later compilations with full *isnād*s.[476] His work also contains quite lengthy sections of legal reasoning with no *ḥadīth*s whatsoever. It is clear that his intention was to produce a discourse on legal topics with supporting *ḥadīth* reports where such were available. But such *ḥadīth*s were neither his sole nor indeed his principal source. The later scholars denied Mālik the dignity of membership of the *Ḥadīth* movement, regarding him rather as an exponent of speculation on legal and ritual questions. When Mālik died, the heyday of *isnād* expertise still lay in the future. Its true founders were men of the generation of Yaḥyā b. Sa'īd (120–98/737–813), 'Abdul Raḥmān b. Mahdī (135–93/752–808), and especially a man like 'Alī b. 'Abdallāh al-Madīnī (161–234/777–848), from whom we have his fragmentary 'Disorders of the *Ḥadīth* and the knowledge of the men' (i.e. mentioned in the *isnād*s).

Schacht suggested that the civil dissension referred to by ibn Sīrīn had been that occasioned by the murder of the Umayyad caliph Walīd b. Yazīd in the year 126/743. Since ibn Sīrīn died in 110/728, Schacht characteristically rejects the attribution of the report to ibn Sīrīn as spurious.[477] Muḥammad b. Sīrīn was born in 35/655, and scholars, looking for an instance of civil strife that had occurred in his days, have suggested the period of the anti-caliphate of 'Abdallāh b. al-Zubayr, between 64–72/683–191. Mālik, we remember, reported the circumstances of ibn 'Umar's *ḥajj* at the time when al-Ḥajjāj came down to Arabia to do battle with 'Abdallāh.[478] It may well be, however, that what the report about the beginnings of the demand for the *isnād* speaks of was not one particular historical event, but rather the Muslims' awareness of the many lines of division that had been opened up on political and theological questions that had had their origins in the older civil commotions. The purpose of the *isnād*, in terms of that report, was to identify which were the reports of 'the people of the *sunna* and the unity', to accept only those and to discard the rest.

The *Ḥadīth* movement took it upon themselves to organise the criteria for the acceptability of such reports as represented political, theological and legal-cum-ritual attitudes with which the Muslim who was neither Shīʿī, not Khārijī, nor an adherent of any other grouping against which they identified 'the people of the *sunna* and the unity', could be comfortable. Their criteria tended to be negative. To be an acceptable 'prop' to a *ḥadīth*, a person must not merely be a Muslim, he should preferably be a *sunnī* Muslim and 'sound' as to his religious views. For example, when it was reported that

> a Basran had consulted ʿAbdallāh b. ʿUmar about a man in their region who was teaching that matters were not divinely predetermined, the venerable Companion of the Prophet had repudiated that view and insisted that Muḥammad had taught the reverse.[479]

One group of speculative theologians reflected that, to reward the good and to punish the evil, if the actions of both groups had been divinely predetermined, led to an imperfect view of divine justice, a thought that caused them to reject all *ḥadīth*s of a predestinarian flavour. Being perfect, God must be perfectly just. If He rewards good, the reward must be deserved; if He punishes evil, the punishment must be deserved. That means that what He rewards and punishes is the choice that Man makes between committing good or committing evil, and that implies the capacity to choose. Man must, therefore, be endowed with freedom to choose. Any *ḥadīth* to the contrary was thus contrary to reason, and Islam is not contrary to reason. Many other *ḥadīth*s were contrary to reason and should also be rejected, such as the *ḥadīth* that

> the Prophet had said, 'There will come a time when people will say, "All right, God created the universe. Now tell us, who created God?"'[480]

The question was improper, not merely to a Muslim, but to any person endowed with intelligence.[481] Many *ḥadīth*s contradicted other *ḥadīth*s. Both sets of *ḥadīth*s could not have come down from the Prophet. Some *ḥadīth*s contradicted the Book of God. No such *ḥadīth* could have come down from the Prophet of God.

The agenda was therefore determined for the *Ḥadīth* party, in part by the internal divisions between the regional schools, and now by the challenge thrown down by the theologians. Their activities were therefore reactive and defensive.

7
The Ḥadīth *Collections*

The scholarly labour on the *isnād* prosecuted during the late second and early third centuries produced its fruit in the first part of the third century when a number of scholars, inspired by Shāfiʿī's assurance that the corporate body of *Ḥadīth* experts possessed between them the entire corpus of the *Sunna* of the Prophet, proceeded to publish the collected *Ḥadīth*. A number of great collections were now compiled. Two techniques were adopted, resulting in two types of collection. One type was arranged 'according to the men'. The *ḥadīth*s traced from different major past personalities formed the individual sections of a collection which was then, in consequence, called a *musnad*. The oldest *musnad* in our hands today is that of Abū Da'ūd al-Ṭayālisī (d. 204/819), while the most celebrated is that of Aḥmad b. Ḥanbal (d. 241/855). A *musnad* has its value to those interested in the views or pronouncements attributed to a specific person, but is of little value when the object is to discover readily answers to specific questions on a single topic. This need explains the rearrangement in a later generation of the contents of a *musnad* into the more manageable form of 'according to the topic', *muṣannaf*. Such rearranging of an earlier work was a frequent occurrence and, in the case of Abū Da'ūd, we have today both forms of his collection . His work consists of 2,767 *ḥadīth*s attributed to 281 of the Companions.[482] He was something of a specialist on the *ḥadīth*s transmitted by Shuʿba, a somewhat severe *isnād* critic, through whom many of the *ḥadīth*s are cited. His work proved popular for several centuries and is still of value, especially for comparative purposes.

Aḥmad's work, although completed only a generation later, is a much vaster undertaking. His *musnad* has been calculated to contain upwards of 30,000 *ḥadīth* reports transmitted from some 700 Companions.[483] His criteria were somewhat more lenient than those of his contemporaries, and he has been criticised for including weak or even fabricated traditions as a result of reproducing reports from men not all of whom were regarded by specialists as wholly reliable. Nevertheless, *Musnad Aḥmad* is today as highly regarded as it has been during the centuries since its appearance, probably because the great repute which its compiler has always enjoyed in Sunnī Islam has, to a high degree, been transferred to his work. The circumstances which led to Aḥmad's acquiring his very special place in the hearts of the Sunnī Muslims, by whom he is revered as saint and victim, lie at the very centre of the explanation of the significance of the *Ḥadīth* literature, the motives for its collection and the reverence paid to those who collected and published it and to their works in subsequent generations.

The anti-*Ḥadīth* attitude of the systematic theologians of whom we spoke earlier was taken up by a caliph who then attempted to force it, as the official faith of Islam, on those over whom he ruled. In 218/833, the then caliph, al-Ma'mūn, captivated by the teachings of the theologians, set up an office of inquisition before which were, at his express instructions to his governors, cited the leading judges and clerics of the Empire and required to answer to the satisfaction of the theologians a series of questions. Those who failed to agree to a list of propositions drawn up by their inquisitors were imprisoned until their fate should be decided. A number of the more conservative-minded scholars, theologians, *Ḥadīth* scholars and popular preachers suffered severely at the hands of their persecutors.[484] Summoned in chains before the caliph's court, some died en route; others were executed for their refusal to acquiesce in the new theology which dealt with recondite matters, such as it had never occurred to the past generations of the believers to discuss. One such thesis was that of the creation of the Quran. The Quran had entered the sphere of matter and time by being revealed to the Prophet. Although all acknowledged that revelation was the speech of God, the distinction was now insisted on which had never occurred to the people or to their unsophisticated teachers: the Quran, they must now acknowledge, was a created object. The ordinary populace could not comprehend these subtleties. What they saw and understood was that their beloved teachers and preachers on whom they relied for the conduct of their daily and weekly devotions in the mosques were thrown into jail to be beaten and tortured, some to be released badly bruised and frightened: weaker spirits, it was thought, who must have surrendered to their jailers' demands or perhaps used prevarication in order to secure their release. Aḥmad, it was said, being of stouter courage and stronger faith, had resolutely withstood the threats and beatings and insisted on defying the innovators and their attempts to interfere with the central tenets of the faith. Not once during the sixteen years that the sufferings of the believers lasted was he seen to waver. Fearing God only, he defied the ruler, his courts and his prisons, his eyes fixed only on that last dread tribunal when he would be called upon to give an account of his faith and his earthly acts to the only sovereign entitled to enquire into both. Ḥaving lasted during the reigns of three caliphs, the inquisition was finally abandoned by a ruler who had no interest in its intellectual subtleties. Aḥmad emerged from the experience as the hero of the masses and the champion of the true believers. Canonised in his own lifetime by public and clerics alike, Aḥmad was compared, in his services to Islam, with Abū Bakr:

> God reinforced Islam by two men – Abū Bakr who confronted the great apostasy, and Aḥmad who confronted the inquisition.
>
> None performed such services to God's religion after the Prophet as those rendered by Aḥmad. Even Abū Bakr had his associates and allies, whereas Aḥmad stood alone.[485]

A modern Muslim writer describes Aḥmad as 'the saviour of Orthodoxy and freedom of conscience and faith in Islam'.[486]

The theologians had attempted to make Islam attractive to the non-Arab intellectual elite of the Empire by ridding it of what they regarded as its major encumbrances. Ibn Qutayba reports that, among these, they numbered the unedifying sight of Iraqi and Arabian jurists divided on most questions of law, yet all appealing to the evidence of the *Ḥadīth*, the ludicrous fables and legends fed to the masses by popular preachers pretending to be qualified to explain the Quran and the religion on the basis of yet another body of popular *ḥadīth* of the kind that lizards were once disobedient Jews who were transmogrified; a wolf was admitted to paradise for eating a tax-collector; and the answer to the conundrum 'Who created God?' was that when God decided to create Himself, He first created fast horses, set them off at a gallop and then made Himself out of their sweat.

> Such idiocies bring Islam into disrepute, reduce non-Muslims to guffaws, and make the religion unattractive to apostate and potential convert alike.[487]

The looseness with which the *Ḥadīth* party spoke of the eternal Word of God, meaning thereby the eternity of the Quran, set up a second eternal existence alongside God and led straight to the sort of dualism from which the theologians in their missionary zeal were attempting to wean the Zoroastrian elite.

The failure of the inquisition ushered in the immediate triumph of the *Ḥadīth* group, determined to steer the populace away from the barbarities of the people of reason and to plant Islam on the firmer foundation of a thoroughgoing Traditional basis. Making the most of their opportunity, they remounted their pulpits, harangued the congregation about the perils of idle speculation and theorising, and demanded a return to the only certainties, the *ḥadīth* reports handed down from the Prophet and the Companions by chains of authority that had been tested and probed to ensure that only the soundest *ḥadīth*s were accepted by the experts and recommended to the believers, to form the sure basis of belief and action alike.

Nor was it only the theologians who had engaged in speculation. Nurtured in the legal circles of Madīna and Kūfa, Shāfiʿī was more concerned than most of his contemporaries about the deep divisions between the jurists of the two centres, and more alert to the dangers posed by the theologians. Noting the reliance of the regional jurists on their own store of *ḥadīth*s from their own Successor and Companion eponyms – ʿUthmān, ʿUmar, Zayd and their respective sons and disciples in the case of Madīna; ʿAbdallāh b. Masʿūd and ʿAlī and their associates and pupils in the case of Kūfa – he had observed the disposition of the scholars at each centre to attribute *ḥadīth*s convenient to their own views to the ancient authorities of the other. He now proposed his solution to their division. There being only one God, one Quran and one Prophet, there could be only one Islam. That would be the Islam of neither Madīna nor Kūfa, of neither ʿUmar nor ʿAlī. It would be the Islam of Muḥammad. It was only the unique person of the Prophet to whom God had granted revelation and authority and to whom He demanded the obedience of the believer. The true Islam could be restored and, with it, not only truth discovered, but also the unity of the Muslims re-established if, in the presence of a *ḥadīth* traced from the Prophet, all other information from all other sources were ignored. Shāfiʿī reserved his most stinging invective for the role that speculation had played in both Madīna and Kūfa in the derivation of rulings in both the legal and ritual spheres when scholars claimed that no more solid information was known to them. The traditional information was available. The jurists had either been remiss in not accepting it from the *Ḥadīth* specialists, or negligent if, knowing of the existence of the *ḥadīth*s, they had failed to accept them, trumping up excuses about their uncertainty as to the attestation of the *ḥadīth*s in circulation. Attestation was the business of the experts. When they had examined the details of the background of the men in the *isnād*s and satisfied themselves as to their characters and competence and paid special regard to the solidity of the connection between them, the non-specialist could make confident use of their *ḥadīth*s. Those expert in these matters had elaborated strict criteria, and their prolonged studies had equipped them to identify the 'sound' from the 'ailing', the 'established' from the 'unknown', the 'connected' from the 'broken off'. All scholars should recognise that there was no longer any excuse for failing to repose complete confidence in the reports from the Prophet that had now been identified. That body of material must now form the sole basis for all pronouncements on legal or ritual questions in the formulation of the Law.

The *Ḥadīth* party was now determined to control the Law as well as the theology of Islam, and two scholars appeared whose aim was to provide the materials for which Shāfiʿī's critique had created the demand.

Muḥammad b. Ismāʿīl al-Bukhārī (194–256/810–70) and Muslim b. Ḥajjāj (203–61/817–74), jointly referred to as 'the two *shaykh*s', each compiled a *Jāmiʿ Ṣaḥīḥ*, that is, a collection of 'sound' *ḥadīth*s only, encompassing all topics of significance. Apart from the Book of God, no more lavish praise has been heaped on any writing in Arabic than that which for 1,000 years has accompanied mention of the twin pinnacles of the *muṣannaf* type of work. They tend to be spoken of as 'second only to the Holy Quran' in terms of authority,[488] as the repositories of the record of the sayings and doings of the Prophet. Although the word 'sound', *ṣaḥīḥ*, in their day laid claim only to the highest degree of probability, owing to the general agreement of the experts on what constituted the very best class of *isnād*, with time the habit has grown of seeing in the word *ṣaḥīḥ* the sense of 'authentic', even 'true'. On its first appearance, each work found critics among the contemporaries, but time has merely added to the reverence with which they have been regarded, in consideration of their aim and their content. The same can be said of their compilers. The intellectual prowess, astonishing powers of assimilation and capacity to reproduce from memory verbatim vast numbers of long *ḥadīth*s with their lengthy *isnād*s without error that have been attributed to each man are the stuff of hagiographic legend. But that is the index of the value that Muslims have attached to the two men's achievements.

Both works are of approximately the same extent, although there are interesting differences in their organisation. Of the two, only Muslim explained in an introduction the aim and plan of his book. He does not propose to include everything that, in his view, is sound, but only what the expert scholars are unanimous as describing as 'sound'. His materials are intended to be of use in the derivation of rules on the lawful and the unlawful, and he proposes to avoid repetition except in certain cases where different sections of a *ḥadīth* may offer rulings on different topics. He proposes to offer three grades of *ḥadīth*, each of which is *ṣaḥīḥ*, but the first class of which consists of *isnād*s whose men are freest of all faults in terms of the transmission of the *Ḥadīth* according to the criteria of the experts. Among their reports, one finds the least degree of difference; in terms of precision and quality of memory, they occupy the front rank. The second and third classes of report are those from men of marginally lower degree who may have slighter powers of memory than those of the first, but are of undoubted honesty and application to the science of *Ḥadīth* and whose *ḥadīth*s show few signs of difference or of error or confusion. Excluded are persons whose reports show frequent differences from better-known versions, or more signs of imprecision; all whose reports regularly do not coincide with those of better-qualified men, or whose reports are less well known among the specialists; and the reports of any persons suspected of lying in their transmitted reports and of all persons of unorthodox views. In addition, Muslim offers, as he proceeds throughout the work, a running commentary on the quality of the *isnād*s which he cites in both second and third classes.

From this, it will already be clear that one is dealing with a self-perpetuating system of doctrines: a man may be honest and truthful in all his dealings, but not known for his application to the study of the *Ḥadīth*. The criteria for the acceptance of *ḥadīth* reports are those which are set out by the *isnād* experts. The degree to which any man meets these criteria is statistically determined on the basis of comparison with *ḥadīth*s which are acceptable to the *Ḥadīth* specialists. A major drawback here, as will be seen, is that the assessment of persons and of *isnād*s is not uniform, but varies from scholar to scholar. The criteria are subjective, rather than objective and demonstrable.

According to ibn Sīrīn, al-Ḥārith was one of the 'Companions of ʿAbdallāh b. Masʿūd'. He refers to him as al-Hamadānī and as al-Aʿwar.[489] The transmitter of the *ḥadīth*s of 'the Companions of ʿAbdallāh', Ibrāhīm Nakhaʿī, may or may not have included Ḥārith in his enumeration of 'the Companions'. According to ʿAlī b. al-Madīnī, al-Ḥārith al-Aʿwar was not among them. He was an associate of ʿAlī's and reported his *ḥadīth*s rather than ʿAbdallāh's. Neither Ibrāhīm nor Shaʿbī 'heard' Ḥārith.[490] Muslim has Shaʿbī say: 'Al-Ḥārith al-Aʿwar al-Hamdānī informed me – and he was a liar!' He also has Ibrāhīm report the words of Ḥārith.[491] Muslim's work is divided into fifty-four books, each dealing with different topics of faith and practice to which he devotes some 4,000 *ḥadīth*s, taking great care to point out differences in the wording of different versions.

The major differences between Muslim's and Bukhārī's compilation lies in the latter's prefacing each section of each chapter with a brief statement indicating his view on the interpretation of the *ḥadīth*s which follow. From these headings, the reader can form an accurate impression of Bukhārī's legal, theological and exegetical attitudes. His intention appears to have been to guide the reader to the meaning or application of each report. One brief example may suffice to show this: *Iʿtiṣām, bāb* 8:

> Section: The Prophet would be questioned on matters concerning which no revelation had come to him, and he would say, 'I do not know', or he would not reply until revelation had come down. He would not reply on the basis of speculation, nor use analogy, since God has said [Q 4.105], 'We have sent down to you

> the Book with truth so that you may adjudicate between the people according as God has shown you'. Ibn Masʿūd said, 'The Prophet was asked about the spirit, but remained silent until the relevant verse was revealed'.

Students of the Law were intended to take to heart the example of the Prophet and desist from indulging in speculation or in arguing by analogy (although Bukhārī's book is not lacking in reports which show the Prophet himself employing analogy).[492]

Bukhārī's work contains some 7,275 individual reports distributed in ninety-seven separate books, but this number can be brought down to 4,000 *ḥadīth*s, for the second major difference between his and Muslim's work is that, determined to distil as many rulings as the different clauses, even individual words, of a *ḥadīth* can be made to yield, he repeats his *ḥadīth*s, at times in a great number of places, depending on how the wording of the reports can be made to respond to his various headings. This degree of repetition can be fascinating for the specialist while trying for the less devoted, making for very disjointed reading. It can also be frustrating for the busy specialist hoping to recheck a particular form of wording for any report.[493] In this sense, Muslim's work is much the easier to use. A further, important distinction between the two men involves their attitudes to *isnād*s. Bukhārī, the stricter of the two, insists on evidence that any two men named consecutively in the *isnād* had actually met. Denouncing this strictness as an innovation, Muslim is content with evidence that the two men were contemporaries who could have met.[494] Technically, this means that Bukhārī, at least, in his theory, would prefer that A said: 'I heard B', or 'B informed me'; Muslim, however, is prepared to accept: 'A told me, on the authority of B', or, 'citing B'.

Although Bukhārī's attitude was more admired by the Muslims as stricter than Muslim's, both men used and knew that their predecessors had used written sources. The two works have much material in common, although Bukhārī recognises 434 persons whom Muslim does not cite, and Muslim cites 625 persons whom Bukhārī does not mention.[495] As each man set out to collect what is *ṣaḥīḥ*, later scholars assure one that what they included is *ṣaḥīḥ*, that is, guaranteed. What is found in the book of either requires no further examination. In this, their two books are unique. But, as neither man aimed at comprehensiveness, it could not be said that what either had not included may be regarded as not *ṣaḥīḥ*. The collection of the Prophet's *ḥadīth*, once begun, was to be pursued. *Ṣaḥīḥ* was defined by those who came after them as:

1. any report found in both Bukhārī and Muslim;
2. any report found in Bukhārī alone;

3. any report found in Muslim alone;
4. any report which matched their criteria, even if they did not include it;
5. any *ḥadīth* in accordance with the criteria of either of the two *shaykhs*.[496]

Together with the two *Ṣaḥīḥ* works, four further collections made up what came to be called 'the six books'. As the four tend to concentrate rather more on the traditions relevant to legal or ritual questions, they are, on this account, referred to as the *Sunan* works, *sunan* being the plural of *sunna*. Abū Da'ūd (203–75/817–88) had studied under Aḥmad b. Ḥanbal. He included in his *Sunan* not merely 'sound' *ḥadīth*s, but also others that he described as 'nearly so', that is, *ḥasan ḥadīth*s, or even 'weak' (*ḍaʿīf*) *ḥadīth*s. The use of 'weak' *ḥadīth*s was inevitable for scholars preferring a thorough Traditional basis for all questions and determined to avoid any hint of speculation.[497] Abū Da'ūd would have the reader understand that lack of comment on any *ḥadīth* indicates that, in his view, it is *ṣaḥīḥ*. His comments are, in fact, both numerous and very useful. For example, he frequently attributes a *ḥadīth* to a particular place, or group, while his notes on his *isnād*s, or on variant wordings of different versions of his *ḥadīth*s, are extremely interesting for the historian, throwing much-needed light on the condition of *Ḥadīth* studies in his time and especially on the discussions among the experts. His arrangement of his material, consisting of some 4,800 reports, is similar to that of Muslim, while his headings are restricted to merely identifying the various topics.

A pupil of both Abū Da'ūd and Bukhārī, al-Tirmidhī (206–79/821–92), compiled his work from the *ḥadīth*s which had been used in the discussions between the regional schools of Law. He shows an intimate knowledge of the detailed arguments 'from the time of the Companions to our own day'. For that branch of Islamic science known as 'the differences between the legal schools', his work is of considerable value, since he appends to each section of his work notes on the use made of the *ḥadīth*s cited by the leading jurists of the different regions in the second and third centuries. His studies with Bukhārī and Abū Da'ūd gave him an expertise in the details of the *isnād*s on which he frequently mentions his discussions with his teachers and others among his elders. As he proceeds from *ḥadīth* to *ḥadīth*, he classifies the *ḥadīth*, showing the advances that had occurred in this field by his generation. His classification range from *ṣaḥīḥ*, *ḥasan*, *ṣaḥīḥ ḥasan*, *ḥasan ṣaḥīh* to *gharīb*, that is, coming down by only a single line of transmission, or reported from a well-known scholar by only one among his known pupils, to *ḍaʿīf*, 'weak', and finally, *munkar*, that is, not acknowledged by the experts. Once established, this classification was taken up by those after him and extended, in terms of the number of lines of transmission reporting, for example *mutawātir*, 'very widespread', and *mashhūr*, 'very widely known'.

EXAMPLES OF PROCEDURE

Abū Da'ūd

a. 'Alī, ibn 'Umar and ibn 'Amr said: A man in a state of major pollution may perform *wuḍū'* [rather than *ghusl*, the major ablution], when about to eat.
   Yaḥyā b. Ya'mur – 'Ammār b. Yāsir – the Prophet granted to such a person about to eat, drink or sleep, this concession.
   Abū Da'ūd: There must be a man between Yaḥyā and 'Ammār.[498]
b. Zuhrī – Abū Salama – Abū Hurayra, 'The Prophet said ...'.
   Abū Da'ūd: Ayyūb, ibn 'Awn and Hishām all report this from Muḥammad b. Sīrīn from the Prophet – i.e. *mursal*.[499]
c. Suhayl – Zuhrī – 'Urwa – Fāṭima ...
   Qatāda – 'Urwa – Zaynab ...
   Abū Da'ūd: Qatāda did not 'hear' one *ḥadīth* from 'Urwa.[500]
d. Abū Da'ūd: In Awzā'ī's report from Zuhrī, there are additional words not present in the reports as transmitted by the other associates of Zuhrī such as: 'Amr b. al-Ḥārith, Layth, Yūnus, ibn Abī Dhi'b, Ma'mar, Ibrāhīm b. Sa'd, Sulaymān b. Kathīr, ibn Isḥāq or ibn 'Uyayna.[501]
   It is essential to point out that the purpose of the *ḥadīth*s being to convey rulings, the wordings of the reports are taken with the highest seriousness by the critics. It is a superficial view of the *Ḥadīth* literature to argue that the weakness it suffers from is the externality of its scrutiny of the *isnād*.
e. Abū Da'ūd: Zuhrī – 'Ubaydallāh b. 'Abdallāh b. 'Utba ...
   Mālik – Zuhrī – 'Ubaydallāh – his father ...
   Ibn 'Uyayna – 'Ubaydallāh – his father
   or, – 'Ubaydallāh – ibn 'Abbās ...
   Abū Da'ūd: Ibn 'Uyayna was confused in his *isnād*.[502]
f. Differing assessments: Abū Da'ūd: Yaḥyā b. Ma'īn regarded Mu'allā b. Manṣūr as *thiqa*; Aḥmad b. Ḥanbal would not transmit from him, since he was known to be interested in speculation (and not only *ḥadīth*s).[503]
g. What the pilgrim may wear: Musaddad and Aḥmad b. Ḥanbal – Sufyān – Zuhrī – Sālim – his father, ibn 'Umar – the Prophet said:
   Mālik – Nāfi' – ibn 'Umar – the Prophet said: do.
   Ḥātim b. Ismā'īl and Yaḥyā b. Ayyūb – Mūsā b. 'Uqba – Nāfi' – ibn

ʿUmar – the Prophet said: do.
Mūsā b. Ṭāriq – Mūsā b. ʿUqba – Nāfiʿ – ibn ʿUmar said: ʿUbaydallāh b. ʿUmar and Mālik and Ayyūb – Nāfiʿ – ibn ʿUmar.
But: Ibrāhīm b. Saʿīd – Nāfiʿ – ibn ʿUmar – the Prophet said: ...
Abū Da'ūd: Ibrāhīm b. Saʿīd is a Madīnan *shaykh* of few *ḥadīth*s.
Aḥmad b. Ḥanbal – Yaʿqūb – his father – Ibn Isḥāq – Nāfiʿ – ibn ʿUmar – the Prophet said: ...
Abū Da'ūd points out, but leaves unresolved, this case of *marfūʿ* versus *mawqūf*.[504]

al-Tirmidhī

Qutayba and Hannād and Abū Kurayb and Aḥmad b. Manīʿ and Maḥmūd b. Ghaylān and Abū ʿAmmār all said: Wakīʿ – Aʿmash – Ḥabīb b. Abī Thābit – ʿUrwa – ʿĀ'isha: 'The Prophet kissed one of his wives, then led the ritual prayer without any ablution'. ʿUrwa said, 'Who could that have been but you?' She laughed.

Tirmidhī: Similar reports have been transmitted from more than one Companion and Successor. The view of Sufyān Thawrī and the Kufans was that there is no need for ablution. Mālik, Awzāʿī, Shāfiʿī, Aḥmad and Isḥāq [b. Rāhawayh] all say: Ablution is necessary after kissing. That was also the view of more than one Companion and Successor.
Our party do not accept this as from ʿĀ'isha from the Prophet. It is not regarded as sound on account of the *isnād*. I have heard Abū Bakr al-ʿAṭṭār of Baṣra report from ʿAlī b. al-Madīnī: 'Yaḥyā b. Saʿīd thought the *ḥadīth* "weak" – indeed, he said, "It's as good as a non-*ḥadīth*".'
I heard Muḥammad b. Ismāʿīl [al-Bukhārī] say it was 'weak'. He argued that Ḥabīb b. Abī Thābit had never 'heard' ʿUrwa. It is also related from Ibrāhīm Taymī that ʿĀ'isha said this. His report is not 'sound' either, since we do not know that Ibrāhīm ever 'heard' ʿĀ'isha. No *ḥadīth* from the Prophet on this topic is 'sound'.[505]

Abū Da'ūd

1. Muḥammad b. Bashshār – Yaḥyā and ʿAbdul Raḥmān – Sufyān – Abū Rawq – Ibrāhīm Taymī – ʿĀ'isha, that the Prophet kissed her and did not perform ablution.
   That is *mursal*. Ibrāhīm never 'heard' from ʿĀ'isha.
2. ʿUthmān b. Abī Shayba – Wakīʿ – Aʿmash – Ḥabīb – ʿUrwa – ʿĀ'isha [as cited by Tirmidhī].
3. Ibrāhīm b. Makhlad – ʿAbdul Raḥmān b. Maghrā' – Aʿmash –

> associates of ours – 'Urwa al-Muzanī – 'Ā'isha [as above].
> It is the Ibrāhīm Taymī and this A'mash *ḥadīth* that were rejected by Yaḥyā b. Sa'īd. Thawrī said, 'Ḥabīb reported to us from 'Urwa al-Muzanī. He reported nothing from 'Urwa b. al-Zubayr.' Abū Da'ūd: But Ḥamza al-Zayyāt does report from Ḥabīb from 'Urwa b. al-Zubayr, from 'Ā'isha a 'sound' *ḥadīth*.[506]

Al-Nasā'ī (214–303/829–915) had two abiding interests: the study of the men of the *isnād*s and the meticulous scrutiny and comparison of the different wordings of the many versions which he collected for each of the *ḥadīth*s that he included in his work. It is his own epitome of an earlier, much larger collection that forms one of 'the six books'. Accumulating the versions of his reports, he occasionally expresses his judgment of their comparative quality and that of their *isnād*s. This gives his work value for those who wish to trace the evolution of the texts of the *matn* of the *ḥadīth*s. It has the further merit of juxtaposing the *ḥadīth*s which document opposing views on a number of topics, while, for the historian, Naṣā'ī's fascination for texts has resulted in his preserving formal documents, such as contracts of various kinds which contain much valuable information for the social history of the time. His death is said to have been brought about as a result of his attempting to impart to the people of Damascus some of the enthusiasm which he personally felt for 'Alī.[507]

The great seventh/thirteenth-century commentator on the *Ṣaḥīḥ* of Muslim, al-Nawawī, and the earlier master ibn Ṣalāḥ, both speak of 'the five books'.[508] The inclusion of the *Sunan* of ibn Māja as one of the 'six' did not occur until after their time. Earlier lists of the 'foundation works on which Islam rests' had included, at least, in the western part of the Islamic world, the *Muwaṭṭa'* of Mālik. The addition of ibn Māja to the 'six' is difficult to account for. He covers as wide a field of topics as Abū Da'ūd, but without the latter's useful insights. It was not the admiration of the native critics that brought about the elevation of his book to canonical status alongside 'the five'. He is said to be alone in reproducing *ḥadīth*s

> from persons suspected of lying, or of stealing other men's *ḥadīth*s. Indeed, some of his reports are not known from any other source.[509]

Others link him with the authors of the *Ṣaḥīḥ* works.[510] Born in 209/824, he died in 273/887.

Perhaps the experts doubted his discretion on seeing him include *ḥadīth*s on the excellence of his hometown of Qazwīn, which many regarded as fabricated. No less a scholar than 'the *shaykh* of Islam', Ibn Ḥajar, commentator on the *Ṣaḥīḥ* of Bukhārī, thought:

> 'The *Musnad* of Dārimī (181–255/797–869) is not of inferior rank to the *Sunan* works and would have had a better claim to be added to 'the five' than that of Ibn Māja.'[511] Ibn Ḥajar had found in the latter many *ḥadīth*s that were not merely 'weak', but even '*munkar*', unknown.[512]

In the manner of Abū Da'ūd, Dārimī makes frequent comments on the *isnād*s, and he refers, in the manner of Tirmidhī, to the schools who uphold or reject particular views. From time to time, he expresses his personal view on what the Law should be.

Many other authors compiled *musnad* or *muṣannaf* works as extensive as those we have mentioned but, for reasons that are unfathomable now, did not achieve the general recognition accorded to the 'six' books, although many of these compilers were noted *isnād* experts at least as learned as those who have achieved canonical status. One of them, the fourth-century critic Dāraquṭnī, devoted a special work to showing the 'weakness' of 200 of the *ḥadīth*s included in the two *Ṣaḥīḥ* works.[513] A second, al-Ḥākim, compiled his work from *ṣaḥīḥ* reports included in neither Bukhārī's nor Muslim's book, yet matching their criteria.[514] Others, having the same aim, greatly extended the scope of what might be regarded by the Muslims as *ṣaḥīḥ* reports.

THE APPLICATION OF THE EXPERTS' RULES

The second Islamic century witnessed a very vigorous intellectual activity that animated a number of schools which had grown up around the personalities of outstanding scholars both in Arabia and in the newly conquered territories outside. Groups of scholars had come together in Makka and Madīna, while the other important centres were those of Iraq, which had grown out of the earlier garrison stations, planted by 'Umar, into the cities of Baṣra and Kūfa. The beginnings of these intellectual activities are obscured from us by the absence of sources. What we can do, however, is to study the brisk exchanges between the second-century schools, note the way their arguments are presented and extract the presumptions that underlie their statements. What strikes one is not simply the universal exploitation of the *Ḥadīth*, but the manner in which the current view of the school is to be made as convincing as possible by tracing it back several generations to prominent Muslim personalities known to have been resident in the region and claimed to have been the first to lay the foundations of the local Islam, and thus the original teachers who had inspired the rise of the local school. More intriguing, perhaps, is the regularity with which, in reacting to each other's arguments, these scholars make a habit of appropriating each other's figureheads, as the backward search for documentation approaches nearer to the time of the Prophet. An illustration of the treatment of one topic (i.e. what necessitates the ritual ablution) will perhaps make the methods employed clearer.

The core of the ideas that had been fermented at Madīna is presented in the surviving writings of one of its great masters, Mālik, who, in his *Muwaṭṭa'*, sums up the thinking that had reached him largely through his teacher, al-Zuhrī, who, in turn, drew upon what he had acquired from the Successors with whom he had been in personal contact: Sa'īd b. al-Musayyab, Hishām b. 'Urwa (son of 'Urwa b. al-Zubayr, nephew of 'Ā'isha, the Prophet's widow), Sālim, son of 'Abdallāh b. 'Umar and al-Qāsim, son of Muḥammad b. Abī Bakr, and a host of others, including scholars in Syria where he latterly made his home. Al-Zuhrī had also had direct contact with at least one Companion, Anas.

> Mālik, reporting from Hishām, notes that he said that 'Urwa had stated: 'He who touches his genitals must renew his ritual purity by performing the *wuḍū'*; he also reports the same words from 'Abdallāh b. 'Umar (through his freedman, Nāfi'). That is confirmed by Zuhrī's report from Sālim to the same effect.
>
> From a descendant of one of the Prophet's agents whose family still retained some of the Prophet's written instructions to his great-grandfather, Mālik reports 'Urwa's telling him of a discussion he had had with Marwān b. al-Ḥakam on the factors thought to breach the ritual purity. Marwān mentioned in his list touching the genitals. 'Urwa declared that he had never heard that. Marwān, however, insisted that his grandmother, Busra, had told him that she had heard the Prophet state that.[515]

We are fortunate in that we also possess the writings of some of Mālik's outstanding pupils. Foremost among them is the Iraqi, al-Shaybānī, who has left us his recension of the *Muwaṭṭa'*, begun while he was studying with Mālik at Madīna, which contains his annotations and comments, from which we learn which of the Madīnan master's views he continued to uphold and which he had come, on his return to Kūfa, to reject, together with his reasons for doing so. Shaybānī's discussion of the above topic involves the citation of no fewer than sixteen *ḥadīth*s.[516]

In addition to the usual appeals to the fathers of Kufan thought, for example to 'Alī's 'I don't care whether I touch my genitals or the tip of my nose [or my ear]'; and 'Abdallāh b. Mas'ūd's 'If the genitals are a source of ritual impurity, then cut them off' – also attributed to Sa'd b. Abī Waqqāṣ, once 'Umar's governor at Kūfa, as ibn Mas'ūd had also been; and Ibrāhīm Nakha'ī's, 'Abdallāh b. Mas'ūd's, 'Ammār's and

Abū 'l-Dardā''s [the last also a noted Syrian figure] 'It's just another part of your own body'; Ḥudhayfa b. al-Yamānī's 'Touching that is just like touching your head' or 'It's just the same as touching your nose', Shaybānī draws upon the noted Makkan authority, ʿAṭā' b. Abī Rabāḥ:

> A Basran who consulted him was reminded by one of ʿAṭā''s other guests that ibn ʿAbbās had said, 'If you think your genitals are impure, then cut them off', while ʿAṭā' can state that in reply to a question he himself had asked him, ibn ʿAbbās had replied, 'I don't care whether I touch my genitals or my nose'. He can report that when a Madīnan consulted Saʿīd b. al-Musayyab, the sage of Madīna had stated, 'Touching the genitals does not involve renewal of the *wuḍū*''.

Pride of place, however, in this battery of ammunition accumulated to be fired off at the scholars in Madīna, is given to the report from the Prophet himself who, when consulted on the same question, had replied, 'Is it anything but just another part of your own body?'

We know that the other major scholar produced in the school of Mālik, al-Shāfiʿī, cares nothing about *ḥadīth* reports from others, Successors or Companions, when a report from the Prophet is available. In addition to Marwān's claim that his grandmother had passed on to him the Prophet's statement, Shāfiʿī had heard a second statement of the Prophet's transmitted by the prolific Abū Hurayra. A version of a similar report shows some uncertainty in the *isnād*, being sometimes reported as coming from the Companion Jābir, at other times failing to mention his name.[517] However, one report only from the Prophet would suffice Shāfiʿī, and he has, as we see, two. On that basis, he is content, on the present topic, to accept the same view as the Madīnans.

The principal Prophet report which occupied central position in Shaybānī's ordnance would appear not to have reached Shāfiʿī, for, if it had, he would most certainly not have failed to react to it. One of Shāfiʿī's major skills, as may be seen in all his writings, had been honed on years of analysing conflict of *ḥadīth*s and of rehabilitating the doctrine involved when any two *ḥadīth*s on a single topic, both traced to the Prophet, clashed. Shāfiʿī was the first author to compile a book devoted solely to reconciling contradictory Prophet reports, as he was also the first to attempt to systematise the theory of abrogation to be applied in the event that reconciliation of the differences proved impossible.

Abū Da'ūd knew both the Busra *ḥadīth* from the Prophet and a second *ḥadīth* which, conflicting with her report, he presents as conveying a relaxation of the ruling.[518] This is none other than the one Prophet report adduced by Shaybānī. With a different *isnād*, Abū

Da'ūd's is the second of two versions to be analysed by later experts. Shaybānī's informant had been the Qāḍī Ayyūb b. 'Utba; Abū Da'ūd's was Mulāzim b. 'Amr. He knows a second route which, however, leads to a *ḥadīth* on the results of deliberately or inadvertently touching the genitals in the course of performing the ritual prayer. Both *ḥadīth*s involve the one Companion, Ṭalq, this second route passing through Muḥammad b. Jābir.

Abū Da'ūd's commentator lists the Companions who insisted on renewal of the *wuḍū'*: 'Umar, Sa'd b. Abī Waqqāṣ, ibn 'Umar, ibn 'Abbās and Abū Hurayra. The scholars who adopted that view were al-Awzā'ī, al-Shāfi'ī, Aḥmad and Isḥāq. Among the Companions, the opposing view had been traced from 'Alī, ibn Mas'ūd, 'Ammār, Ḥudhayfa and Abū 'l-Dardā'. The scholars who championed this contrary view included Abū Ḥanīfa, his pupils, and Sufyān Thawrī i.e. the Iraqis.[519]

Since Abū Hurayra's conversion to Islam occurred only in AH 7, whereas the alternative report stems from a man who came in a tribal delegation to Madīna as the Prophet was engaged in constructing his mosque, his must be a report from 'the early period of Islam'. Alternatively, this second report has been subjected to interpretation. Some versions of this report refer to touching the genitals while performing the ritual prayers. When at prayer, the Muslim will be clothed, from which it follows that the Prophet's reply that it was not necessary to renew the *wuḍū'* referred in fact not to touching one's genitals but to touching the intervening fabric.[520]

> It is said that, in one of their regular scholarly sessions, Aḥmad and Yaḥyā b. Ma'īn reviewed the *ḥadīth*s on this topic. Aḥmad's position was that the *wuḍū'* must be renewed; Yaḥyā's that that was not necessary. Failing to convince each other, they agreed to ignore the Prophet reports on the subject and consider only what the Companions had taught. Aḥmad now insisted on the ibn 'Umar reports, to which Yaḥyā discovered that he had no reply.[521]

Another expert commentator on *isnād*s, al-Tirmidhī, introduces the *isnād*: Isḥāq b. Manṣūr – Yaḥyā b. Sa'īd Qaṭṭān – Hishām b. 'Urwa – 'Urwa – *Busra* – the Prophet.[522] He mentions parallel *ḥadīth*s reported by Umm Ḥabība, Abū Ayyūb, Abū Hurayra, 'Ā'isha, Jābir, Zayd b. Khālid and 'Abdallāh b. 'Amr. A second *isnād* to which he refers is: Isḥāq b. Manṣūr – Abū Usāma – Hishām b. 'Urwa – 'Urwa – Marwān b. al-Ḥakam – *Busra*. Complementary to his first *isnād* is a third: 'Alī b. Ḥujr – 'Abdul Raḥmān b. Abī 'l-Zinād – Abū 'l-Zinād – 'Urwa – *Busra*. The greatest of all experts on the *isnād*s of *ḥadīth* reports, his teacher, al-Bukhārī, judged that the 'soundest' of all *ḥadīth*s on this side of the dispute was that relayed by Busra.

A second great expert on *isnād*s, Abū Zurʿa, had declared that the Umm Ḥabība *ḥadīth* was 'sound'. It had been reported by al-ʿAlā' b. al-Ḥārith – Makḥūl – ʿAnbasa b. Abī Sufyān – Umm Ḥabība. But al-Bukhārī contradicted this: Makḥūl did not 'hear' from ʿAnbasa, as is shown by the fact that all Makḥūl's other reports run: Makḥūl – a man – ʿAnbasa. Tirmidhī deduces from this remark that al-Bukhārī did not consider the Umm Ḥabība *ḥadīth* to be 'sound' at all.

Tirmidhī next cites the report from Mulāzim b. ʿAmr reaching back to Ṭalq, as first given by Abū Da'ūd. This is the best *ḥadīth* on this side of the dispute which reflects the views of several Companions and some Successors, and was adopted by the Kufans. The Ṭalq report had come down through Ayyūb b. ʿUtba and Muḥammad b. Jābir. Some of the *Ḥadīth* experts had expressed doubts on the qualifications of both of these men as bearers of *ḥadīth* reports. The version through Mulāzim b. ʿAmr is adjudged to be 'sounder' and better in the technical sense. Ayyūb b. ʿUtba had been the informant of al-Shaybānī, and Muḥammad b. Jābir's report had concerned touching the genitals in the course of performing the ritual prayers.

Shāfiʿī appeared not to have encountered the Ṭalq *ḥadīth* and used the Abū Hurayra report to complement and reinforce that of Busra. In his version of this Abū Hurayra report occur the words: 'with no intervening material of any kind'.[523]

Among the later writers on abrogation, the author of the *Iʿtibār* knew both positive and negative *ḥadīth*s, and his account provides an insight into the application of the rules of the mature science of the *Ḥadīth*.[524]

He adduces the Shaybānī, the Sufyān b. ʿUyayna and an Abū Da'ūd version of the Ṭalq *ḥadīth* attributing to the Prophet the reply that renewal of the *wuḍū'* is uncalled for. His lists of Companions, Successors and scholars who adopted this opinion is an amalgam of those of Shaybānī and Khaṭṭābī with, in addition, the warning that *both* positive and negative attitudes had been attributed to Saʿd b. Abī Waqqāṣ, Saʿīd b. al-Musayyab and ʿAbdallāh b. ʿAbbās. In both the negative and the positive camps, some additional names appear. In the latter, for example, he mentions Awzāʿī and the majority of the Syrian scholars.

It had been asserted that the Ṭalq *ḥadīth* had been abrogated by the *ḥadīth* from Busra. Shāfiʿī had mentioned in his *ḥadīth*s one in which ʿĀ'isha applied the rule that the *wuḍū'* be renewed to females. Ḥāzimī discusses at length a report from ʿAmr b. Shuʿayb – his father – his grandfather – the Prophet which extends the rule to both males and females. This *isnād*, he says, is 'sound' for the following reasons: first, the report is cited in his *Musnad* by Isḥāq b. Ibrāhīm, who is an indisputable imām; although the report comes via Baqiyya, who has been criticised by several scholars, in this instance criticism does not arise, since Baqiyya is trustworthy in himself, especially when, as here, he reports from well-known persons. In such circumstances, he is relied on by Muslim and others. Second, here, Baqiyya cites Zubaydī, a reliable Syrian, recognised by all experts. Third, in the same way, ʿAmr is acknowledged by all experts, especially when, as here, he reports from his father and he from his grandfather. This *isnād* is continuous, showing no break in the chain.[525] Fourth, Tirmidhī reports in his section on the 'weakness' of *ḥadīth*s that Bukhārī had judged ʿAmr's *ḥadīth* on the topic under discussion to be 'sound'. Fifth, since this present ʿAmr *ḥadīth* has come down by a variety of paths, none may suppose it unique to Baqiyya who might, if that had been the case, be presumed, as happens in the absence of parallel versions, to be reporting from some person unknown to the *Ḥadīth* experts.

Those who say that touching the genitals does not entail the renewal of the *wuḍū'* allege that the Ṭalq *ḥadīth* is the more reliable of the reports. First, Ṭalq is well known to have been a Companion of the Prophet. Second, his association with the Prophet had been a lengthy one. Third, there are many *ḥadīth*s from Ṭalq in circulation. By contrast, Busra is less well known. The transmitters are disagreed as to her tribal affiliation. Fewer *ḥadīth*s are associated with her name than with that of Ṭalq. In consequence, it would appear that her association with the Prophet had been 'weaker' than his. Besides, in general, the testimony of women is weaker than that of males.[526] The great *Ḥadīth* expert, ʿAlī b. al-Madīnī, asked Yaḥyā b. Maʿīn: 'Why do you insist on the Busra *ḥadīth*, when it reached Marwān only through one of his guards?' The other expert, Fallās, thought the Ṭalq *ḥadīth* 'firmer' than that of Busra. Even admitting that Busra's *ḥadīth* is sound, there is in it no evidence for abrogation. Why not harmonise the *ḥadīth*s? – for Luwayn reports from ibn ʿUyayna that the interpretation of her report is 'Now, wash your hands' – that is, it was a mere matter of personal hygiene.

Those who insist on the renewal of the *wuḍū'* reply as follows:

> None disputes that Busra was a Companion of the Prophet, nor the quality of her *ḥadīth*, except only the ignorant. Shāfiʿī said, 'We have reported our view from other than Busra. Those who challenge our reliance on Busra, cite *ḥadīth*s from other females, any number of whom are less well known to the non-expert. How can Busra be regarded as 'weak', having regard to the earliness of her conversion and of her *hijra*? She uttered her *ḥadīth* in the midst of numerous *muhājirūn* and *Anṣār*, none of whom rebutted it. Indeed, we know that some of them adopted her view on the strength of her report, such as ʿUrwa, who had

earlier taken the opposite view. Ibn ʿUmar heard her *ḥadīth* and never ceased acting on it until he died.

This is the way in which legal and religious knowledge should be treated.

As for the supposed differences in the wording of the versions of the Busra report, the same or even more applies to the Ṭalq *ḥadīth*. But, if one chain of a *ḥadīth* is sound, and factors that would justify criticism are absent, then the report must be accepted, with no regard paid to the parallel chains. Mālik's version is indisputably sound in its transmission. The story told about ʿUrwa's challenging Marwān's account which obliged Marwān to despatch one of his guards to question Busra and return with her reply is not a flaw in the *ḥadīth*, since we see that ʿUrwa accepted her report, which he would not have done unless the guard, in his view, was wholly reliable. Further, there are reports that ʿUrwa himself had questioned Busra, who confirmed the report. Thus, there are several *isnād*s of the form: Hishām – ʿUrwa – *Busra*.

The Ṭalq *ḥadīth* does not equal the Busra report in quality. The *sanad* is unknown and the wording inept. Shāfiʿī said, 'Our opponents claim that the Qāḍī of Yamāma [Ayyūb b. ʿUtba] and Muḥammad b. Jābir reported from Qays, from his father, from the Prophet, words indicating that *wuḍū*' need not be renewed. We have enquired about this Qays, but found none to know him to possess the qualities that would render his report acceptable. His report has been challenged by a report from a person whose qualities we have set out and whose capacity and accuracy as transmitter is greater.' Here, Shāfiʿī is said to have in mind the reports of Ayyūb and Muḥammad, both of whom are considered by *Ḥadīth* experts to be 'weak'.

The Ṭalq *ḥadīth* has also been transmitted by Mulāzim b. ʿAmr – ʿAbdallāh b. Badr – Qays – his father, Ṭalq. Yet the authors of the two *Ṣaḥīḥ*s have not relied on either of the first two men's transmissions. ʿIkrima b. ʿAmmār reported it from Qays – the Prophet. That transmission is *mursal*, yet he is the 'strongest' of all those who report it from Qays, but in an unacceptable form, as one sees. It is also reported that Yaḥyā b. Maʿīn stated, 'The scholars have discussed the reports of Qays b. Ṭalq at length and repose no confidence in them'.

Ibn Abī Ḥātim said, 'I asked my father and Abū Zurʿa about this report. Both said Qays b. Ṭalq is not evidential. Both declared him "weak" and inaccurate.'[527]

The Qays b. Ṭalq *ḥadīth* is reproduced in neither of the two

*Ṣaḥīḥ*s, nor have the two *shaykh*s relied on any of his reports, nor the reports of most of those who transmit his other *ḥadīth*s.

Now, whereas they do not reproduce the Busra *ḥadīth* either, on account of the disagreements as to whether ʿUrwa actually heard from her directly, or only indirectly through Marwān, they nevertheless rely on all the men mentioned in the *isnād* of her report, from Marwān to those later in date than he.

This is how one establishes that the Busra *ḥadīth* is to be given preference over the Qays *ḥadīth* on grounds of *isnād* consideration. Preference is determined by the conditions governing the 'soundness' of reports and the qualifications of the transmitters, as against those who appear in the parallel *isnād*s.

That there is in this question no abrogation is shown by the dates. Ṭalq's report refers to the early days of Islam. Busra, Abū Hurayra and ʿAbdallāh b. ʿUmar's reports are later, given the later date of their respective conversions.

All cases of contention affecting what the scholars regard as serious matters and the relevant conflict of the evidentiary *ḥadīth*s tend to be treated at this degree of length and with this degree of attentive comparison of the details of the parallel *isnād*s and of the parallel wording. But, as neither Busra nor ʿAbdallāh b. ʿUmar was a late convert to Islam, the suspicion arises that the extreme utility of the name of Abū Hurayra lies in the repeated motif of his converting only at the time of the Khaybar expedition in AH 7. He thus seems to figure in the present dispute simply to protect the Busra report from the allegation that, being an early report, it might be the one that had been abrogated. Shāfiʿī will be found now to emphasise earliness of conversion and length of association with the Prophet; now, lateness of conversion as indicating information from the later period, namely abrogation.

CONFUSED *ḤADITHS*

The three elements of confused *isnād*s, confused *matn* and rationalisation are represented in full on the single topic of the status of lizard flesh.

ʿAbdallāh b. ʿUmar reports that, when asked about this, the Prophet replied, 'I don't eat it myself, but I don't say that it is unlawful'.[528]

Versions of this report make it more solemn by having the Prophet consulted and replying when in the pulpit.[529] Further versions describe a meal at which, offered lizard meat, the Prophet declined to eat but did not say it was unlawful.[530] Circumstantial details begin to be added:

> The Prophet was in a company of his followers and they were offered meat. A woman of the Prophet's household called out, 'It's lizard meat!' The Prophet said to the group, 'Eat it, it's quite lawful, but not part of my normal diet'.[531]

Sha'bī, who had associated with ibn 'Umar for the best part of two years, declared that that was all that ibn 'Umar had reported from the Prophet on the subject.[532]

'Abdallāh b. 'Abbās, whose reports are even more confused, states:

> *I accompanied* the prophet and Khālid b. al-Walīd to Maymūna's. Offered roast lizard, the Prophet stretched out his hand, when one of the women present said, 'Tell him what he is about to eat'. The Prophet stayed his hand. I asked, 'Is it unlawful?' He said, 'No, but it is not available in our country, and I feel a certain aversion'. Khālid said, 'I pulled it across and ate it, as the Prophet looked on'.[533]

Now

> 'Abdallāh reports, 'Khālid b. al-Walīd told me that *he accompanied* the Prophet to Maymūna's, his aunt and the aunt of ibn 'Abbās also. He found a roast lizard had been brought from Najd by her sister, Ḥafīda. She put the dish before the Prophet, who rarely stretched his hand before being told what he was about to eat and it was identified for him. On this occasion, he stretched out his hand, when one of the women said, 'Tell the Prophet what you are offering him'. They said, 'It's lizard', and he raised his hand. Khālid said, 'Is lizard unlawful?' The Prophet said, 'No, but it's not found in our country, and I find that I feel a certain aversion'. Khālid said, 'So I pulled it across and ate it, as the Prophet looked on, and he did not forbid me'.[534]

> Ibn 'Abbās reports that Khālid told him that he had accompanied the Prophet ... [as above]. Maymūna, who was his aunt, put before him lizard meat brought by Umm Ḥafīd from Najd. The Prophet never ate anything until he knew what it was ...[535]

> Ibn 'Abbās: When *we were* at Maymūna's, the Prophet was given two roast lizards ...[536]

To one version is added: 'This was also reported by Yazīd'.[537] A second version makes no mention of Yazīd b. al-Aṣamm.[538] In a further version, ibn 'Abbās was not present. The point of this version is that he reached his conclusion by inference.

> My aunt, Umm Ḥafīd, presented the Prophet with some fat, cheese and several lizards. He ate some of the fat and the cheese, but left the lizard, thinking it 'unclean'. But, it was eaten at his table, which would never have happened had it been unlawful.[539]

> Yazīd b. al-Aṣamm reports, 'We were at a wedding feast in Madīna and were offered 13 lizards from which some ate but others didn't. The following day, meeting ibn ʿAbbās, I told him this. Those with him started discussing this at length. Some said, "The prophet said, 'I don't eat it myself, but I don't say that it is forbidden, or that it is unlawful'". Ibn ʿAbbās disagreed. "There never was a prophet but that he was sent to declare some things lawful and other things unlawful. At Maymūna's, accompanied by *al-Faḍl* b. ʿAbbās and Khālid, and another of his wives, they were offered lizard. As the Prophet was about to eat, Maymūna said, 'It's lizard'. The Prophet stayed his hand, saying, 'That's something I've never had before. Eat up.' Al-Faḍl, Khālid and the other woman had it, but Maymūna said, 'I won't if he doesn't'."'[540]

The reports stemmed from an original which said merely 'ibn ʿAbbās', with no further identification.

> Jābir b. ʿAbdallāh reports, 'The Prophet, brought some lizard, declined to eat it, saying, "I don't know. It could be some past generation transmogrified".'[541]

> Abū 'l-Zubayr consulted Jābir about lizard. Jābir said, 'Don't eat it, it's unclean'. ʿUmar intervened, 'The Prophet did not ban it. God benefits more than one person with it. It's the food of most herdsmen. If I had any, I'd eat it.'[542]

> A man consulted the Prophet, asking for a ruling. 'Our place is full of lizards. What do you recommend, give us a *fatwā*.' He replied, 'I've been told that a tribe of Israelites was transmogrified'. He neither recommended nor forbade it. Later, ʿUmar said, 'God benefits more than one person with it. It's the food of most herdsmen. If I had any, I'd eat it. The Prophet merely felt a personal aversion to it.'[543]

> An Arab consulted the Prophet. 'I'm from a lowland full of lizards, which are the staple food of my people.' Three times he said this, and three times got no answer. Finally, the Prophet said, 'God cursed, or He was angry with a tribe of Israelites and changed them all into reptiles. I don't know if these are they. I don't eat them myself, but I don't prohibit them.'[544]

It was reported that the Prophet had banned the flesh of the domestic donkey at the time of the Khaybar raid. Some men reasoned that that was probably because they were 'unclean'.[545] One can see them eating garbage. Others thought that he may have banned them precisely because they were domesticated. Ibn ʿAbbās was uncertain whether it was because they were the people's mode of transport.[546] One man would not eat chicken because he had seen chickens eating litter. He was prevailed upon to eat only when a Companion assured him that the Prophet had eaten chicken.[547]

It was not difficult for the theologians to find instances of 'idiocy' in the *Ḥadīth*. ʿAbdallāh b. ʿUmar, it was claimed, had attended the stoning of the two Jews; a similar claim has been entered on behalf of Jābir b. ʿAbdallāh. One traveller had an even more interesting contribution to make to the literature. He had witnessed a troop of monkeys stoning two of their number who had breached the sexual code.[548] In a work which reads remarkably like a satirical review of the *Ṣaḥīḥ*, one wag asked whether these monkeys had, perhaps, stoned on the basis of the Tora.[549] We have seen the attempts made to argue that there had, in fact, been a revelation brought to Muḥammad which resulted in the presence of a stoning-'verse' in the Quran. The absence of a stoning-'verse' from their copies of the Quran had to be explained to the Muslims of the post-Prophetic age.

> The verse, it is alleged, had been written down on a sheet that was kept under the bedding in the Prophet's apartments. Unfortunately, a domestic goat got in one day and gobbled up that sheet. The sheet had, in addition, contained the record of a revealed verse stating that five acknowledged breast-feeding sessions erected a lifelong barrier to the marriage of the suckled infant with the nurse or any of her female descendants, or any female child suckled by the same wet-nurse.[550]

That was a Quran verse essential to Shāfiʿī's rulings on marriage.[551] It was referred to in a *ḥadīth* from the Prophet's widow ʿĀ'isha, who insisted that it was still being recited as part of the Quran at the time of the Prophet's death. Mālik curtly dismissed that *ḥadīth*.[552]

A rather more subtle way of accounting for the absence of these two vital items of revelation from the written Quran texts was to argue that whoever may first have collected the texts into a book (*muṣḥaf*), it must have been someone other than the Prophet himself, who would have noticed the omission.[553] Other difficulties attending the *Ḥadīth* concerned mistaken identities, such as, for example, the confusion of differing sons of ʿAbbās, or the attribution of a single view to a multiplicity of Companions, who happen to share the same forename, ʿAbdallāh. The word means merely 'a believer' and could refer to any monotheist. To the student of *Ḥadīth*, it was important to identify further which ʿAbdallāh was meant: ibn ʿUmar (Madīna); ibn ʿAbbās (Makka or Baṣra); ibn Qays (Baṣra), or ibn Masʿūd (Kūfa). Similarly, conflicting views are attributed to one and the same person – especially serious when that person is the Prophet. One protest against the proliferating *ḥadīth*s from Muḥammad took the form of 'Ā'isha's criticism of the stream of *ḥadīth*s attributed to the late convert, Abū Hurayra, with whom she crossed swords on numerous topics. She insisted that the number of *ḥadīth*s actually spoken by the Prophet had been so small that they could be counted.[554] Attacks by others on the probity of the man were based on his sheer prolixity. The response was framed to their question:

> 'How is it that Abū Hurayra has so many *ḥadīth*s to relate from the Prophet, when the major Companions have so few?' The reply is either that trading in the markets or tending to their plantations kept many of the Companions for quite long periods out of the Prophet's presence, whereas Abū Hurayra, who had no other vocation but religion and learning, grew inseparable from the Prophet with the intention of harvesting the crop of religious instruction which flowed from his lips.[555]

Even more characteristic is the reply framed in the form of another *ḥadīth*: the miracle of the cloak.

> The Prophet had promised that whoever threw open his coat as soon as he began his discourse, and pulled it to him when he had done, would never forget a word that he had uttered. Abū Hurayra claimed that he had implicitly followed this instruction and had been rewarded with the fulfilment of the Prophetic promise.[556]

> 'None of the Companions', boasted Abū Hurayra, 'possesses as many of the Prophet's *ḥadīth*s as I do – except perhaps only 'Abdallāh b. 'Amr. But then, he wrote down everything, whereas I memorised everything I heard.'[557]

On the question of the legitimacy or illegitimacy of writing down the Prophet's teachings, a vast body of material came into existence on each side of the argument. Proponents and opponents alike of the recording of the *Ḥadīth* attributed their view on the matter, in what I should call 'technical' *ḥadīth*s, to the Prophet himself.

Considerable scope for the further application of the *Ḥadīth* lay in the field of Quran commentary. That, indeed, is very likely to have been a very ancient activity, preceding by several generations the deliberations of the legal scholars. Mālik himself had heard that the stoning penalty had originated in the Book of God. He no longer understood what that meant. Ignorance of the historical source of the first discussions on the penalty had already, before Mālik's day, led to the separation of stories about the Prophet's supposed practice from a possible origin in the Book of God, leading to the formation of a body of *Ḥadīth* inspired by the supposition that stoning was something that

Muḥammad had done; that it was *sunna*. By Mālik's time, from the *sunna* materials discussed in preceding generations, it had already long been assumed that this *sunna* was connected, this being a legal topic, with Muḥammad's role as magistrate of Madīna. The unanimity on this stoning penalty, not merely of the Muslims of all the regions, but as between Shī'ī and Sunnī Muslims alike, may suggest a rough date for those discussions in the period before there was any Sunnī-Shī'ī rift, as well as before the hardening of the demarcation lines between the schools of Baṣra, Kūfa, Makka and Madīna. It might even have lain in the pre-Conquest days, thus predating the diaspora.

Goldziher searched for an explanation of the wide divergences between the provincial centres on most points of the Law and the doctrine. He overlooked the equal necessity to explain the startling fact of unanimity on certain points of Law and doctrine, such as stoning, or that the number of the daily ritual prayers is five, or that the Muslims were concerned to observe any fast on the day of 'Āshūrā'. None of these matters can be directly derived from a Quran text. All have been traced to the *sunna* of the Prophet. Unanimity on the stoning penalty was not, however, total. Mālik mentioned its rejection by one group of Muslims who had failed to find it in the Quran. The later scholars identify this group as some of the Khawārij, or Khārijites, to whom, intriguingly, some of the later commentators add the Mu'tazila. These are the very *ahl al-kalām*, or systematic theologians, that Shāfi'ī had to work so hard to convince that it was the Quran that insisted on the religious obligation to obey God *and* the Prophet, that is, to accept the *Sunna* of the Prophet as well as the Book of God. It had been the Mu'tazila who had instigated the inquisition whose cruel persecution of the *Ḥadīth* group had made a saint of Aḥmad and called forth the powerful public reaction against the appeal that reason be allotted a role in the derivation of Law and doctrine. When the day of triumph for the forces of conservatism dawned, tables were overturned and reason driven forth from the temple. The *Ḥadīth* group captured not only the fields of the Law and the doctrine. Their victory extended also into the field of Quran commentary. Only interpretations handed down by approved chains of authority tracing them back to the pious forebears would be listened to. The Prophet is made to put this into words:

> 'He who comments on the holy texts on the basis of reason and arrives at the correct interpretation, arrives at the wrong interpretation.'[558]

The insistence that the exegesis must be based exclusively on that one source which alone guarantees truth, being quite incapable of error – that based on the *manqūl*, what has been handed down, and the *ma'thūr*, that which is traced by an *isnād* in an *athar*, or report – was extended by Shāfiʿī to the Arabic of the Quran. Only one man in all of history possessed all of the *sunna*, and only one man possessed the global knowledge of the Arabic language. Knowledge of the language was now in the possession only of the entire collective of native Arabic speakers; the entire *Sunna* was the preserve only of the entire corporate body of scholars of the *Ḥadīth*. This was meant to exclude exegesis based only on evidence drawn from linguistics. Reliance on an individual's knowledge of the language could lead only to arbitrary interpretations. But, on examination, it will be found that that is precisely the shortcoming of an interpretation based on *ḥadīth* reports from the Companions.

> 'They turn away from the Reminder as though they were startled asses fleeing from a qaswara.'

In the exegesis, we find a number of explanations for the unfamiliar terms that occur frequently in the Quran.

qaswara: means

1. 'archers' – ibn ʿAbbās; Abū Mūsā; Mujāhid.
2. it means 'a party of hunters with bow and arrow' – Qatāda; Mujāhid.
3. it means 'a lion' – ʿIkrima.
4. it means 'arrows' – Qatāda.
5. 'hunters' – ibn ʿAbbās; Saʿīd b. Jubayr.
6. a party of men – ibn ʿAbbās, who said, 'I know of no Arabic dialect in which the word means a lion. It means: a party of men.'
7. human voices – ibn ʿAbbās.
8. a lion. Abū Hurayra; Zayd b. Aslam; Zayd b. Aslam from Abū Hurayra; ibn ʿAbbās: in Arabic, the lion is *asad*; in Persian, it is *shār*; in Nabataean, it is *arbā*; the word *qaswara* is Ethiopic.[559]

We have heard that a number of the Prophet's followers had been despatched from Makka to Ethiopia. On occasion, the Prophet himself is reported as using Ethiopic words, and, when he is furious and wishes to curse, so also Abū Hurayra.[560] Nothing is known of any visit that Abū Hurayra is supposed to have made to that territory. There is no trace of such a report.

At the level of the conditional clause, an indifferent interpretation of a Quran verse is attributed to Muḥammad. Q 9.80, speaking of certain unnamed nominal Muslims, says:

> Pray that they be forgiven, or do not pray that they be forgiven; if you pray seventy times that they be forgiven, God will not forgive them.

> Ibn ʿUmar reports: When ʿAbdallāh b. Ubayy [the leader of opposition to Muḥammad at Madīna] died, his son begged the Prophet to give him his shirt for his father's shroud. That Muḥammad did. He next asked the Prophet to pray over the body. As the Prophet made to do so, ʿUmar went over and seized his clothing and dragged the Prophet away, saying, 'Do you propose to pray over him, when God has forbidden you to?' Muḥammad explained, 'God did not forbid me. He gave me a choice, "Pray that they be forgiven, or do not pray that they be forgiven; if you pray seventy times for their forgiveness, God will not forgive them". I propose to pray for ʿAbdallāh more than seventy times.' ʿUmar expostulated, 'But he is only a nominal Muslim!' The Prophet, however, insisted on praying for him and God then revealed, 'Do not pray over any of them that dies and do not stand by his graveside'. (Q 9.84)

This verse refers to those who decline to accompany Muḥammad on an armed raid. The above *ḥadīth* is traced to the Prophet indifferently through (ʿAbdallāh) b. ʿUmar and (ʿAbdallāh) b. ʿAbbās.[561]

Further, account must be taken and explanation offered for the very numerous occasions on which *ḥadīth*s terminate with the words, 'then the confirmation of that was revealed by God', or with, 'now go back and check verse such-and-such, if you please'.

THE FABRICATING OF *ḤADĪTHS*

The *Ḥadīth* specialists were well aware that many fabricated *ḥadīth*s were in circulation. To combat this, the utmost they could do was to issue stern warnings; and, typically, these warnings were themselves, ironically, cast into *ḥadīth* form.

> Thus, ʿAlī is represented as reporting that the Prophet himself had had to issue the warning, 'Do not father lies on me, for he who does so will enter Hellfire'.[562]
>
> ʿAlī himself proclaimed, 'I would sooner fall from Heaven to Earth than father lies on the Prophet'.[563]
>
> ʿAbdallāh b. al-Zubayr asked his father, 'Why is it that I do not hear you relating *ḥadīth*s from the Prophet in the way that so-and-so and ʿAbdallāh b. Masʿūd, for example, do?' Zubayr replied, 'By God! I was never out of the Prophet's company from the day I converted to Islam, but I did hear him say, "He who fathers lies on me may here and now select his resting place in Hell"'.[564]
>
> Mughīra had heard the Prophet announce, 'To fabricate lies in

> my name is not like using another's name for this purpose. He who deliberately fathers lies on me may here and now choose his resting place in Hell.'[565]

The Companions have not all been credited with a like prolixity in their transmission of *ḥadīth*s from the Prophet, and, although Anas is by no means an uncommon name in the *isnād*s of *ḥadīth*s,

> he is reported to have said, 'What prevents me from relating many *ḥadīth*s to you is that I heard the Prophet say, "He who goes out of his way to father lies on me may here and now select his resting place in Hell"'.[566]

Precisely the same sentiment is reported from the Prophet by the most prolific of all the Companions, Abū Hurayra.[567] That one *ḥadīth* may contemplate another is shown by the following:

> Zubayr said to his son in the course of the above reported conversation, 'I note that they are adding the word "deliberately" to this Prophet *ḥadīth*. By God, he did not even say "deliberately".'[568]

It was possible to convey instructions from the Prophet on any topic, yet to bypass the restrictions which the scholars placed upon precision in the matter of the *isnād* by reporting a meeting with the Prophet in a dream and then relaying his words. This was acceptable, since

> Abū Hurayra had reported the Prophet's saying, 'The Devil cannot assume my guise, so he who sees me in a dream has really seen me in truth – but he who then deliberately fathers lies on me may here and now select his resting place in Hell'.[569]

It could thus well be that the minatory formula applied in so sweeping a way to the transmission of *ḥadīth*s in the ordinary way may represent merely the generalisation of a warning that had originally been intended to have a more specific reference to a particular class of *ḥadīth*s. How the Prophet's warning came to be generalised is shown in the fact that some scholars can trace it back to forty Companions, others to sixty and some to as many as between seventy and eighty, including among them all the ten men who had been promised in advance that they would certainly be going to Heaven.[570] It will be, however, for God to make the final determination as to whether those who deliberately lied against His Prophet are consigned to Hell or forgiven by divine grace, especially if they never wavered in their adherence to the formula that 'there is no god other than God and Muḥammad is in truth His Prophet.'[571] Insertion of the word 'deliberately' is important, for without it the term used in the Arabic, *kadhaba*, can mean quite simply 'to get something wrong', a hazard from which no human is immune.[572] The scholars were divided as to whether detection of untruth in one *ḥadīth* rendered only that *ḥadīth*, or every *ḥadīth* by that transmitter, liable to rejection. Scholars were particularly severe on *ḥadīth*s which concerned 'the lawful and the unlawful'. *Ḥadīth*s on other topics had to be treated with more indulgence.[573] The sterner critics might be disposed to treat all fabrications to outright condemnation, but the countless *ḥadīth*s which incited the masses to acts of piety although admittedly offering them grossly inflated rewards for what appear to be the most trifling acts of devotion or filling their heads either with the most glowing accounts of the seductive luxuries awaiting the believers in Paradise or reducing them to terror by graphic descriptions of the horrors awaiting the wicked in Hell, while deplorable in their unbridled exaggeration, probably did no harm, and might even do some good. Among the worst offenders in this respect were the popular preachers and the pious promoters of asceticism and religious enthusiasts who interpreted the Prophet's warning to mean:

> 'Those who deliberately father lies on me with the aim of misleading the Muslims in their religion may here and now select their resting places in Hell'.[574]

These are people who cheerfully admit that they fabricate their *ḥadīth*s, not against the Prophet, but in his service. In this, they merely show their ignorance and their extreme gullibility.

Fulminate they may do against those who take the slippery slope, but the experts proved ineffective against those who fed the public appetite for thrills and who ministered to their emotional needs. When asked about the problem of the forgeries and fabrications in circulation, the *Ḥadīth* specialists were inclined to reply complacently that there were experts who were alive to the problem and had things under total control.[575]

> In a sermon, Muʿāwiya claimed that the Prophet had told them that the religions before Islam had split into seventy-two sects. The Muslims would split into seventy-three sects, of which seventy-two would end up in Hell, and only one sect could look forward to getting into Heaven, i.e. the people who maintained the unity of the Muslims.[576]

In an alternative version,

> 'There will not cease among my people one party upholding God's affair. They will be nowise harmed by those who let them down, nor by those who oppose them. Thus they will remain until God brings things to a close.' At this, a man prompted Muʿāwiya, 'Muʿādh said, "They will be in Syria"'. 'There you are,' said Muʿāwiya, 'Muʿādh said, "They will be in Syria"'.[577]

We have spoken already about the versatility of the *Ḥadīth*. The fact that the *Ḥadīth* party emerged intact from the severe trial to which they had been subjected owed more to the indifference of one ruler than to their own brilliance did nothing to prevent them luxuriously wallowing in a warm glow of triumphalism. When a second man by the name of Muʿāwiya reported that

> the Prophet had said, 'A group of my people will not cease to triumph, unharmed by those who let them down, until the Last Hour strikes', they were quick to apply these words to themselves. Asked to what the Prophet's words referred, their hero Aḥmad b. Ḥanbal replied, 'If this triumphant party is any other than the *Ḥadīth* party, I do not know who else they can be'.[578]

8
The Western Approach to the Ḥadīth

Goldziher's major achievement was undoubtedly his recognition that the mass of contradictions in the *Ḥadīth* was traceable to the competition between disputing political interests, Umayyads, Shīʿa and Khawārij; regional groups of scholars with interest in legal questions, and disagreements among the theologians on questions such as free will versus predetermination. The weaknesses in his procedure arose from his acceptance of the description of the Damascus dynasty circulated by their political enemies, the Shīʿa, the Khawārij and ultimately by the Abbasids who overthrew and succeeded them, in which they were painted as worldly, autocratic and not simply indifferent, but actively hostile to religious enquiry. The picture which he accepted in 1889, he realised some years later had been painted too black and white, and he was to modify his earlier view.[579] That the picture was less stark than he had originally thought and considerably more subtle and complex was brought out some fifty years later by Schacht, who, taking Goldziher's overall thesis that much of the *Ḥadīth* was the result of mere fabrication, and applying his considerable erudition to the contents and to the *isnād*s of the special class of *ḥadīth*s on legal questions, opened up the vista of regional groups of scholars working out a programme of Islamic Law as they understood it to be in their separate areas. Schacht showed the degree to which the older generations of 'lawyers' shared much material in common, although they were also divided on many issues. His studies on the details of the *isnād*s led to some useful insights on how information can be derived from the confusions apparent in the attribution of specific legal propositions to a range of individual personalities in the different regions and in the different generations. His provocative studies on the increasing sophistication shown by the *isnād*s, as they acquired wider 'spread' and obtained surer and more secure routes to prominent personalities of the past, to Successors, Companions and eventually to the Prophet, make it certain that the *isnād* itself had consciously been seen and exploited as a weapon of debate in its own right.[580] The data recoverable from the literary period lend considerable support to his suggestions on the evolution of the *isnād* instrument. Schacht improved upon Goldziher's findings in his observation that the representatives of the legal 'schools' in the generation preceding that of Shāfiʿī had come under increasing pressure from the *Ḥadīth* party, whose insistence on strict documentation forced upon the 'lawyers' the adoption of the *ḥadīth* as the principal means of expressing their conclusions on all topics. That, in turn, led to the obfuscation of the historical source of those conclusions themselves. The content of their legal codes altered little as a result, but their presentation had to change to conform with a new orthodoxy, thus obscuring the actual nature of the thinking that had first produced the conclusions.

A major weakness detectable in the work of both these pioneers was the failure of each to take adequate account of the underlying pressure exerted on all branches of Islamic intellectual activity in the earliest period by the looming presence of the Quran – or, rather, of the preparatory work on the interpretation of the sacred texts that had already reached quite advanced positions on questions of cult, ritual and theological attitudes and even legal questions, before the appearance of what Schacht called 'the ancient schools of law'.

We took note that, in his endeavours to locate the source of the legal penalty for adultery which formed part of the law that he had inherited, Mālik, author of the oldest surviving Sunnī law work, demonstrated that, in the middle of the second century, men no longer knew where that had come from. Mālik had heard that it had come from 'the Book of God', but could not make the mental connection with any text known to him in his Quran. A similar inability faced the scholars in their discussions on the fast of ʿĀshūrā'. In these and other cases which divided them, such as opinions on *tamattuʿ* of the *ḥajj*, or 'temporary marriage', or washing/wiping the feet in the *wuḍū'*, and, developing from that, the arguments on making do with merely wiping the footwear, questions on shortening the ritual prayers on a journey, or of combining two of the ritual prayers in certain conditions, scholars, the heirs to these and a host of other questions, failing to connect any of these matters with the Quran, or with its interpretation, took refuge in attributing them to a second source, 'the *sunna*'.

> ʿUthmān invited ʿAlī to punish a breach of the ban on drinking wine. ʿAlī delegated the actual application of the penalty to another and counted out the strokes as they fell. He stopped him at forty. The Prophet had applied forty lashes; Abū Bakr had applied forty lashes. ʿUmar had imposed eighty lashes, and each is *sunna*.[581]
>
> The population swelled in ʿUmar's day, and drinking became a common habit among the people. ʿUmar consulted the Prophet's Companions and ʿAbdul Raḥmān b. ʿAwf suggested use of the 'lightest penalty', so ʿUmar adopted eighty lashes.[582]
>
> Abū Hurayra (and Muʿāwiya) reported the Prophet as ordering

> the flogging of drinkers. For a man's fourth such offence, the Prophet ordained execution.[583]

The scholars, however, did not adopt this death penalty for the persistent drinker. They took the view that it had been repealed.

> Shāfiʿī had heard the Prophet's report from only one man – a man of virtue who transmitted *ḥasan* reports. He is uncertain whether, in this instance, the man's memory was to be relied upon. He knew of a second report mentioning either death or banishment, in a parallel to which a man was brought to the Prophet charged with the fifth offence of drinking, yet was merely sentenced to be flogged. If any of the previous *ḥadīth*s are, in fact, 'sound', this last report indicates their repeal. Those other reports on the subject are *mursal*. Further, ʿUthmān had conveyed from the Prophet a celebrated general statement on the penal law: 'no Muslim may be put to death except for one of three causes – apostasy, adultery and unjustifiable homicide'. As to the 'soundness' of this report, the *Ḥadīth* specialists entertain no doubt. The attempt may be made to argue that this general statement does not contradict the reports on the death penalty for persistent drinking, but Shāfiʿī knows of no scholar who calls for other than repeated flogging of the incorrigible drinker, on the fifth or the sixth charge. No drinker was ever executed. So, if the reports on the Prophet's institution of a death penalty for persistent drinking prove to be sound, it must have been rescinded. In the Quran, God has specified which acts merit killing and which flogging. Killing may not replace flogging[!] except on the basis of information 'soundly' reported from the Prophet, in the absence of contrary Prophet statements or an indication of abrogation.[584]

> When ʿUmar consulted the Companions on this problem of a penalty for drinking, ʿAlī spoke up: 'A man drinks, he gets drunk; he gets drunk, he rants; he rants, he is bound to slander somebody. I think you should flog them eighty strokes of the lash.' ʿUmar adopted the suggestion.

Mālik adds:

> The *sunna* in our region is that whoever consumes any intoxicant, *whether or not he gets drunk*, incurs the flogging penalty.[585]

> ʿAlī declared, 'I will compensate the heirs of anyone who dies as a result of undergoing a legal penalty, except in the case of drinking, for it was not the Prophet who instituted it; we did'.[586]

Whoever instituted the penalty for drinking did it on the analogy of the penalty of the eighty lashes imposed in Q 24.4 for the unjustifiable slander of innocent females. Despite the Muslim insistence that the Quran prohibits wine, there is no provision in the Quran of any penalty for any breach of the prohibition.

> Mālik was informed by Rabīʿa b. ʿAbdul Raḥmān (often dubbed 'Rabīʿat *al-ra'y*' for his supposed reliance on speculation, as opposed to *ḥadīth*s) that he had asked the great Madīnan expert, Saʿīd b. al-Musayyab, about the compensation for a woman's loss of a finger by the criminal act of another. Saʿīd said that for one finger, it was ten camels; for two fingers, it was twenty camels; for three fingers, it was thirty camels; and for four fingers, it was twenty camels. 'What?' exclaimed Rabīʿa, 'the greater the injury she sustains, the less the compensation she obtains?' Saʿīd asked him if he were an Iraqi. 'No,' said Rabīʿa, 'a scholar seeking confirmation, or a beginner seeking instruction.'
>
> 'Well, anyway,' said Saʿīd, 'that is the *sunna*.'[587]

Shafiʿī was at first attracted to this *ḥadīth* for two reasons.

> Saʿīd had claimed that it was the *sunna*. There was a parallel *ḥadīth* from the Companion, Zayd b. Thābit, a confidant of the Prophet. Second, the ruling was irrational and so could not have resulted from human ratiocination.
>
> The Iraqis held that a woman's compensation was always half that payable to a male, and they could adduce a *ḥadīth* from ʿAlī to that effect. This, they said, was supported by a *ḥadīth* from ʿUmar. This Iraqi view was also attractive. If the life of a female is always compensated for at half the weregeld paid for a male life, the idea that all injuries received by females should be compensated on the same scale was unexceptionable from the analogical angle. It was not a conclusion which an intelligent person could be mistaken about. But Saʿīd had said, 'That is the *sunna*'. The doctrine which he so described could not have been arrived at by the application of legal reasoning. It could not arise from faulty application of analogy, since such mistakes have to be at least plausible, which this Madīnan view self-evidently is not. It must, therefore, have been reached on the basis of some precedent which the Madīna scholars felt they had no option but to follow. Saʿīd did say it was the *sunna*. That probably means that it comes from the Prophet, or from the general body of the Prophet's Companions. To the objection that it is contrary to the reports from ʿAlī and ʿUmar, it can be said that neither of their reports is 'sound'. Had they been satisfactorily transmitted, it is probable that their conclusions had been reached through the

> application of rational methods which would have produced no other result. Saʿīd's declaration, on the other hand, being non-analogical and contrary to reason, can be based only on precedent. On that basis, and for that reason, I once accepted it and agreed with it, but have since abandoned it. That is because one finds scholars from time to time saying, 'Such-and-such is the *sunna*', but *they fail to trace it to the Prophet* by an acceptable *isnād*. That being the case, one has no option but to declare that analogy provides the better solution.

The Iraqis produced a *ḥadīth* from Zayd in which the thinking processes of the Madīnans are reconstructed:

> the rates of compensation payable to the female equal those paid to the male until they reach one third of the male rates, at which point the female rates drop to one half of the male rates. But this Zayd *ḥadīth* is less satisfactorily transmitted than the *ḥadīth* from ʿAlī. There being no satisfactory *ḥadīth* from the Prophet, resort to analogy is preferable.[588]

> ʿUmar determined that the compensation for the loss of a thumb should be fifteen camels; for the forefinger, he awarded ten, and ten also for the middle finger; he awarded nine for the next finger and six for the little finger. Doubtless, ʿUmar would have been aware that for the loss of an entire hand the Prophet had set the compensation at fifty camels. There being five differently shaped fingers of varying utility, ʿUmar seems to have applied his discretion to arranging them in order of usefulness, declaring the appropriate compensation. ʿUmar's ruling was accepted and acted upon for a time until there came to light a document written by the Prophet for ʿAmr b. Ḥazm in which Muḥammad stated that the compensation for any of the fingers was to be ten camels. When ʿAmr's descendants produced this document, the Muslims abandoned ʿUmar's ruling and adopted that of the Prophet. ʿUmar, too, would have abandoned his own ruling if he had known that of the Prophet.

– or so Shāfiʿī insists. To reinforce the technical point at issue, in another place, it is reported that ʿUmar had said: 'But for the statement made by the Prophet to which attention has now been drawn, the matter would have been decided on the basis of our own reasoning'.[589]

What all the scholars who engaged in these studies were doing was to attempt to account for the present state of the Law. What the *Ḥadīth* scholars were engaged in was the conscious attempt to link the present state of the Law in its details to identifiable personalities in the community's past. Shāfiʿī sought to simplify this process by tracing the present state of the Law, wherever possible, to a single personality of the past, the Prophet himself. Here, we witness the deliberate smashing of the smooth chronological line from the Prophet on to the latest period. What happened in the years following the Prophet's death, in the time of ʿUmar, is rejected in favour of 'turning the clock back' to what has been reported as having been the ruling issued by the Prophet.

SHĀFIʿĪ AND THE 'SOURCES OF KNOWLEDGE'

Shāfiʿī speaks of the four ways of acquiring knowledge of the divine will: Quran, *Sunna*, analogy and *ijmāʿ*.[590] What he means by the last principle, consensus, tends to vary with the audience which he chances to be addressing. It changes also on the accident of whether or not a *ḥadīth*, and preferably one transmitted as from the Prophet, happens to be available. Shāfiʿī declines to interpret *ḥadīth*s from the Prophet in the light of *ḥadīth*s from the Companions, or later figures. But he invariably interprets the Quran in the light of his *ḥadīth*s from the Prophet, which renders his alleged 'hierarchy of sources' somewhat suspect.[591]

We have seen him, on the question of the penalty for the persistent drinker, interpret *ḥadīth*s from the Prophet in the light of the general view adopted by the specialist scholars. The case showed that *isnād* guarantees did not always suffice to satisfy 'the general body of the scholars'. In the face of *ḥadīth*s of unwelcome content (*matn*), they were always receptive to ready presumption of repeal (*naskh*). Officially, according to the theories, *naskh* is indicated by the content of a contrary *ḥadīth* – in Shāfiʿī's case, a *ḥadīth* from the Prophet. But, repeal is actually indicated by this majority scholarly view.[592] That represents the older meaning of the term '*sunna*', for which others were beginning to use the alternative term *ijmāʿ*, that is, scholarly consensus. For many of the specialists, Iraqi and Madīnan, '*sunna*' had meant past precedent, exhibited in the discussions on the compensations payable to females. There being no clear-cut Quran guidance at the level of detail, nor any satisfactorily transmitted statement that had been traced from the Prophet, then in such cases, for Shāfiʿī, analogical derivation from such general principles as were thought to be based on Prophetic precedent came into play. In theory at least, analogy exerts priority over *ijmāʿ*. In the second case which we considered, that of the compensation payable for loss of fingers, analogy appears to have given rise to a Prophetic statement. The conclusion at issue was, however, presented as an analogy derived from the same *ḥadīth*. That *ḥadīth*, being from the Prophet, was permitted to override the considered judgment attributed to the caliph ʿUmar, removing the refinement of consideration of the position of the finger or its supposed greater or less utility. The compensation for the entire hand being fifty camels, and there being five fingers, the compensation for any one of the fingers was set at ten.

We stated that Shāfiʿī's attitude to appeals made to *ijmāʿ* was ambivalent. In other cases, he himself seems to have no other suggestion to offer concerning the origin of certain of the rulings of the inherited Law. For example, it was generally noted that, in instituting his tax regime, the Prophet had had in mind Arabian conditions. Taxes on agricultural produce had focused on the crops grown locally, namely wheat, barley and maize.

> 'The Muslims before our time taxed, in addition, a range of other crops, concentrating on what people grew for personal consumption. The tax base was thus extended. They both imitated in this those before them, and argued by analogy with what the Prophet had introduced, since he had taxed crops used as food sources.'[593]

Similarly, it is ascertained that the Prophet taxed financial resources held in silver. Mālik stated that the undisputed *sunna* in his region was that tax must also be paid on resources held in gold, just as it must be levied on silver.[594]

> For Shāfiʿī, the Prophet had taxed silver. That the Muslims taxed gold must be presumed to have been either based on a *ḥadīth* from the Prophet, although that *ḥadīth* has not come down to us, or derived by analogy from the tax on silver, on the principle that gold, like silver, is a means of exchange.[595]

For Shāfiʿī, there were two grades of consensus: the *ijmāʿ* of the entire Muslim populace on the general duties of the believer; and the expressed views of the general body of specialist scholars on specific points of the Law. Apparently resistant to the urgings of others that the general agreement of the scholars must be based ultimately on statements of the Prophet, even if these have not been handed down to us, he swung between now acknowledging the force of that general scholarly agreement and the countervailing realisation that it was precisely specialist knowledge that caused disagreement. Only the Quran and *ḥadīth*s from the Prophet acknowledged by the entire Muslim public guaranteed absolute certainty.[596] Only the *ḥadīth*s in the possession of the specialists alone were liable to give rise to different conclusions or were susceptible to *ta'wīl*, or minute reinterpretation. But the accomplished scholar, by the application of a series of rules, could arrive at a conclusion as to which of the competing *ḥadīth*s was the more deserving of acceptance. For example, on the much-debated question of how precisely to define 'usury', which all Muslims agreed had been denounced by God and His Prophet in the strongest terms, two views had come down from the Companions.

> Usury arises when the exchange of two commodities of like kind is marked by unequal quantities; or usury arises when the facility to defer payment is reflected in the agreed price.

Both views are reported as from the Prophet by Companions of equal eminence. One view had been adopted by the Makkans, and the other by the Madīnans. For Shāfiʿī, the two opinions were either potentially reconcilable or potentially irreconcilable.

> They were reconcilable on the presumption that the Makkan authority had either misheard the question that the Prophet had been asked, or had heard only the reply and not the question. However, given the Makkan attitude, it is more likely that the reports are irreconcilable, and the scholar is obliged to choose between them. Whereas those who report the *ḥadīth* favoured at Madīna are not regarded as of greater powers of retention than the transmitter of the form preferred at Makka, they are not reputed to have had weaker powers of retention either. Among the transmitters of the Madīnan version are, however, persons much older in years and of much longer association with the Prophet than those reporting the Makkan version. Indeed, one of them, Abū Hurayra, is regarded as having been the most outstanding memoriser of his day. The number of the transmitters of the Madīnan form of the *ḥadīth* is greater. The greater number is more likely to be more retentive and less exposed to error than the smaller number, and the older than the younger transmitter.[597]

Thus, the mechanical criterion of number may be applied. Other criteria expressed by Shāfiʿī contain a high degree of interpretative judgment.

> One chooses the *ḥadīth* which is closer in spirit to the Quran; if there is no Quran text, one prefers the better-attested in terms of the *isnād*, that is, the *isnād* that contains the better-known names or names of those known to be better memorisers; or the *ḥadīth* that is accompanied by the greater number of *isnād*s, since that is more likely to have been better memorised; or the *ḥadīth* that is more in keeping with the sense of the Quran in general, or the sense of the *sunna* of the Prophet in general; or more in keeping with what the scholars recognise, or more correct in terms of analogy with parallel matters, or the view espoused by the greater number of Companions.[598]

As 'to what is more in keeping with what the scholars recognise', Shāfiʿī's interlocutors would allege that that was sufficient evidence that what the scholars acknowledged must have been based on an ascertained utterance of the Prophet whether or not they had transmitted the relevant report. Shāfiʿī was not willing to go as far as that. What he would say was that

> what the scholars agreed had been transmitted from the Prophet had indeed been transmitted from him. Where they were agreed but did not assert that that had been transmitted from the Prophet was open to the two possibilities: that it had been transmitted from him, and that it had not been formally transmitted from him. We may not, however, presume that it had been transmitted from him in the absence of the formal apparatus of transmission. We used to hold what they hold, imitating their attitude in this respect. We realise that where there are *sunna* reports from the Prophet, they cannot fail to be known to some of them, although not known to all of them. We further know that collectively they could not agree on something not in conformity with the *sunna* of the Prophet – nor upon an error.[599]

The Prophet had demanded that men adhere to the community of the Muslims. That must mean that the consensus of the Muslims is binding.[600]

9

Conclusions: ijmāʿ *(Consensus) versus* sunna

From all the discussions we have considered, a number of conclusions may be drawn. Shāfiʿī's aim to achieve a full statement of the Law of Islam on the basis of two primary sources was not attainable, although he very nearly succeeded.

Many of his contemporaries, for example, Mālik and those he had taught, were still at the stage of being impressed by the general agreement of those scholars around them. What was so generally agreed by the Muslims might be regarded as the very stuff of Islam. They might not always be able to say precisely where it had come from, but it was spoken of as 'the *sunna* of the Muslims', or simply 'the *sunna*'. Faced in his own day with 'the *sunna* of Madīna' and 'the *sunna* of Kūfa', Shāfiʿī sought, with the aid of the unifying principle of 'the *sunna* of the Prophet', to locate and to impose a less localised '*sunna* of Islam'. Objections had been raised to individual theses of an inherited Law on the grounds that they were not in conformity with the Quran, the Book of God. Observing that the protesters were scholars sceptical of the competing claim to 'the *sunna*' made by quarrelling groups of Arabians and Iraqis each appropriating the term to their own particular regional stock of *Ḥadīth*, and realising that these objectors were deaf to any but evidence derived from the Quran itself, Shāfiʿī attempted to satisfy both his own aims and this novel demand. He thus restricted his response to drawing from the Quran the arguments which it had addressed to the Prophet's contemporaries: to obey the Prophet is to obey God; to disobey or ignore the Prophet is to disobey and ignore God. Obedience to God can be demonstrated solely by obedience to Muḥammad and, after his death, obedience to his *sunna*. That religious obligation solemnly imposed upon men in the Quran could, in Muḥammad's lifetime, be fulfilled either by asking the Prophet oneself, or by accepting the word of another man who had approached the Prophet and asked him and could now pass on his instruction.[601] This, according to Shāfiʿī, continues to be possible on the basis of the *ḥadīth*s collected by and found to satisfy the *isnād* criteria of the specialist scholars. When it was objected that the specialist scholars appeared to be content to accept their very significant information on the basis of *isnād*s from, at best, two or three individuals, at worst even from a single person, Shāfiʿī insisted on drawing the parallel with the contemporaries of the Prophet who had not shown any reluctance to accept their information from single persons who had questioned the Prophet and whose reports on the Prophet's replies the other Muslims were prepared to trust. Shāfiʿī is here defending the special situation where important information required by him and his contemporaries had been discovered only in *ḥadīth*s transmitted by only a single person, the so-called *akhbār al-āḥād*. *Isnād*s, he says, which can be trusted are accepted. *Isnād*s which cannot be trusted may be ignored. No-one appears to have made the point that what was possible for the Prophet's contemporaries, that is, to satisfy themselves as to the truth of any statement by checking with him directly, was no longer possible following his death. It is, however, standard practice for Shāfiʿī to draw this parallel between the single-person report which he and other *Ḥadīth* specialists accepted and the trust that individual Companions had shown to each other in their day. Attempts to introduce some minimum number of transmitters for each generation through which the *ḥadīth*s had passed since the death of the Prophet could always be dismissed as arbitrary. Citing the reports on the fate of those who deliberately imputed to the Prophet words he had not uttered, Shāfiʿī is complacent in supposing that the knowledge of that class of *ḥadīth* had sufficed to deter men from incurring such dreadful risks.[602] Besides, the business of the *Ḥadīth* scholars is to achieve probability rather than certainty.[603] Thus, to accept a command or a prohibition from the Prophet on the basis of a formally correct *ḥadīth* is to act in complete conformity with the demands of the Quran. If satisfactorily reported as from the Prophet, no *ḥadīth* can ever be in conflict with the Book of God, communicated to us by the same generation from the same source, the Prophet, who had been charged with the additional responsibility of clarifying to men the precise meaning of what God intended by His revelations in the Quran.[604]

That the scholars of the various regions have disagreed is to be imputed to their having relied on reports from ordinary men, rather than on those from the inspired lawgiver. However, in the presence of a report from the Prophet, reports from any other quarter need not even be considered. Such reports neither reinforce nor weaken Prophet reports.[605] Companion reports often clash. That happens because the Companions had not all been equal in their knowledge of the prophet's teachings. Some had been more frequently in his company than others, so that the oldest of his associates might well be unaware of something he had done and said, if they chanced to be absent on an occasion when others were present and able to report. The report from one or more Companions to which no other Companion has been reported as dissenting has a strong claim on our consideration. But a report from a single Companion from the Prophet has an even stronger claim to be considered, no matter how many other Companions may be reported as having done or said differently. Those who place great reliance upon Companion reports and who cite them to counter reports from the Prophet transmitted as from other Companions frequently excused their procedure on the plea that 'the Companions knew the mind of the Prophet best'. Shāfi'ī rejects this line of argument: only the Prophet knew the mind of the Prophet best.[606] Thus, in opposition to any *ḥadīth* from the Prophet, only a second report from the Prophet may be considered. Only if two or more Companions report from the Prophet anything in opposition to another report also from the Prophet are these reports to be considered. There are frequent such instances of conflicting information. But only if both items are explicitly traced to the Prophet are they to be investigated. Consideration must then be given to the dates of the acts or words reported, as indicated in the *isnād*s of the relevant *ḥadīth*s, if not from the texts of the reports. As is the case with the *asbāb* of the Quran, knowledge of the historical situation which provoked the Prophet's words or actions on a particular occasion is invaluable for removing a conflict which will prove to be merely apparent. If it is a question of repeal, only the information on the later of the two situations is followed. But Shāfi'ī himself is not always consistent in his application of this principle, and other instances are seen in which his references to repeal are mere presumption.

The *Ḥadīth* movement was daily unearthing much fresh material on the views of earlier generations of the Muslims. Nor was it only in Iraq that the group which formed around the person of Mālik had its competitors. He was opposed on many questions by the scholars in Makka. He had, besides, rivals and enemies in Madīna itself. Having studied not simply with Mālik but also with his contemporaries in Makka, Iraq and Madīna itself, Shāfi'ī was armed with a much vaster bulk of *ḥadīth*s than those acknowledged by Mālik, and many of these had *isnād*s reaching back either to older Arabian authorities, or to Iraqi authorities and to the Prophet himself. Many of these Shāfi'ī could use to challenge what Mālik referred to as the 'agreement of the scholars' of Madīna and, where that conflicted with information reported as from the Prophet, he could question the legitimacy of the appeal to that 'agreement', or, where it conflicted with the *ḥadīth* material traced to older Madīnan authorities, he could question the very reality of that alleged 'agreement'.[607]

'Agreement', consensus, *ijmā'*, as a principle of verification of the theses of the Law, was still very much alive in the time of Shāfi'ī. His references, however, to the principle itself, were equivocal, even inconsistent. We have seen him, on the question of the treatment of the persistent drinker, use the agreement of the legal scholars as an argument to dismiss a *ḥadīth* report from the Prophet in which he had been alleged to propose the death penalty. It had been that *ijmāʿ* that he had used to decide between the two reports from the prophet. Elsewhere in his writings, Shāfiʿī, for polemic reasons, denies what others call *ijmāʿ*. The representative scholars of the Islamic regions not having ever met or been brought together, it was idle, he would insist, to allege that there could exist any consensus.[608] Only what the entire body of the Muslims, the unlearned and the learned together, were agreed upon, such as the number of the daily ritual prayers, the obligation to observe the fast of the month of Ramaḍān, and a few other general matters of the kind, of which no Muslim was ignorant, could be graced with the name of *ijmāʿ*. Otherwise, Law derived from the work of specialists skilled in the meanings of the Quran and its interpretation and who, between them, possessed the *sunna* of the Prophet, the knowledge of the criteria of the *isnād*s and were skilled in its interpretation also.

Shāfiʿī's great rival, Shaybānī, had 'heard', on the other hand,

> that the Prophet had said, 'Whatever the Muslims regard as good is good in the sight of God; whatever the Muslims regard as bad is bad in the sight of God'.[609]

This report had reached Shaybānī, but for it he had no *isnād*. Ṭayālisī knew the same statement, but as a pronouncement uttered by the Companion, ʿAbdallāh b. Masʿūd.[610] Ibn Māja, with an *isnād* passing through Abū Hurayra, produces it as a statement of the Prophet's, specifically directed at people who, in exactly the same way as the anti-*Ḥadīth* group addressed by Shāfiʿī, had shown their reservations about the *'sunna'*.

> 'Let me not find any of you ensconced at his ease saying, when a *ḥadīth* from me is reported to him, "Recite the Quran rather than this" – whatever good thing is uttered, it is I who have said it.'[611]

The growing principle of *ijmāʿ* is appealed to by Ibn Qutayba in his debate with the theologians. One of them had scoffed at the notion that sleep breaches a man's ritual purity and necessitated the renewal of the *wuḍū'*. As far as he was concerned, the agreement that the Muslims had achieved on the point was erroneous. Nor did it matter which posture was adopted for sleep, sitting up or lying flat out.

> The Muslims perform their morning *wuḍū'* since they had seen their elders do so. That had nothing to do with sleep. Most people rising in the morning usually have to relieve themselves. They generally have dried, crusty scales on their eyes and stale mouths. That is why they prefer to wash first thing each day.

This kind of argument enrages Ibn Qutayba, since it is contrary to the *sunna*. The Prophet had said: 'My people will never agree on an error'.[612] The theologians prided themselves on their skill in rational argument and sought to bring the entire Law onto strictly rational bases, yet there are elements of the Law and the *sunna* which are not susceptible of rational explanation. No logic could explain, for example, why it is that the woman who is not permitted to perform any of the prayers when she is menstruating, nor to observe the ritual fast, is not required to 'make up' any prayer missed for this cause, and yet is required to 'make up' the fast. The fact that that is so is simply because that is the *sunna*.[613]

> One man reported from Qatāda, who traced it to Abū Hurayra, that the Prophet had said, 'When you receive from me a *ḥadīth* which accords with the Truth, accept it, whether I said it or not'.[614]

On this, one expert comments:

> 'For this statement, there is no *ṣaḥīḥ isnād*. He who transmitted it has been responsible for more than one unrecognised *ḥadīth*.'

According to a second expert, the *ḥadīth* was fabricated by persons hostile to Islam, while Khaṭṭābī said it had no basis. The transmitter of a report parallel to this is described as quite unknown, or 'weak', or probably acceptable, or a legal specialist to whom no suspicion attaches, who was in contact with those from whom he transmits reports. Perhaps his memory was poor. In a variant to the Ibn Māja *ḥadīth* above, we find an addition:

> 'Whatever good thing reaches you from me, whether I said it or not, I said it; whatever bad thing reaches you – I do not say bad things'.[615]

In the period between Mālik and his pupils, Muḥammad and Shāfiʿī, there occurred a veritable explosion of *isnād*s. We noted the large number of reports that Muḥammad could introduce on the question of *wuḍū*' after touching the penis. On another matter, the validity in certain types of case of the testimony of only one witness plus the oath of the claimant, Mālik could muster very few reports, not one of which would satisfy the *isnād* experts. The reports are *munqaṭi*ʿ, yet Mālik pronounces that they express the *sunna*.[616] Shaybānī has a report to the effect that Zuhrī (Mālik's teacher) had denounced the view that Mālik defends as 'an unwarrantable innovation'. The Iraqis attribute its introduction to the Umayyads.[617] On the same topic, Shāfiʿī alleges no fewer than twenty-two separate *isnād*s.[618]

The production and the 'improvement' of *isnād*s proceeded in the period after Shāfiʿī and is especially noticeable in cases like the above which were the subject of discussion or debate. A few examples of the completion of *isnād*s will illustrate this.

1. Mālik – Yaḥyā b. Saʿīd – ʿAmr b. Shuʿayb – ʿUmar – the Prophet. Shāfiʿī – Mālik – Yaḥyā b. Saʿīd – ʿAmr b. Shuʿayb – the Prophet.
   Cf. Abū Da'ūd: 'I find in my book from Shaybān, but I did not hear this from him – Abū Bakr, an associate of mine, informed me – Shaybān – Muḥammad (b. Rāshid) – Sulaymān (ibn Mūsā) – ʿAmr b. Shuʿayb – his father – his grandfather: the Prophet used to do so-and-so, and apropos of this, he said:[619]
2. Mālik: Nāfiʿ said, 'I do not think ʿAbdallāh b. ʿUmar reported this other than from the Prophet'.
   Shāfiʿī – Mālik – Nāfiʿ – ibn ʿUmar, I think from the Prophet. Shāfiʿī – a man – Ibn abī Dhi'b – Zuhrī – Sālim – his father, ʿAbdallāh b. ʿUmar – the Prophet. Sālim had no doubt that this was his father's report and that it was *marfūʿ* (raised) to the Prophet.[620]

Mālik's report had been cited extensively in the form of ʿAbdallāh b. ʿUmar's *opinion*, given in reply to a question:

cf. Muslim: ʿAbd b. Ḥumayd – ʿAbdul Razzāq – Maʿmar – Zuhrī – Sālim – ʿAbdallāh b. ʿUmar: the Prophet prayed ...
Muslim – Abū Bakr b. abī Shayba – Yaḥyā b. Ādam – Sufyān – Mūsā b. ʿUqba – Nāfiʿ – ibn ʿUmar – the Prophet ...[621]
Ibn Māja: Muḥammad b. al-Ṣabāḥ – Jarīr b. Ḥāzim – ʿUbaydallāh b. ʿUmar – Nāfiʿ – ibn ʿUmar – the Prophet ...[622]

There are many examples of this same phenomenon of Shāfiʿī's *ḥadīth*s, either *mursal* or *munqaṭiʿ* as cited in the *Risāla*, yet recoverable in the classical collections as fully connected, *marfūʿ ḥadīth*s. There are even instances in which the modern editor and commentator on the *Risāla*, Shaykh Shākir, either rejects Shāfiʿī's arguments or the *ḥadīth*s on which they are based, or even declares in some instances that the *ḥadīth*s are mere fabrications.[623]

Shāfiʿī himself was inclined to be severe on the subject of the impeccability of the *isnād*, although he also points out that he has yet to meet another who maintained these very high standards that he himself insisted on.[624] Whereas he alleges that the past generations in his region had been free of the habit, he has noted the recent trend towards *tadlīs*. From those known to practise *tadlīs* (dissimulation), he declares that he would insist that they use the correct formula of transmission, that is, *ḥaddathanā*, or *samiʿtu*, before he will agree to accept a single *ḥadīth* from them.[625] The *mursal ḥadīth* is also common. But, if acknowledged by known specialists, and reported by them, in formally correct fashion, *mursal ḥadīth*s acquire a degree of strength. Or, if a second *mursal ḥadīth* is found, coming down from a second transmitter, that also tends to confirm the first. If Companion statements support what the *mursal ḥadīth* reports, that shows that the *mursal* has a 'sound' foundation. So also does the view expressed by the generality of the scholars.[626] Companion statements, even if based on opinion, can indicate the 'soundness' of a *mursal*, for the transmitter may have mistaken that statement (*qawl*) for a *ḥadīth* report.[627] The *mursal* reports of the older Successors who had met some of the Companions do not pose the same problems as the *mursal* of the younger Successors who had met none of the Companions. Their *mursal* reports are subject to stricter control. But scholars differ in approach. Some, wishing to accumulate a large stock of *Ḥadīth*, accept reports from men who are best ignored. The less careful scholars accept from weak transmitters who happen to agree with their views, while rejecting the reports of others who happen to disagree with their views. Shāfiʿī has expressed his amazement at the number of *mursal* reports that have been accepted from the younger Successors.[628]

The reasons that would justify a scholar's rejection of any *ḥadīth* the like of which he had already accepted are:

> that he knows a contrary *ḥadīth*; that what he hears and the person from whom he hears it are more reliable than is the case with the *ḥadīth* which it opposes; or the person who informed him of one of the *ḥadīth*s has greater powers of memory; perhaps his informant may in his eyes be suspect, or he may entertain suspicions about the informant's informant; or perhaps the *ḥadīth* may be susceptible to more than one interpretation and he opts for one of the interpretations, abandoning the alternative.[629]

No other cause will justify the rejection of a formally correct transmission. When the general body of scholars is satisfied with a *ḥadīth*'s credentials, no man may reject it. If it comes from the Prophet, it is *sunna* and it alone, together with the Quran, provides absolute certainty.[630]

From the subsequent development of Islamic literature, it may appear that Shāfiʿī's insistence on the primacy of the *sunna* of the Prophet has triumphed. In a sense that is true, but in another sense the triumph has been that of the *Ḥadīth* experts. Shāfiʿī considered that, in the sphere of the *Ḥadīth*, 'the general agreement of the scholars' was *ijmāʿ*, and, in the period after his death, the principle of *ijmāʿ* continued to gather strength. In the generation following his, it was the *ijmāʿ* of the *Ḥadīth* party that guaranteed for al-Ṭabarī not merely the details of the orthography and the pronunciation of the Quran texts, so that if more than a single reading had been proposed in the different centres in *ḥadīth*s of equal strength between which it was not possible to decide, each of the readings must be declared valid and acceptable provided they were handed down by the Muslims as

> 'their heritage from their Prophet by a known, open transmission which gives no man any excuse either to allege ignorance, or reluctance to accept it. What comes down in a manner that is probative among the Muslims is the truth. It cannot be doubted that it comes from God. What is attested in this manner can never be opposed by opinions, suppositions, nor the isolated views of the smaller number.'[631]

The text having been settled, the interpretation of the text is determined in precisely the same fashion, on the basis of precisely the same guaranteed transmission.

It was *ijmāʿ* that determined the community's rightful ruler. *Ijmāʿ* determined which *ḥadīth*s were unquestionable, therefore, what the Law and the theology of Islam would be. On their appearance, the general scholarly welcome accorded to the *Ḥadīth* collections of Bukhārī and Muslim, who had included not every *ḥadīth* that, in their personal opinion was 'sound', but what the *Ḥadīth* experts were unanimous was 'sound', guaranteed that, in turn, their works would be sanctified by the *ijmāʿ* and thus placed in the highest category, beyond questioning. We also saw that the aim of the leading *Sunan* collectors was to include, in addition to what was regarded as 'sound', those *ḥadīth*s of the *ḥasan* class, identified as those which the *Ḥadīth* experts had not unanimously rejected on one ground or another. Thereafter, the *ijmāʿ* had selected which of the *Sunan* works should be selected to join the two *Ṣaḥīḥ* works to form 'the six books'.

In an interesting passage, Ibn Qutayba explains this emerging preference for the *ijmāʿ*:

> In our view, Truth is established by *ijmāʿ* more frequently than by the transmission [of *ḥadīth*s] since the *ḥadīth* can be exposed to the mischance of forgetfulness or carelessness. It can be affected also by ambiguities, reinterpretation and abrogation. The reliable also accept information from unreliable persons. There are also parallelisms, with one report saying one thing and another another thing, both of which may be acceptable. One man might report a Prophet command but be absent when it is later rescinded. So he reports the command in good faith, but not its cancellation since he does not know anything about it.
>
> *Ijmāʿ* is exempt from these hazards. That is why Mālik can report a *ḥadīth* from the Prophet and then say 'But what is done in Madīna is something different', on a basis other than that particular *ḥadīth*. Mālik's town was the Prophet's town. When something was done in the Prophet's day, the same thing would

> be done in the second generation, and in the third and subsequent generations. The Madīnans would not all abandon something done in the Prophet's day in his town and adopt something different. What is transmitted by an entire generation outweighs what is transmitted by one man from one man. Men have transmitted connected *ḥadīth*s yet disregarded them. For example, it is correctly reported that the Prophet combined two prayers when safe in Madīna and in no fear of enemy attack. All scholars have, however, agreed not to act on this, either because it may have been repealed, or because Muḥammad had done that for some compelling reason, such as rain, or his being preoccupied with affairs of state.
>
> Another *ḥadīth* reports that a man died without leaving any heirs, apart from a man he had manumitted to whom the Prophet assigned his property. The scholars do not act on this, possibly because they do not repose sufficient trust in one man named in the *isnād*. Equally, it could be on account of a problem of interpetation. The words might be interpreted: 'apart from the man who had manumitted him'. Alternatively, the ruling may have been as first stated, but later that ruling was replaced by the one represented in the second interpretation.
>
> Despite its having been reported by a satisfactory *isnād*, the scholars ignored the report that, in the *wuḍūʿ*, the Prophet wiped his headgear (and not his head). That, too, may have been abrogated, or perhaps the transmitter, having seen the Prophet wipe his head-covering and his head, reported only the more remarkable of the two situations and ignored the obvious one. At any rate, they prefer the other *ḥadīth* in which it is reported that the Prophet wiped his turban and his hair. The obligation to wipe the head is imposed in the Quran and is not cancelled by a *ḥadīth* worded to the contrary.[632]

Other *ḥadīth*s had fared better. Among these were the reports that, when travelling, the Prophet had set the precedent that the Muslim might wipe his boots instead of having to remove them to wash his feet in the *wuḍūʿ* before praying. That shows a continuation of the old wipe/wash controversy. The traveller was permitted, in addition, instead of periodically having to keep dismounting for the prayer and remounting after it, to combine two of the ritual prayers. An effort to extend the same facility to the non-traveller proved unsuccessful. For some, however, the facility to wipe the boots rather than the feet had been successfully passed on to non-travellers. The performance of *wuḍū'* itself had shrunk to only once a day, unless the ritual purity were breached by some factor other than sleep – and what the other factors might be was much debated. The inheriting of two sets of traditions reporting the Prophet's precise timing of his ritual prayers, proving incapable of an agreed solution, had led to general agreement that for each prayer there was an extended time-band between the external limits of which each of the prayers must be completed.[633] The question of whether the traveller or the sick must observe, or even may observe, the fast of Ramaḍān proving equally impossible to resolve, it was left open on the argument that the prophet had done both: when travelling, he had sometimes fasted and, at other times, had broken his fast.[634] Similarly, when travelling, he had sometimes curtailed the ritual prayers and at other times had performed the complete ritual.[635] Although Muḥammad is known to have performed only one pilgrimage in Islam, he has been credited with four different types of performance and with uttering four different kinds of *ihlāl*: he had declared his intent to perform the *ḥajj* alone (*afrada*); to combine his *ḥajj* with an *ʿumra* (*jamʿ*; *qirān*); he had *tamattaʿ*, said to mean the performance of a *ḥajj* and an *ʿumra* on a single visit; he had countenanced *mutʿa*; he had shown the validity of *faskh*, or cancellation of one's *ihlāl* and the substitution of another declaration; he had permitted the performance of an *ʿumra* in the season set aside for the *ḥajj*; the *ʿumra*, during the 'ten days', might precede or might follow the *ḥajj*. On this question, the scholars argued that each of the Companions had reported within the limits of what he had seen or heard the Prophet either say, himself do, or permit to others.[636]

It is even conceded that the Prophet had permitted temporary marriage, either on expeditions or on the pilgrimage expedition; but that establishes no precedent, since he immediately stated that that practice was prohibited for all future generations. In his penal system, the Prophet is reported to have applied a penalty for drinking wine that had not been supplied by the Quran, and, although he is stated to have imposed forty lashes, the Companions have been imitated in their preference for the analogy with the penalty supplied by the Quran for the slander of believing females. Muḥammad is further suggested to have inclined towards the execution of the persistent drinker, but continued flogging for the fourth and subsequent offences has been preferred. By contrast, execution by stoning for the offence of adultery has prevailed, overwhelming the objection that no such penalty is mentioned in the Quran and that, indeed, it runs counter to the penalty that is there established.

Legal regulations that depart from the meaning of the relevant Quran statements were rationalised, as we have seen, on the argument that there were two historical bases for regulation: the Quran and what, at a given moment, was called '*sunna*'. The post-Prophetic generations had inherited, it was thought, from the time of the Prophet, full documentation supplied, first, by the Prophet's associates to the rising generation that would succeed them. The second generation had preserved the sacred materials in trust and had faithfully handed them on to those coming after them and so on, generation after generation, until they reached the major experts of the *Ḥadīth*. Checking the credentials of the several links in the transmission, the experts had issued their guarantee that it was possible to organise, collect and continue to pass on undimished and uncontaminated this national heritage into the hands of the succeeding generations of Muslims.

Several observations militate, however, against this neat model of the history of the *Ḥadīth*. We have seen that the Muslim analysis of the Tradition was directed at reassuring the believers that they might take this deposit of the *Ḥadīth* on trust. They show themselves to have been perfectly well aware of the many hazards to which the *Ḥadīth* had been exposed in the course of its passage. They saw clearly that confidence in their reports could be demanded only if the links back to the generation surrounding Muḥammad could be shown to have been unbroken and reliable at each stage of the transmission. The *ḥadīth*s must be supported by connected *isnād*s. The individual links in their chains of authorities must be shown to be men of probity and undoubted reliability. It is at this point however, that the outside observer takes note of the absence of unanimity in the assessment of the qualities of the individual transmitters. To give but one example before proceeding, the assessments uttered by the experts on a single *ḥadīth* concerned with the topic of the permissibility of the use of the cupping technique to relieve pain and disorder when one is fasting, range along the entire length of the spectrum of 'quality control'.

> Aḥmad b. Ḥanbal described the *ḥadīth* in question as 'the soundest of all the reports on the question'; his associate, Ibn Maʿīn, thought it the 'weakest of all'; Bukhārī suspected that it had not been competently memorised, while Abū Ḥātim is said to have thought the report 'groundless'.[637]

One is left with the impression that the experts assert rather than demonstrate their evaluations of the reports and the men.

To emphasise their own insistence upon examination of the *isnād*, the experts show that scholars of the generation of, for example, Zuhrī had already insisted on the production of *isnād*s for all statements made. To place that insistence at the turn of the first/second century may be thought somewhat self-defeating. We have seen that Zuhrī's follower, Mālik, had not yet had access to impeccable *isnād*s, and from him we learn that that had also been the case with his teacher. Mālik himself is nonetheless cited by the later scholars for his cautious and critical scrutiny of his *isnād*s, and hailed as an outstanding example of the practices which they themselves emphasised. In the time of Mālik's pupils, classification of the *isnād*s had made some advance, but justification of the use still being made of the *munqaṭi'* and the *mursal ḥadīth*s and the acceptability of the *khabar al-wāḥid*, or *ḥadīth* transmitted from a single authority, remained necessary precisely because of the imperfect nature of the instrument held to guarantee the materials used in the scholarly debate. The visible replacement in a later day of the incomplete *isnād*s that earlier scholars had had to rely on by the completed connections more in keeping with the taste of a later scholarship suggests the victory of theory over fact. It also, incidentally, added a further principle to the scholars' growing list of 'rules'. That the same *ḥadīth* may be cited both in *mursal* and in *muttaṣil*, or connected form, did not justify criticism of either the transmitter whose *isnād* was incomplete, or of him whose *isnād* was complete. Some men have better memories than others, and any addition, whether to the text (*matn*) of a *ḥadīth* or to its *isnād*, made by a man who was recognised as *thiqa*, reliable, and *ḥāfiẓ*, blessed with a sound memory, must be accepted on trust. The principle is worded thus: *ziyādat al-thiqa maqbūla*.[638]

This triumph of theory over fact is even more clearly illustrated in the evolution of the meaning of the term *sunna*. The contrast between an earlier understanding of the term as 'past precedent' underlined by occasional sporadic references to 'the *sunna* of the Prophet' marked the transitional nature of Mālik's thought from the anonymous to the more precisely specific use of the term that blossomed only in the writings of Shāfi'ī, whose ceaseless repetition of the theme that '*sunna*' is meaningless unless it is shown to be reported exclusively from the Prophet shows that this usage is something novel. The narrower reference forced upon the term had, as we saw, been consciously adopted by Shāfi'ī for technical, jurisprudential reasons. That restriction was seen to be radically different from what the term had meant to Mālik, to Zuhrī and, before him, to his informant, Sa'īd b. al-Musayyab (d. 95/713). Born of controvery, Shāfi'ī's definition was radically new, it was revolutionary and it could never be reversed. His tireless repetition of the definition shows that it was not generally self-evident in the second half of the second century, nor in the first half of the third, to judge by Ibn Qutayba's stated preference for the *ijmā'* as against *ḥadīth*s of satisfactory *isnād*. It was to be the *ijmā'* that, by taking the *Ḥadīth* under its wing, would set the stamp of approval on the individual reports. Shāfi'ī himself had insisted that *ḥadīth*s which were generally approved by the corporate body of the competent experts might not be questioned.

THE ASSESSMENT OF THE *ḤADITH*

A further difficulty that arises is that such general acknowledgement proved to be not at all a common phenomenon. Standards of assessment of individual transmitters vary very widely indeed from expert to expert and from generation to generation, leaving the outside observer often very confused. The standards applied vary also with the topic dealt with in a *ḥadīth*, being at their most severe whenever a question of Law, 'the lawful and the unlawful', arises, and at their most lenient when ethical or edificatory material designed to affect the behaviour of the masses by appeal to the emotions of fear or hope is involved. The latter includes the frequent lavish descriptions of the seductive luxuries awaiting in the Hereafter those who volunteer to undertake seemingly trivial supererogatory acts of simple piety, or the horrifically graphic details of the tortures awaiting the damned. Also included under this heading are many *ḥadīth*s designed to magnify the virtues and self-denial of the great personalities of the community's past. A common Western complaint that, in the assessment of the *ḥadīth*s, too much emphasis has been placed by the critics on the external factor of the *isnād* to the disregard of the content of the reports, can be seen to be overstated from a study of the literature on the fabricated *ḥadīth*s, where there has been an attempt to purge the most extravagant reports. However, it remains true that such a study brings out even more clearly the varying standards applied by the critics in different centres and in different periods. The Muslim critic who entertained any reservation about the content of such reports might tend more usually to express some dissatisfaction with one or other element in the *isnād*, but criticism of the *matn* is not so rare as is sometimes claimed. One instance of this would be the following tale in which

> a female jinn is reported to have discussed with the Prophet a strange encounter with Satan. Seeing him stand in prayer, she accosted him, demanding to know why he prayed, he being who he was. The Devil replied that he still hoped that God would keep His promise to forgive him in the end.[639]

That report was rejected out of hand, on the grounds that it was intellectually unacceptable. Only then was the *isnād* discussed, as if for the sake of form.

Conversely, if the content appears attractive, attacks on the *isnād* will meet with a vigorous response. Delicate questions are occasionally met with in the *Ḥadīth* on the fate of the Prophet's parents. The reply that can usually be anticipated is that since they pre-dated his mission, his parents must presumably be languishing in Hell. The continuing process of apotheosis of the Prophet that is natural in religions made the thought intolerable to Muslims imbued with their own personal filial piety, which they automatically transferred to Muḥammad.

> The Prophet's widow recalled a day when Muḥammad went out looking forlorn and distressed but returned beaming with joy. He informed her that he had petitioned God concerning his mother. God, in His limitless mercy, had brought her back to life so that she could hear and accept her son's message. After she had declared her belief, God had then returned her.

The attack on this report concentrating on the *isnād*, the reply was that the *ḥadīth* was not, as alleged, a fabrication, although this particular form might be said to be 'weak'. Al-Suyūṭī vigorously defended the report, referring to his own composition on the revivification of both noble parents. The greatest of the *Ḥadīth* critics, Ibn Ḥajar, defends the *isnād*.

> Two men had been rejected as 'unknown'. On the contrary, both were known. One, a Madīnan, had come to Egypt, dying there in 258/871. Although 'weak', he had never been accused of lying in his transmissions. The second, if not a noted *Ḥadīth* transmitter, was a celebrated Quran scholar, highly spoken of by Quran and *tafsīr* experts.
>
> The report is known in two versions, both transmitted from a man recognised as one of Mālik's transmitters, to whom no criticism had ever been attached.

> The commentator on the Prophet's biography, al-Suhaylī, related a report, coming from only one chain of transmission, which he thought might have been *ṣaḥīḥ*, 'sound', that he had found in his grandfather's handwriting. The *isnād* involved some unknown names, but the grandfather stated that he had copied it from a book whose author traced it to the same source as the above Mālik version. This form of the *ḥadīth* involves the restoration to life of both parents – but God is all-powerful, nothing is beyond His mercy and His capability. His Prophet merits being singled out for whatever signal sign of His favour God wishes to bestow on him.
>
> Qurṭubī declared that there was no contradiction between the reports on the resurrection of the Prophet's parents and the Quran's withholding permission to pray for them. Their resurrection was the later of the two events. In his book on the Prophet, Ibn Munīr stated that the restoration to life 'that occurred in favour of our Prophet is the equivalent of the restoration to life that occurred in favour of Christ'.[640]

From this, it is apparent that factors additional to the quality of the *isnād*s had their role to play in deciding whether any *ḥadīth* would be upheld or rejected.[641] To return to the differing assessments made of the individuals in the *isnād*s, we cite:

1. Aḥmad and others abandoned Layth. But Suyūṭī can point out that Muslim and 'the four' cite him.[642]
2. Warqā' is 'worthless'. Suyūṭī: 'He is *thiqa*, a scholar cited by 'the Six'.[643]
3. Al-Qāsim is 'abandoned'. Suyūṭī: He is cited by 'the four'; Ibn Ma'īn said he is *thiqa*; Juzjānī said, 'Outstanding', he had met forty Companions; Tirmidhī: *thiqa*. But others characterised him as 'weak', *ḍa'īf*.[644]

Arabic names can be very confusing, and it is important not to allow oneself to be muddled.

4. Isḥāq b. Wahb is a liar. Suyūṭī: God forbid! Isḥāq is neither a liar, nor yet 'weak'. He is *thiqa*. The Isḥāq who was a liar was Isḥāq b. Wahb al-Ṭaharmasī.[645]

Here, the author has confused two men. A further instance of muddle is the transmuting of 'Abdul 'Azīz b. Abī Rawād into 'Abdul 'Azīz b. Muḥammad al-Darāwardī.[646]

The book of Ibn al-Jawzī is a mine of information on the varying assessments proffered by the *isnād* experts. It is not unusual to find entries such as:

> Of this same person, Ibn Ma'īn in one place says *thiqa*; in another place, he says 'weak'.[647]
>
> Accompanying a very remarkable *isnād*: ... al-Mas'ūdī – 'Āṣim – Abū Wā'il – 'Abdallāh b. Mas'ūd – the Prophet – Gabriel – Michael – Isrāfīl – the Elevated One – God – God's Book of Decrees, one finds al-Baghdādī's comment: 'All the men named in this *isnād* are known bar one, 'Abdallāh b. Muḥammad. I am persuaded that my informant invented this name and then attached to it this *ḥadīth*.' The invented person's supposed informant has left a book from which this *ḥadīth* is absent.

Al-Dhahabī's comment is more concise: both *matn* and *isnād* are fabrications.[648]

One, 'Abdallāh b. Jarrād alleged that both he and his uncle were Companions of the Prophet. When asked what his uncle had heard from the Prophet, he solemnly answered: 'The *Muwaṭṭa*' of Mālik, Sufyān's Collection and other things'.

> Ibn Ḥajar: There were two men: 'Abdallāh b. al-Jarrād who was a Companion and who is listed by Bukhārī and others. His name was: 'Abdallāh b. Jarrād b. al-Muntafiq b. 'Āmir. 'Abdallāh b.

Jarrād b. Muʿawiya was no Companion.[649]

Spurious *ḥadīth*s are recognised despite acceptable *isnād*s; other *ḥadīth*s described by al-Ḥākim as *ṣaḥīḥ* on the criteria of the Two *Ṣaḥīḥ*s are dismissed as 'fabrications'. On other occasions, both descriptions are rejected if the *matn* is attached to an *isnād* which is merely 'weak'.[650]

> ʿAbdul Raḥmān b. Sharīk may be 'weak' to Abū Ḥātim, but to others he is *thiqa*. Bukhārī cites him in the *Ṣaḥīḥ*.
>
> Ibn ʿUqda may be an extreme Shīʿī who has been accused of lying, but, in fact, he is a major *ḥāfiẓ* on whose quality they merely disagreed. Dāraquṭnī said: 'Those who call him a liar, I call liars. The *imam*s, leaders and conservators of the *Ḥadīth* pronounce this *ḥadīth ṣaḥīḥ*.'[651]

Baghdādī neatly exposes one *ḥadīth* by pointing out that the *isnād* had been 'overcorrected'.

> Muḥammad b. Mazyad reported once from Qābūs – his father – his grandfather – Jābir ... On a second occasion, this had become: Qābūs – his father – Jābir ... The informant had noticed the absurd error he had committed. The father of Qābūs was a Muslim who had been in contact with certain Companions, for example, ʿAlī. We have no knowledge of the conversion of the grandfather of Qābūs. He was born in the pre-Islamic age and, for all we know, he may have died a heathen. At all events, the man reporting from Qābūs lived too late to have met even him.[652]

The dismissal of the *ḥadīth* as having been fabricated, *isnād* and *matn*, does not appear to have been provoked by the report's containing the Prophet's curse on the man responsible for the killing of his grandson. Many another accepted *ḥadīth* shows the Prophet foretelling the dreadful circumstances of that event.

The foregoing examples are admittedly drawn from late sources. But a similar range of assessments can be seen to be recorded from the earliest stages of the development of the sciences of the *Ḥadīth*. In the *ʿIlal*, for example,

> ʿAlī b. ʿAbdallāh, on comparing two versions of a *ḥadīth* from the Prophet, declares a preference for the Zuhrī version tracing the *ḥadīth* to ʿAbdul Raḥmān b. ʿAwf. The other version, he says, is wrong. He rejects Muḥammad b. ʿAmr's transmission from Abū Salama, reporting via Abū Hurayra.[653]

One of Bukhārī's two versions is that reported by Abū Hurayra.[654] In his *ʿIlal*, Tirmidhī reports:

> Some experts criticise some of the leading scholars, describing them as 'weak' on account of their memories. Other experts

> describe these men as *thiqa*, having regard to their status and their truthfulness, although they may make the occasional error. Yaḥyā b. Sa'īd criticised Muḥammad b. 'Amr, and then transmitted from him. 'Alī b. 'Abdallāh informed me that he had questioned Yaḥyā about Muḥammad b. 'Amr. 'Do you mean to be lenient, or to be severe?' asked Yaḥyā. 'Alī said he meant to be severe, and as Yaḥyā said, 'He's not one of those you want. He used to say, "Our teachers said – Abū Salama and Yaḥyā b. 'Abdul Raḥmān b. Ḥāṭib".' According to Yaḥyā, Mālik b. Anas had said much the same about Muḥammad b. 'Amr. Yaḥyā, however, was prepared to concede that Muḥammad b. 'Amr was superior to Suhayl b. abī Ṣāliḥ and 'Abdul Raḥmān b. Ḥarmala.[655]

'Alī knows the latter from a report transmitted from 'Abdallāh, but 'Abdul Raḥmān is not known as an associate of 'Abdallāh's.[656]

> 'Alī reports that Yaḥyā did not accept from Sharīk, nor from Abū Bakr b. 'Ayyāsh, nor al-Rabī' b. Ṣubayḥ, nor al-Mubārak b. Faḍāla. But 'Abdallāh b. al-Mubārak, Wakī' b. al-Jarrāh, 'Abdul Raḥmān b. Mahdī and other *imams* transmitted from them.[657]

> Some scholars impugned transmitters such as Suhayl b. abī Ṣāliḥ, Muḥammad b. Isḥāq, Ḥammād b. Salama and Muḥammad b. 'Ajlān. They had noticed lapses of memory in some of their reports. But, among those who did accept from these and their like were 'Alī b. 'Abdallāh and Sufyān b. 'Uyayna, who described both Suhayl and Ibn 'Ajlān as respectively *thabit* and *thiqa ma'mūn* [reliable, trustworthy].[658]

> Yaḥyā was somewhat confused about Ibn 'Ajlān's *ḥadīth* from Sa'īd al-Maqburī which is sometimes reported, Sa'īd – Abū Hurayra, and at other times, Sa'īd – a man – Abū Hurayra. Yaḥyā said, 'I simplify this by saying: Sa'īd – Abū Hurayra'.

The Maqburī *ḥadīth*s are a constant source of confusion.[659]

'Alī reports that it was common for Successors to name now one Companion, now another, in their reports. Tirmidhī thought that was to be put down to the fact that they had not written their *ḥadīth*s but trusted too much to memory. Some of them added to, some of them omitted from their *isnād*s, even changed their *isnād*s or their *matn*.

> Muḥammad b. Sīrīn would say, 'I might hear the same *ḥadīth* from ten men. The wording would not be the same twice, although the meaning was always the same.'[660]

That concerns us less at this point than the remark about the changes made in the *isnād*s. Great difficulty is caused to the student of the *Ḥadīth* by the practice of these early experts who state, or at least are reported as stating, their views on the *isnād*s in the form of simple lists of names of those whose *isnād*s they approve of and those whose *isnād*s they disapprove of, without any hint of a general principle. They thus appear as mere statements of unaccountable personal preferences. For example,

> ʿAlī reports from Yaḥyā: 'I prefer Mujāhid's *mursal* reports to ʿAṭā''s; I prefer Ibn Jubayr's *mursal* to ʿAṭā''s; Mujāhid and Ṭāwūs are on a par. Abū Isḥāq's *mursal ḥadīth*s, those of Aʿmash, Taymī, Yaḥyā b. abī Kathīr, Ibn ʿUyayna and Thawrī's are all as good as non-reports. I prefer Mālik's *mursal* reports above all others.'[661]

It is difficult to know what to make of such statements unless to conclude that, by the time they were being made, Mālik had acquired some reputation among these scholars. Tirmidhī suggests that the *imām*s criticised the *mursal* since a scholar is as capable of reporting from an unreliable as he is from a reliable informant. How is one to know if he does not name his immediate informant?[662] Ḥasan Baṣrī, who criticised Maʿbad's theological views, nevertheless cites him for other matters. Shaʿbī denounced Ḥārith al-Aʿwar as a liar, yet relied on him for legal information, indeed praising him for the quality of that particular branch of information as the best-informed on legal topics.[663]

When Aʿmash questioned Ibrāhīm Nakhaʿī as to who his intermediary was for the information he cited as from ʿAbdallāh, Ibrāhīm replied somewhat loftily:

> If I name my intermediary, that is who told me. But when I say, "ʿAbdallāh said", that is something I heard from several persons reporting from ʿAbdallāh.'[664]

Under the powerful influence of Shāfiʿī's seemingly unshakeable arguments, modern Muslim writers on the *Ḥadīth*, arguing from the figure of the Prophet onwards, state in their presentation of the development of the *Ḥadīth* a 'must have been' case. Hesitation is caused in the case of the non-Muslim writer by a series of factors. The arbitrary nature of the assessment of the men named in the *isnād*s and the way it can vary from expert to expert, and from time to time, inspires doubt. Rejection of one man's reports on account of his views on other matters, we have seen, accompanies acceptance of another man's reports, despite his views on other matters. The frequency of single-line transmission where one might have expected multiple reporting and the prevalence of accusations of *irsāl* or *tadlīs* and the scholarly tendency to seek to minimise their implications, are further factors which prevent acceptance of the simple view that the *Ḥadīth* represents information deposited by the Prophet with his Companions, lovingly preserved by that generation to be passed on, unchanged, unchanging and eternal in an unbroken, continuous transmission, generation after generation until it reached the hands of the compilers of the great third/fourth-century collections. This reads as altogether too ahistorical an approach, taking no account of the major commotions and social dislocations caused by the civil wars and the external conquests that occupied the Muslims during the forty years following the death of the Prophet, and wholly disregarding the impact on the Muslims arriving in the conquered territories of the developed cultures of the pre-existing populations among whom they would settle, many of whom in time, on converting to Islam, would furnish it with its most prominent figures participating in creating the new cosmopolitan Islamic culture to which they brought their own religious, legal, political and theological contributions. These men were not guided by Arabian institutions and presuppositions, of which they knew nothing. Nor do modern Muslim writers consider the competitive atmosphere in which the *Ḥadīth* flourished, the debates which nourished and exploited it. Above all, they take no account of development. Too many bland rationalisations are attempted when even the medieval experts mention negative features. Perhaps the most negative feature affecting the history of the *Ḥadīth* is *irsāl*. The demand for *isnād*s shows the absence of *isnād*s. The prevalence of *irsāl* and *tadlīs* and their discussion and then rationalisation point in precisely the same direction. The generation that deserves most attention in future studies of *Ḥadīth* is that of the younger Successors. Ḥasan Baṣrī (20–110/641–728); Muḥammad b. Sīrīn (33–110/653–728); the Madīnan, Sa'īd b. al-Musayyab (13–95/634–714); the Kūfan, Ibrāhīm Nakha'ī (50–95/670–714); the Makkans, 'Aṭā' (27–113/648–731), Ṭāwūs (d. 106/724), Ibn Jurayj (86–150/705–68) and Mujāhid (21–104/642–722). For Madīna, other important figures would be al-Qāsim b. Muḥammad (d. 107/725), Sālim b. 'Abdallāh (d. 106/724) and Sulaymān b. Yasār (34–107/654–725).

These are the names most commonly cited for *irsāl* and *tadlīs*, and that suggests a break in the continuity of the transmission. It might, on the other hand, point to yet another factor. This concerns not oral transmission but the transmission of written records. In *Ḥadīth* circles, there appears to be a permanent tension between the knowledge that materials had been circulated in written form and the scholars' wish that that had not been the case. The experts declare their strong preference for *samā'*, that is, the strictly oral reception and dissemination of all *ḥadīth*s. Possibly influenced by the preference for exclusively oral testimony in the law-courts (in sharp contrast to the Quran – see Q 2.282), this declared preference for oral reception and transmission of the *Ḥadīth* may equally have been engendered by genuine fear of the inadequacies of the script. In any event, the *Ḥadīth* experts always retained strong reservations about the role, if any, that writing be admitted to have played in *Ḥadīth* circles. The rationalisation of what was a known practice has tended to obscure the facts. One notes the frequency with which one reads, in deference to prejudice,

> 'Most of the older authorities did not write their *ḥadīth*s – or, if they did, they did so only after having first heard them'.[665]

Those who wrote stood more chance of preserving the *ipsissima verba* of their informants, but they also ran the serious risk of misreading from their notes. Those who did not write avoided the perils of *taṣḥīf* (misreading), although they ran the risk of forgetting. Two opposing views on the writing of *Ḥadīth* were reflected in the celebrated conflicting statements relayed as from the Prophet. The same division is voiced in the scholarly debates over the demand for precise, verbatim reports as against the transmission of *ḥadīth*s 'according to the sense'. The latter has been seen in the earlier Ibn Sīrīn statement which has its parallel in a statement from his contemporary, ʿUrwa b. al-Zubayr, citing, it is said, ʿĀ'isha.[666] We heard Abū Hurayra's supposed boast about his infallible memory. The only Companion who might match him for volume of *ḥadīth*s was ʿAbdallāh b. ʿAmr – but ʿAbdallāh had written his. When asked why his reports were not so complete as those of Sālim, Ibrāhīm Nakhaʿī supposedly replied: 'Sālim wrote his, whereas I memorised mine'.[667] The strictures of the scholars are later than an activity which has not been wholly effaced by theory. In transmitting any *ḥadīth*, a man was supposed to say: 'I heard so-and-so say ...'. The preferred terms to be used should be *samiʿtu/ḥaddathanī/akhbaraniī/anba'anī*, which were all meant to indicate audition. Again, rules about vocabulary do not completely conceal the practice, since these terms can be reported as having been recommended for use in circumstances in which audition was known not to have been the method of acquisition.[668] Observation obliged the theorists to adapt their demands to a range of teaching methods that had long been in vogue in scholarly circles. Having recited their own notebooks to a group of students, or had them recited to them by one of the students, teachers licensed the learners to transmit the contents to others. A busy teacher might simply hand a book of his *ḥadīth*s to an intelligent student, or give him the freedom of his library, or even furnish him with some of his *ḥadīth*s in the course of correspondence. In all such cases, whatever the method employed, the elders would license their juniors to transmit their materials, using whichever of the above terms they preferred. It follows that the expert of later date could never be absolutely certain by which means a man had acquired his stock of *ḥadīth* reports. Ibn ʿAbbās, ʿAṭā', Sufyān Thawrī, Manṣūr b. al-Muʿtamir, Ḥasan Baṣrī, Hishām b. ʿUrwa, Zuhrī, Mālik – even Abū Hurayra – are only a few of the names of the celebrities credited with having adopted and even skilfully defended such methods of disseminating knowledge. In many cases this is no longer easily detectable, given the habit of the transmitters of citing, in good faith, the names of the authors as opposed to the titles of their books. For his own day, Shāfiʿī could speak of this as the normal thing. For the earlier stage, it is detectable from the negative judgments uttered against men who, in a later stage of the *Ḥadīth*, had become 'household names' whose reports were to be accepted without demur. The later period's hunger and thirst after information had overcome the earlier period's pompous strictures.

> ʿAlī b. ʿAbdallāh asked Yaḥyā b. Saʿīd how he evaluated the *ḥadīth*s which Ibn Jurayj had transmitted from ʿAṭā' al-Khurāsānī. The highly respected expert replied, 'Weak'. ʿAlī protested, 'But he says, "*akhbarani* ʿAṭā'"'. Yaḥyā assured him that that meant nothing. ʿAṭā' had given him a book.[669]

Similar reports about any number of other transmitters abound. Yaḥyā himself found the same justification for accepting the *mursal* reports of Ḥasan that Shāfiʿī later found for accepting the *mursal* reports of Saʿīd b. al-Musayyab:

> 'When Ḥasan says, "the Prophet said ..." one can usually find a basis for his *ḥadīth*s'.[670]

The responsibility in the transmission of *ḥadīth*s is, in the end, that of the transmitter. The recipient seeks to establish probability rather than certainty, and, even from those known to practise *tadlīs* , Shāfiʿī is prepared to accept *ḥadīth*s providing they use the approved formally correct vocabulary of transmission, *ḥaddathanā* or *samiʿtu*. Matters are determined not on the basis that they come from the Prophet, but on the grounds of the consensus of the *Ḥadīth* specialists that they probably come from the Prophet.

Epilogue

In the compressed perspective that hindsight imposes, of the many personalities engaged in creating the Islamic Tradition, Shāfiʿī and Aḥmad have emerged as key figures. Although the tone of Mālik's *Muwaṭṭa'* is preponderately Arabian, he was open to Iraqi views on legal topics, as is clear from the scattering of Iraqi *isnād*s that one encounters in his work. We have seen that he counted among his many pupils Muḥammad al-Shaybānī, the future spokesman of the Kūfan school who, although endorsing much of Mālik's materials, would also produce major works in refutation of the legal positions adopted at Madīna. Mālik's second major pupil, Shāfiʿī, was probably, from his wide travels, even more expertly informed on the opinions of the legal schools of his day. Among his works would be several refutations of the conclusions of his chief rivals, both Madīnans and Kūfans. A significant result of the incessant polemic waged in the latter half of the second century was the firm establishment of the *Ḥadīth* as the chief vehicle of scholarly debate. That set the *Ḥadīth* on solid foundations as the currency of scholarly interchange, thus reinforcing its significance in the minds of the Muslims generally. It was, however, not the debating victories which they scored over each other that marked the major achievement of these scholars. Far more significant for future developments were Shāfiʿī's dazzling arguments for the primacy of *ḥadīth*s from the Prophet. These had been directed at two main targets. First was the older, informal and unsystematised deference to past precedent, 'the *sunna* of the Muslims', which was still, at the outset of Shāfiʿī's career, the tradition inherited from the forebears, including teachers and parents and, behind them, the local Successors, thought to have passed on the teachings and opinions of their predecessors, the Companions of the Prophet. Once publicly declaimed, Shāfiʿī's insistence on the uniqueness of the figure of the Prophet and the clear superiority of statements reported from or about him was so obvious that it could never thereafter be challenged. That was especially the case since Shāfiʿī's second target was those who, seeking to reject the *Ḥadīth* as a legitimate source of religious or legal knowledge, and demanding recognition of the Quran as the exclusive basis of the Law, forced Shāfiʿī to respond both to them and to the lawyers on the basis of exclusively Quranic evidence. It was God who had demanded uncomplaining adherence in all matters to the word of the Prophet alone. Reacting in defence of an existing Law against those who protested that they 'could not find two penalties in the Book of God', Shāfiʿī was himself well aware of the consequences of the line of argument that he had introduced. 'Had the Muslims judged on the basis of the Quran alone, without taking account of the indications of the *sunna* of the Prophet, they would have cut off the hand of every thief and they would have flogged every fornicator.' In founding the claims which he made for the *sunna* on the Quran, Shāfiʿī had simultaneously used the Quran to declare the *sunna* independent of the Quran. It would never again be possible to cite the Quran to restrain or to challenge the *sunna*. This created the illusion that there were two sovereign, independent sources underlying the Law: the Book of God and the *sunna* of the Prophet. The impression was given that, being parallel, *sunna* and Quran at no point touched. Each had to be considered in its own sphere and on its own terms. It was said that the Quran could not judge the *sunna*. Rather, it was the *sunna* that judged the Quran. Shāfiʿī spoke of three categories of *sunna*. The first of these concerned matters regulated in the Quran with which the *sunna* 'coincided precisely'. In that case, the regulation is the Quran's and the *sunna* becomes wholly redundant. We can therefore surely ignore such *sunna* as historically insignificant. His second category consists of matters introduced in the Quran in general language, with the detailed clarification delegated to the Prophet. This category Shāfiʿī illustrates with reference to Q 5.6. The Prophet had demonstrated the ablution. Two reports are known. In one, Muḥammad had washed once; in the other, he had washed thrice. The Prophet's conduct is said to establish that the minimum required to satisfy the regulation is one washing. Thus, by inference, one perceives that the threefold washing is optional. Given, however, the wording of the verse, the nature of language and the coexistence of the two reports, it is clear that these are two competing reports. They are not, however, presented as such, but as the inevitable result of interpretative potential, resolved only by knowledge of the *sunna*. The elucidatory function of *sunna* is additionally illustrated in the Prophet's insistence that the ankles are to be washed – not wiped. Further aspects of the ablution, not mentioned in the verse but supplied only in the *sunna*, include illustrations of what occasions the need for *wuḍū'*-renewal. Similarly, while their obligatoriness is baldly stated by the Quran, knowledge of the number, frequency and manner of performance of the ritual prayers, or the kinds of property to be taxed, the rates of taxation and the dates on which tax is payable, or the detailed practices of the *ḥajj* and the *ʿumra*, is wholly *sunna*-based.

Shāfiʿī had illustrated his first category by the Quran's imposition of the rule to face the Kaʿba when performing the ritual prayer. Since only those in the immediate vicinity of the building can be assured of the correct direction to face, the obligation of those not in its immediate vicinity must be to make every effort, using all available means such as the position of the sun or the stars, local landmarks and the known directions of the various winds, and so on, to ascertain the direction to face. Their obligation is not to hit on the precise direction, merely to make the effort to discover what they believe to be the correct direction. Thus Shāfiʿī lays the foundation stone of his programme of the relation between human effort (*ijtihād*), the exercise of the intellect and the fulfilment of the divine commands. In his second and third categories, the *sunna* takes the place of physical landmarks. The *sunna* functions not merely to elucidate but to supplement the Quran's regulations, supplying the details needed to implement divine commands; and, by a species of analogy, Shāfiʿī adds to the first and second categories the third, in which the *sunna* addresses matters quite unmentioned in the Quran. For this category, his evidence is Quran.

> Q 53.3–4: The Prophet 'does not speak from whim, but on the basis of revelation imparted to him'.
>
> Q 59.7: 'What[ever] the Prophet brings you, that accept; from what[ever] he prohibits, desist.'

Although by training and background Shāfiʿī belonged to the legal school, his whole approach shows that he had thrown in his lot with the *Ḥadīth* party. Both his arguments in principle and the Quran verses by which he sustained them have remained the staple of Muslim writers on the *sunna* from his time to the present day.

The *Ḥadīth* specialists gloated over their supposed victory over the party of Reason. In the charged atmosphere engendered by the persecution of the pious conservatives at the hands of the devotees of Greek logic and metaphysics, the essentials of Shāfiʿī's spirited argumentation furnished, together with the powerful emotions of the victims of the onslaught on Tradition, a formidable combination of feelings coloured by fearful suspicion of an excessive dependence upon rational method and an unforgiving hatred of its alien, un-Islamic origin. God was believed to have intervened to deliver His people and to rescue His religion. Their strong sentiments fostered in the *Ḥadīth* circles an anti-intellectual bias and antipathy for anything foreign. *Ḥadīth* scholarship opted for isolationism. Building a defensive wall around the Law and the theology, they became increasingly inward-looking, inclined to self-congratulation and determinedly indifferent and oblivious to all but their own concerns.

For more than 1,000 years, the conservatives have maintained the mood and the arguments of Shāfiʿī and Aḥmad, offering the stoutest resistance to any internal or external critique of the *Ḥadīth*. Having done so once before, they denounce the studies of Goldziher and Schacht as alien and dismiss them as 'unscientific in method' and based on nothing more than mere spite and jealousy of Islam which, alone of all the major religions, has been blessed with the institution of the *isnād*.

Some Western scholars, too, have expressed reservations about the hypotheses of Goldziher and Schacht. My own position is that the wholesale rejection of the *ḥadīth*s as mere invention and fabrication misses the point that many of the *ḥadīth*s can be shown to spring from an ancient source in the primitive exegeses. Were that argument accepted, then part of the *Ḥadīth* at least could be said to reach back to the first attempts to understand the Book of God. Such *ḥadīth*s would preserve some material on the thinking of Muslims, if not precisely in the age of the Prophet, then very soon after, in what might be called the age of the Quran.

Notes

1. Q 23.84–9.
2. Q 43.31.
3. Q 72.8–9.
4. al-Bukhārī, Muḥammad b. Ismā'īl, *Jāmi' al-Ṣaḥīh*, bad' al-khalq, bāb: idhā waqa' al-dhubāb ...
5. Ibid., Ṭibb, bāb: al-'ayn ḥaqq.
6. Q 6.29.
7. Q 10.16.
8. Q 17.49; 36.78.
9. Q 16.24; 27.68.
10. Q 8.32.
11. Q 6.7; 17.93.
12. Q 21, passim.
13. Q 16.43; 21.7.
14. A. Guillaume, *The Life of Muhammad*, Oxford, 1955, p. 198.
15. The History of al-Ṭabarī, vol. VI, *Muḥammad at Mecca*, trans. and annotated by W. M. Watt and M. V. McDonald, New York, 1988, p. 159.
16. 'The Sunna jāmi'a pacts ...', R. B. Serjeant, *BSOAS*, vol. XLI, pt 1, 1978, pp. 1–42.
17. Q 3.123.
18. Q 7.157; cf. Q 2.140, 146, 159.
19. Q 3.187.
20. Q 7.157.
21. Q 2.47–105.
22. Q 2.101.
23. Q 4.76, 84.
24. Q 3.165–75.
25. Badr – Qaynuqā', AH 2.
26. Uḥud – Naḍīr, AH 3.
27. The 'battle of the trench', AH 5.
28. Qurayẓa.
29. Q 9.30.
30. Q 6.101; 72.3.
31. Q 3.68.
32. Q 37.102.
33. Q 37.102–7.
34. Q 2.127.
35. Q 2.144.
36. Guillaume, op. cit., p. 499ff.
37. Ibid., p. 540ff.
38. Ibid., p. 566ff.
39. Bukhārī, manāqib al-Anṣār.
40. Guillaume, op. cit., p. 627.
41. Q 9.2–8.
42. Q 12.2.

43. Q 2.97.
44. For example, Aḥmad Amīn; Abū Rayya.
45. Muṣṭafā al-Sibā'ī, *al-Sunna*, Damascus/Beirut, 1398/1978, p. 187ff.
46. M. Z. Ṣiddīquī, *Ḥadīth Literature*, Calcutta, 1961, pp. xviii–xix.
47. Abū Da'ūd, *Sunan*, 2 parts in 1, Cairo, 1348/1929, 1, p. 3.
48. al-Ṭayālisī, *Manḥat al-Ma'bud*, 2 parts in 1, Cairo, 1372/1952, 1, p. 34.
49. 'Abdul Raḥmān al-Tha'ālibī, *al-Jawāhir al-Ḥisān fī tafsīr al-Qur'ān*, 2 vols, Algiers, 1905, 1, p. 95.
50. Abū Da'ūd, op. cit., Ṣalāt, bāb: idhā ṣallā khamsan.
51. Mālik b. Anas, *al-Muwaṭṭa'*, Ṣalāt, al-'amal fi-'l-sahū.
52. Bukhārī, Buyū', bāb: al-khurūj fi-'l-tijāra.
53. Ibid., isti'dhān, bāb: al-taslīm wa-'l-isti'dhān thalāthan.
54. Q 24.58.
55. Bukhārī, I'tiṣām, bāb: al-iqtidā' bi sunan rasūl allāh.
56. Abū Da'ūd, Ṣalāt, bāb: al-sakta 'inda 'l-iftitāḥ.
57. *Muwaṭṭa'*, mā jā'a fi-'l-ṣadāq; *Muwaṭṭa' Muḥammad*, p. 182.
58. *Muwaṭṭa'*, Ṭahāra, tark al-wuḍū' mimmā massat al-nār.
59. See J. Burton, 'The Qur'ān and the Islamic practice of wuḍū'', *BSOAS*, vol. LI, pt 1, 1988, p. 22.
60. See J. Burton *The Collection of the Qur'ān*, Cambridge University Press, 1977, pp. 146–7, 166–75.
61. Bukhārī, al-ashkhāṣ, wa-l-khuṣūma, kalām al-khuṣūm ...
62. Muḥammad b. 'Abdallāh, Abū Bakr b. al-'Arabī, *Aḥkām al-Qur'ān*, 4 vols, Cairo, 1376/1957, 4, pp. 1,870–1.
63. *Collection of the Qur'ān*, p. 145.
64. 'Abdallāh b. abī Da'ud, *Kitāb al-Maṣāḥif*, ed. A. Jeffery, Cairo, 1355/1936, al-tanqīṭ wa-'l-tashkīl.
65. Bukhārī, Wuḍū', al-wuḍū' min ghayr ḥadath.
66. Ibid., lā yatawaḍḍa' min al-shakk ḥattā yastayqin.
67. See n. 65.
68. *Muwaṭṭa'*, wuḍū' al-nā'im idhā qāma.
69. Muslim b. al-Ḥajjāj, *Jāmi' al-Ṣaḥīḥ*, Ṭahāra, bāb: jawāz al-ṣalawāt kullihā bi-wuḍū' wāḥid.
70. *Muwaṭṭa'*, loc. cit.
71. Bukhārī, loc. cit., al-istijmār witran.
72. *Muwaṭṭa'*, Ṣalāt, ṣalāt al-nabī fi-'l-witr.
73. Bukhārī, loc. cit., bāb: man lam yara 'l-wuḍū' illā min al-makhra jayni.
74. Ibid., Ṣawm, bāb: al-ḥijāma wa-'l-qay'.
75. Ibid., Tafsīr, Q 96.
76. Ibid., Q 74.
77. Ibid.
78. Ibid., Adab, bāb: raf' al-baṣr.
79. Ibid.
80. Ibid., Tafsīr, Q 53.
81. Bukhārī, Bad' al-khalq, bāb: idhā qāla aḥadukum 'amīn'; cf. Abū Ja'far, Muḥammad b. Jarīr al-Ṭabarī, *Jāmi' al-bayān 'an ta'wīl āy al-Qur'ān*, 30 parts in 10, Cairo, 1903, 27, p. 25.
82. Bukhārī, loc. cit.
83. Ibid., al-mi'rāj; Ṭabarī, loc. cit.
84. See J. Burton, 'Those are the high-flying cranes', *JSS*, vol. 15, 2,

1970, pp. 246–65; Q 22.52.
85. Cf. A. Guillaume, *Islam*, 1954, p. 187; W. M. Watt, *Muḥammad at Mecca*, Oxford, 1953, p. 103.
86. *Collection*, pp. 82–4.
87. Bukhārī, Ṣawm, bāb: ʿĀshūrā'.
88. Ibid.
89. *Muwaṭṭa'*, Ṣiyām: yawm ʿĀshūrā'.
90. Bukhārī, Ṣawm, bāb: wujūb ṣawm Ramaḍān.
91. *Muwaṭṭa'*, loc. cit.
92. I. Goldziher, *Muslim Studies*, London, 1971, 2, pp. 18–19.
93. Bukhārī, Riqāq, mā yuḥdhar min zahrat al-dunyā wa-'l-tanāfus.
94. Bukhārī, Fitan, sa-tarawna baʿdī umūran …
95. Bukhārī, Manāqib al-Anṣār, bāb: qawl al-nabī 'iṣbirū'.
96. Bukhārī, Faḍl Abī Bakr, 3.
97. *Muwaṭṭa'*, mā jā'a fi-'l-ṭāʿūn.
98. Bukhārī, Manāqib Quraysh.
99. Ibid.
100. Bukhārī, Manāqib al-muhājirīn, bāb: qiṣṣat al-bayʿa.
101. Q 49.9.
102. Bukhārī, ʿalāmāt al-nubuwwa; cf. Diyāt, qawl al-nabī 'lā taqūm al-sāʿa'.
103. Muslim, Imāra, bāb: al-amr bi-wafā' al-bayʿa, 4.
104. Bukhārī, Fitan, bāb: man ḥamal ʿalaynā al-silāḥ.
105. Ibid.
106. Ibid., bāb: lā tarjiʿū baʿdī kuffāran.
107. Ibid., bāb: idhā iltaqa 'l-muslimāni bi-sayfayhimā.
108. Ibid., Ṣalāt, al-taʿāwun fī banā' 'l-masājid.
109. Ibid., Shahādāt, bāb: kayf yuktab 'hādhā mā ṣālaḥ' …
110. Aḥmad b. Ḥanbal, *Musnad*, 6 vols, Beirut, 1389/1969, 1, pp. 118–9.
111. Muslim, Faḍā'il al-Ṣaḥāba, min faḍā'il ʿAlī b. abī Ṭālib.
112. Ibid., 13.
113. Ibid., 9.
114. Mālik, *Muwaṭṭa'*, bāb: al-nahy ʿan al-qawl bi-'l-qadar.
115. Bukhārī, Libās, bāb: al-sikhāb li-'l-ṣibyān.
116. Ibid., mā jā'a fi'l-iṣlāḥ, bāb: qawl al-nabī li-'l-Ḥasan.
117. Ibid.
118. Ibid., ʿalāmāt al-nubuwwa.
119. Ibid., mawt al-nabī.
120. Ibid., Iʿtiṣām, bāb: mā yukrah min al taʿammuq …
121. Ibid., Faḍā'il aṣḥāb al-nabī: Abū Bakr.
122. Ibid., Ṣalāt, bāb al-adhān li 'l-musāfir; bāb: ahl al-ʿilm wa-'l-faḍl aḥaqq bi-'l-imāma.
123. Abū Da'ūd, Kitāb al-sunna, bāb: fi-'l-tafḍīl.
124. Ibid.
125. Ibid.
126. Bukhārī, Ḥajj, bāb: al-khuṭba ayyām minan; cf. Tafsīr, Q 5, 'kuntu ʿalayhim shahīdan mā dumtu fī-him'.
127. Ibid., bāb: al-khuṭba ayyām minan.
128. Abū Da'ūd, loc. cit., bāb: fi-'l-khulafā'.
129. *Musnad* Aḥmad, 1, p. 148.
130. Abū Da'ūd, loc. cit.
131. Ibid.

132. Ibid.
133. Ibid., bāb: fi-'l-tafḍīl.
134. Bukhārī, Adab, bāb: raḥmat al-walad wa-taqbīlihi.
135. Ibid., Aḥkām, bāb: al-umarā' min Quraysh.
136. Muslim, Imāra, bāb: wujūb ṭā'at al-umarā'.
137. Bukhārī, Bad' al-khalq, bāb: mā dhukir 'an B. Isrā'īl.
138. Bukhārī, Fitan, bāb: kayf al-amr idhā lam takun jamā'a.
139. Ibid., Manāqib al-muhājirīn, bāb: dhikru Mu'āwiya.
140. Ibid., Aḥkām, al-sam' wa-'l-ṭā'a.
141. Ibid., Bad' al-khalq, bāb: 'wa-ilā 'Ād akhāhum Hūdan'.
142. Ibid., Ghazawāt, bāb: ba'th 'Alī b. abī Ṭālib.
143. Ibid., Diyāt, bāb: man tarak qitāl al-Khawārij.
144. Muslim, Imāra, bāb: al-amr bi-luzūm al-jamā'a.
145. Ibid.
146. Bukhārī, Fitan, bāb: lā ya'tī zamān illā alladhī ba'dahu.
147. Muslim, loc. cit.
148. Ibid., bāb: fī ṭā'at al-umarā' wa-in mana'ū 'l-ḥuqūq.
149. Bukhārī, Ghazawāt, bāb cit.: cf. Diyāt, bāb: 'wa-man aḥyāhā'.
150. Mālik, *Muwaṭṭa'*, Buyū', bāb: mā taqa' fīhi 'l-shuf'a.
151. Ibid.
152. Ibid., bāb: mā yajūz min al-sharṭ fi-'l qirāḍ.
153. Ibid., mā lā yajūz ...
154. Ibid., end.
155. Ibid., mā jā'a fi-'l-li'ān.
156. Ibid., I'tikāf, end.
157. Ibid., Farā'iḍ, mīrāth al-jidda.
158. Ibid.
159. Ibid.
160. Ibid., end.
161. Ibid., 'Uqūl, 'aql al-jirāḥ fi-'l-khaṭa'.
162. Ibid., al-ḥammāla fi-'l-kitāba.
163. Ibid., mā yukrah an yunbadh jamī'an.
164. Ibid., 'Uqūl, 'aql al-jirāḥ fi-'l-khaṭa'.
165. Ibid., labs al-thiyāb al-muṣabbagha fi-'l-iḥrām.
166. Ibid., i'ādat al-junub al-salāt wa-ghusluhu.
167. Ibid., mā jā'a fi-'l bawl qā'iman.
168. Ibid., mā jā'a fi-'l-nidā' li-l-ṣalāt.
169. Ibid., mā jā'a fī qiyām ramaḍān.
170. Ibid., Ṭalāq, mā jā'a fi-'l-khiyār.
171. Abū Da'ūd, Janā'iz, al-muḥrim yamūt, kayf yuṣna' bihi.
172. *Muslim Studies*, 2, pp. 41–2.
173. Ibid., pp. 46–8.
174. Al-Khaṭīb al-Baghdādī, *Taqyīd al-'ilm*, ed. Y. al-'Ishsh, Damascus, 1949; 1974, p. 107.
175. N. Abbott, *Studies in Arabic Literary Papyri*, II, Chicago, 1967, p. 20.
176. *Muslim Studies*, 2, pp. 43–6 and passim.
177. J. Schacht, *Origins of Muhammadan Jurisprudence*, Oxford, 1950, pp. 156–7.
178. Ibid., pp. 166, 171–2.
179. Ibid., p. 140ff.
180. Ibid., pp. 30, 33, 150, 163, 165.

181. Ibid., pp. 2, 63.
182. Ibid., p. 190ff.
183. Cf. *Middle East Studies*, 3, 1966–7, pp. 195–203 (N. J. Coulson).
184. Mālik, *Muwaṭṭa'*, Ṭahāra, al-wuḍū' min mass al-farj.
185. Ibid., 3.
186. Ibid., 2.
187. Ibid., 3.
188. Ibid., al-amr bi-'l-wuḍū' li-man mass al-Qur'ān.
189. Ibid., al-rukhṣa fī qirā'at al-Qur'ān 'alā ghayr wuḍū'.
190. Bukhārī, Tafsīr, sūrat al-qiyāma; cf. sūrat al-nūr.
191. See J. Burton 'The Interpretation of Ḳ 87, 6–7', *Der Islam*, Band 62, Heft 1, 1985, pp. 5–19.
192. Bukhārī, loc. cit.
193. Ibid., al-tartīl fi-'l-qirā'a.
194. 'The Interpretation', p. 6.
195. Mālik, *Muwaṭṭa'*, Ṣalāt, mā jā'a fi-'l sa'y yawm al-jumu'a; cf. *Muwaṭṭa' Muḥammad*, p. 55.
196. Muḥammad b. Idrīs al-Shāfi'ī, *Umm*, Ṣalāt, al-mashyu ilā 'l-jumu'a; cf. Bukhārī, Ṣalāt, bāb: lā yas'ā ilā 'l-ṣalāt.
197. Bukhārī, Tawḥīd, bāb: qawl allāh 'faqra'ū mā tayassar'.
198. *Collection*, p. 138ff.
199. Mālik, *Muwaṭṭa'*, Ṣalāt, bāb: qaṣr al-ṣalāt fi-'l-safar.
200. al-Ṭabarī, op. cit., 9, pp. 128–9.
201. Muslim, Ṣalāt, bāb: ṣalāt al-musāfirīn wa-qaṣruhā.
202. Mālik, *Muwaṭṭa'*, loc. cit.
203. Muslim, loc. cit.
204. Ṭabarī, loc. cit., p. 126.
205. Muslim, loc. cit.
206. Ṭayālisī, loc. cit., p. 124.
207. Ṭabarī, loc. cit., p. 127.
208. Q 48.27.
209. Ṭabarī, loc. cit., p. 125.
210. Muslim, loc. cit., qaṣr al-ṣalāt bi-Minan.
211. Ibid.
212. Ṭayālisī, loc. cit., p. 125.
213. Mālik, *Muwaṭṭa'*, ṣalāt al-musāfir idhā kān imām.
214. Muslim, loc. cit.
215. Ibn Ḥajar, *Fatḥ al-Bārī*, 17 vols, Cairo, 1378/1959, 3, p. 223ff.: Ḥajj, bāb: al-ṣalāt bi-Minan.
216. Shāfi'ī, *Ikhtilāf al-Ḥadīth*, p. 67ff.
217. Mālik, *Muwaṭṭa'*, al-jam' bayn al-ṣalātayn fi-'l-ḥaḍr.
218. Shāfi'ī, *Umm* I, Ṣalāt: ikhtilāf al-waqt.
219. Mālik, *Muwaṭṭa'*, faḍl ṣalāt al-jamā'a 'alā ṣalāt al-fadhdh.
220. Ibid., cf. jāmi' al-ṣalāt; jāmi' al-targhīb fi-'l-ṣalāt.
221. *Muwaṭṭa' Muḥammad*, p. 79; cf. Muslim, al-ṣalāt fi-'l-riḥāl.
222. *Umm*, loc. cit.; cf. ibid., p. 67.
223. Al-Tirmidhī, *al-Ṣaḥīḥ*, 10 vols, Cairo, 1350/1931, 1, p. 303, mā jā'a fi-'l-jam' bayn al-ṣalātayn.
224. Mālik, *Muwaṭṭa'*, al-jam' bayn al-ṣalātayn fi-'l-ḥaḍr.
225. *Muwaṭṭa' Muḥammad*, p. 82.
226. Ibid., cf. n. 223.
227. Ibn al-'Arabī, *Sharḥ Ṣaḥīḥ al-Tirmidhī*, 3, pp. 13–14.

228. *al-Mudawwana al-Kubrā*, 1, p. 116.
229. *Umm*, 1, pp. 69–70; Tirmidhī, 1, p. 304.
230. Ibn Ḥayyān, *al-Baḥr al-Muḥīt*, 8 vols, Riyāḍ, 1969, 2, p. 34; Al-Rāzī, *al-Tafsīr al-Kabīr*, 32 parts in 16, Teheran, 1970, 5, pp. 80–2.
231. Ṭabarī, op. cit., 3, pp. 434–5.
232. Ibid., pp. 443–4.
233. Rāzī, loc. cit.; Ibn Ḥayyān, loc. cit.
234. Bukhārī, Ṣawm: bāb: 'wa 'ala alladhīn yuṭīqūnahu'.
235. Mālik, *Muwaṭṭa'*, Ṣiyām, mā jā'a fi-'l-ṣiyām fi-'l-safar; cf. Muslim, Ṣawm, jawāz al-ṣawm wa-'l-fiṭr li-'l-musāfir.
236. Bukhārī, Nikāḥ, bāb: mā yukrah min al-tabattul; Muslim, Nikāḥ, nikāḥ al-mut'a.
237. *Encyclopaedia of Islam*, E. J. Brill, Leiden, 1936, 3, p. 775.
238. *Origins*, p. 266.
239. See J. Burton 'The meaning of iḥṣān', *JSS*, 19 (1974) 1, pp. 47–75.
240. al-Ṭabarī, 8, p. 177.
241. Al-Suyūṭī, *al-Durr al-manthūr fī tafsīr al-ma'thūr*, 6 vols, Cairo, 1314/1896, 2, p. 141.
242. Ibid.
243. Ibid.
244. al-Rāzī, op. cit., AD. Q 4.24.
245. Muslim, Ḥajj, bāb: jawāz al-tamattu'.
246. Ibid.
247. Ibid.
248. Ibid.
249. Ibid., Nikāḥ, nikāḥ al-mut'a.
250. Ibid.
251. Ibid.
252. Ibid., bāb: fī naskh al-taḥallul min al-iḥrām.
253. Ibid.
254. Ibid.
255. Bukhārī, Ghazawāt, bāb: ba'th 'Alī etc.
256. Ibid., I'tiṣām, bāb: nahyu 'l-nabī 'alā al-taḥrīm ...
257. Muslim, Ḥajj, bāb: fi-'l-mut'a bi-'l-ḥajj wa-'l-'umra.
258. Ibid., Nikāḥ, bāb: nikāḥ al-mut'a.
259. Ibid., Ḥajj, bāb: jawāz al-tamattu'.
260. Ibid.
261. Ibid.
262. Bukhārī, Dhabā'iḥ, bāb: luḥūm al-ḥumur.
263. Muslim, nikāḥ al-mut'a.
264. Mālik, *Muwaṭṭa'*, Ḥajj, bāb: mā jā'a fi-man uḥṣir bi-'adū.
265. Muslim, Ḥajj, bāb: jawāz al-tamattu'.
266. Mālik, *Muwaṭṭa'*, ifrād al-ḥajj.
267. Mālik, *Muwaṭṭa'*, Ḥajj, bāb: al-qirān fi-'l-ḥajj.
268. Ibid., mā jā'a fi-'l-tamattu'.
269. Ibid.
270. Ibid., mā jā'a fī man uḥṣir bi-'adū.
271. Ibid., mā jā'a fī man uḥṣir bi-ghayr 'adū.
272. Ibid.
273. Ibid., mā jā'a fi-*l-tamattu'.
274. Ibid., jāmi' mā jā'a fi-'l-'umra.
275. Ibid., mā jā'a fi-'l-tamattu'.

276. Ibid., al-ʿumra fī ashhur al-ḥajj.
277. Ibid., mā yunhā ʿanhu min al-thiyāb fi-'l-iḥrām.
278. Ibid.
279. Ibid., labs al-thiyāb al-muṣabbagha fi-'l-iḥrām.
280. Ibid.
281. Muslim, Ḥajj, mā yubāḥ li-'l-muḥrim wa mā lā yubāḥ.
282. Ibid.
283. Mālik, *Muwaṭṭa'*, Ḥajj, bāb: mā jā'a fi-'l-ṭīb fi-'l-ḥajj.
284. Ibid.
285. Ibid.
286. Bukhārī, Ḥajj, bāb: al-ṭīb ʿinda 'l-iḥrām.
287. Mālik, loc. cit.
288. *Ikhtilāf*, p. 290.
289. Shāfiʿī, *Ikhtilāf Mālik, Umm*, 7, p. 200.
290. Mālik, *Muwaṭṭa'*, Ḥajj, bāb: nikāḥ al-muḥrim.
291. Ibn Saʿd, *al-Ṭabaqāt al-Kubrā*, 8 vols, Beirut, 1380/1960, 8, p. 134.
292. Mālik, loc. cit.
293. Ibn Saʿd, loc. cit., p. 135.
294. Ibid., p. 134.
295. Ibid.
296. Ibid., p. 135.
297. Ibid.
298. Ibid., pp. 134–5; cf. Muslim, Nikāḥ, bāb: taḥrīm nikāḥ al-muḥrim wa karāhat ...
299. Ibid., pp. 142–3; Muslim, loc. cit.
300. *Ikhtilāf*, p. 238.
301. Ibid., p. 240.
302. *Muwaṭṭa' Muḥammad*, p. 149.
303. Ibid., p. 140.
304. Al-Khaṭīb al-Baghdādī, *al-Kifāya*, Hayderabad, 1357/1938, p. 48.
305. Q 5.46.
306. Q 2.79.
307. Q 7.157.
308. Q 2.75, 4.46, 5.13, 5.41.
309. Mālik, *Muwaṭṭa'*, Ḥudūd, mā jā'a fi-'l-rajm.
310. Bukhārī, Muḥārabīn, bāb: aḥkām ahl al-dhimma.
311. Mālik, *Muwaṭṭa'*, loc. cit.
312. Ibid.
313. Ibid.
314. Ibid.
315. Q 4.14, 4.80, 33.36, 72.23.
316. Q 4.65.
317. Q 59.7.
318. *Umm*, 7, p. 250ff.
319. *Risāla*, p. 84 (279).
320. *Umm*, 7, p. 271.
321. *Risāla*, pp. 72–3.
322. Ibid., pp. 67, 128.
323. Ibid., pp. 133–4.
324. Ibid., pp. 67, 133.
325. Ibid., p. 132.
326. Ibid., pp. 245–51.

327. *Umm*, 6, pp. 124–30.
328. Ibid., 4, pp. 129–30.
329. *Risāla*, p. 129, 247.
330. Muslim, Ḥudūd, ḥadd al-zinā.
331. *Risāla*, pp. 132, 247.
332. Ibid., pp. 132, 248.
333. Ibid., pp. 89–90.
334. Ibid., pp. 89, 403.
335. Ibid., pp. 91–2.
336. Ibid., p. 87.
337. *Mudawwana*, 1, p. 107.
338. Ṭabarī, op. cit., 2, p. 479.
339. Abū Da'ūd, Ṣalāt, idhā ṣallā khamsan.
340. Mālik, *Muwaṭṭa'*, Ṣalāt, al-'amal fi-'l-sahū.
341. Muslim, Qadar, 1.
342. Ibid., 4.
343. Ibid., 16.
344. Ibid., 17; Q 92.5–10, 91.7–8: 'The soul and He Who created it and inspired in it its evil and its piety'.
345. Ibid., Ḥijāj Ādam wa Mūsā, 3.
346. Abū Da'ūd, Ṣalāt, mā yu'mar bihi min al-qaṣd fi-'l-ṣalāt.
347. Bukhārī, Riqāq, bāb: al-qaṣd wa-'l-mudāwama 'alā 'l-'amal.
348. Ibid., Ṣalāt, bāb: fi-'l-janā'iz.
349. Ibid.
350. Ibid., Adab, bāb: idhā ajāba bi-'labbayka wa-sa'dayka'.
351. Ibid., Tawḥīd, bāb: qawl allāh 'yuḥadhdhirukum allāh'.
352. Ibid., bāb: 'limā khalaqtu bi-yadayya'.
353. Ibid., bāb: 'wujūh yawma'idhan nāḍira'.
354. Ibid., bāb: 'inna raḥmat allāh qarīb min al-muḥsinīn'.
355. Ibid., Ṣalāt, bāb: faḍl al-sujūd.
356. Ibid., Tawḥīd, bāb: qawl allāh 'yuhadhdhirukum nafsahu'.
357. Ibid., 'alāmāt al-nubuwwa.
358. Ibid.
359. Ibid.
360. Ibid.
361. Ibid.
362. Ibid.
363. Ibid.
364. Ibid.; cf. al-Dārimī, *Sunan*, 2 parts in 1, Cairo, 1387/1966, 1, p. 22ff.
365. Muslim, Ḥadīth Jābir al-ṭawīl wa-qiṣṣat Abī 'l-Yusr.
366. Ibid., bāb: inshiqāq al-qamr.
367. Bukhārī, I'tiṣām, bāb: bu'ithtu bi-jawāmi' al-kalim.
368. Ibid., Tafsīr, Q 96.
369. Ibid., hijrat al-nabī wa-aṣḥābihi.
370. Ibid., Adab, bāb: faḍl al-ṣalāt li-waqtihā.
371. Ibid., bāb: 'uqūq al-wālidayn (note assonance and rhyme).
372. Ibid., 3.
373. Ibid., 4.
374. Ibid., 16.
375. Ibid., 4.
376. Ibid., bāb: qawl allāh 'yā ayyuhā 'lladhīn āmanū ittaqū allāh wa-kūnū ma'a 'l-ṣādiqīn'.

377. Ibid.
378. Ibn Qutayba, *Ta'wīl mukhtalif al-Ḥadīth*, Cairo, 1387/1966, p. 34.
379. Mālik, *Muwaṭṭa'*, Jāmi' al-Ṣalāt.
380. Bukhārī, Adab, bāb: al-kibar.
381. Ibid., bāb: raḥmat al-walad wa-mu'ānaqatuhu.
382. Ibid., bāb: ja'al allāh al-raḥma mi'a juz'.
383. Ibid., bāb: al-sā'ī 'ala 'l-armala.
384. Ibid., bāb: ḥaqq al-ḍayf.
385. Ibid., Nikāḥ, 1.
386. Ibid., bāb: idhā bātat al-mar'a muhājira firāsh zawjihā.
387. Ibid., Adab, raḥmat al-nās al-bahā'im.
388. Ibid.
389. Ibid., bāb: lā yaḥill li-rajul an yahjur akhāhu ...
390. Ibid., bāb: man kān yu'min bi-'llāh wa-'l-yawm il-ākhir; cf. bāb: ithm man lā ya'man jāruhu bawā'iqahu.
391. Cf. n. 390.
392. Ibid., bāb: al-waṣāt bi-'l-jār.
393. Ibid., bāb: ifshā' al-salām.
394. Ibid., Da'awāt, bāb: al-du'ā' bi-'l-mawt wa-'l-ḥaiya.
395. Ibid., Adab, bāb: ṣilat al-wālid al-mushrik.
396. Ibid., bāb: al-ḥadhar min al-ghaḍab; cf. Mālik, *Muwaṭṭa'*, mā jā'a fi-'l-ghaḍab.
397. Bukhārī, Adab, bāb: man akhbar ṣāhibahu bimā yuqāl fīhi.
398. Ibid., bāb: al-ḥayā'.
399. Ibid., istitābat al-murtaddīn, 5.
400. Ibid., I'tiṣām, bāb: al-iqtidā' bi-sunan rasūl illāh.
401. Ibid., Ṣalāt, bāb: man adraka rak'a min al-'aṣr.
402. Ibid., bad' al-khalq, bāb: mā dhukir fī B. Isrā'īl.
403. Ibid., Ṣalāt, bāb: al-ijāra min al-'aṣr ila 'l-layl.
404. Ibid., bāb: al-ijāra ilā ṣalāt al-'aṣr.
405. Ibid., Faḍā'il al-Qur'ān, bāb: faḍl al-Qur'ān 'alā sā'ir al-kalām.
406. Ibid., Ṣalāt, bāb: al-ijāra ilā niṣf al-nahār.
407. *Muwaṭṭa' Muḥammad*, pp. 345–6.
408. Al-Suyūṭī, *al-Itqān fī 'Ulūm il-Qur'ān*, 2 parts in 1, Cairo, 1354/1935, 1, p. 38.
409. Muslim, Introduction, bāb: al-isnād min al-dīn.
410. Ibid.
411. Ibid.
412. Ibid., bāb: al-nahyu 'an al-ḥadīth bi-kulli mā sami'a.
413. Ibid.
414. Ibid., bāb: fi 'l-ḍu'afā' wa-'l-kadhdhābīn wa-man yurghab 'an ḥadīthihi.
415. Ibid.
416. Ibid.
417. Ibid.
418. Ibid.
419. Bukhārī, Manāqib, 'Alī b. abī Ṭālib.
420. Muslim, loc. cit.
421. Ibid., bāb: al-kashf 'an ma'āyib ruwāt il-ḥadīth.
422. Ibid.
423. Ibid.
424. Ibid.

425. Ibid.
426. Ibid.
427. Bukhārī, Ṣawm, bāb: al-ḥijāma wa-'l-qay' li-'l-ṣā'im.
428. 'Alī b. 'Abdallāh al-Madīnī, *'Ilal al-Ḥadīth wa-ma'rifat al-rijāl*, Aleppo, 1400/1980, p. 69ff.
429. Ibid., p. 74.
430. Ibid., p. 99.
431. Ibid., p. 77.
432. Muslim, loc. cit.
433. Ibid.
434. Ibid.
435. Ibid.
436. Abū Da'ūd, Ṭahāra, bāb: wa idhā aqbalat al-ḥayḍa tada' al-ṣalāt, end.
437. *Kifāya*, p. 129.
438. Muslim, loc. cit.
439. Ibid.
440. Ibid.
441. Ibid.
442. Ibid.
443. Ibid.
444. Ibid.
445. Ibid.
446. *Risāla*, pp. 370–1.
447. Ibn al-Ṣalāḥ, *'Ulūm al-Ḥadīth*, Madīna, 1386/1966, p. 31.
448. Ibid., pp. 89–90.
449. *'Ilal*, 7.
450. *'Ulūm al-Ḥadīth*, pp. 47–51.
451. *Kifāya*, p. 358.
452. Ibid., p. 348.
453. *Kifāya*, p. 358ff.
454. Ibid., p. 361.
455. Ibid., p. 125.
456. Ibid., pp. 54–65.
457. See J. Burton, *Sources of Islamic Law*, Edinburgh University Press, 1990, ch. 5.
458. Mālik, *Muwaṭṭa'*, Ḥudūd, mā jā'a fi-'l-rajm, 10.
459. Al-Qurṭubī, *al-Jami' li-aḥkām al-Qur'ān*, 20 parts in 10, Cairo, 1369/1950, 2, p. 66.
460. Al-Ghazālī, *al-Mustaṣfā*, 2 vols, Cairo, 1322/1904, 1, p. 124.
461. *Muslim Studies*, 2, p. 32.
462. *Origins*, p. 16.
463. *Mukhtalif*, p. 195ff.
464. Ibid., p. 199.
465. Ibid., p. 313.
466. Mālik, *Muwaṭṭa'*, jāmi' mā jā'a fi 'l-riḍā'a.
467. *Mukhtalif*, p. 314.
468. *Umm*, 7, p. 208.
469. *Risāla*, p. 263; *Ikhtilāf*, p. 240.
470. J. Robson, 'The *isnād* in Muslim Tradition', *Tr. GUOS*, xv, pp. 15–26.
471. *Kifāya*, p. 391.

472. Bukhārī, Ghazawāt, Ḥadīth al-Ifk.
473. *Origins*, p. 22; al-Suyūṭī, *Comm. Muwaṭṭa' Mālik*, Introduction, p. 9, i.e. *Tanwīr al-Ḥawālik*, al-fā'idah al-khāmisa; cf. *Comm. Muwaṭṭa' Muḥammad*, Introduction, p. 13.
474. *Origins*, loc. cit.; *Comm. Muwaṭṭa' Muḥammad*, Introduction, p. 25.
475. Muslim, Introduction, al-Kashf, n. 16.
476. *Comm. Muwaṭṭa' Muḥammad*, Introduction, p. 13. Mālik's balāghāt are said to consist of 'what he had read', *not* heard.
477. *Origins*, p. 37.
478. See above, p. 74.
479. Abū Da'ūd, bāb: fi 'l-qadar.
480. Bukhārī, I'tiṣām, bāb: mā yukrah min kathrat il-su'āl.
481. Al-Suyūṭī, *al-La'āli 'l-maṣnū'a fi 'l-aḥādīth al-mawḍū'a*, 2 vols, 1352/1933, Tawḥīd, 2, p. 3.
482. Al-Ṭayālisī, op. cit., Introduction, p. 7.
483. Ṣiddiquī, op. cit., p. 82.
484. See *Encyclopaedia of Islam*, 1st edn, s.v. 'miḥna'; cf. W. M. Patton, *Ahmed b. Hanbal and the Miḥna*, London, 1897.
485. 'Alī b. al-Madīnī, op. cit., Introduction, p. 6.
486. Ṣiddiquī, p. 79.
487. *Mukhtalif*, pp. 7–8.
488. Ṣiddiquī, pp. 89, 96.
489. *'Ilal*, pp. 44–6.
490. Ibid., pp. 46–7.
491. Muslim, Kashf, nos. 14–16.
492. Bukhārī, Ḥajj, bāb: al-ḥajj wa-'l-nudhūr 'an il-mayyit.
493. See now A. J. Wensinck, *Concordance et indices de la tradition musulmane*, 8 vols, E. J. Brill, Leiden, 1936–88.
494. Muslim, ṣiḥḥat al-iḥtijāj bi-'l-ḥadīth il-mu'an'an.
495. Al-Nawawī, *Sharḥ Ṣaḥīḥ Muslim*, on margin of al-Qasṭallānī, *Irshād al-Sārī*, 12 vols, Cairo, 1326/1908, Introduction, p. 23.
496. *'Ulūm al-Ḥadīth*, pp. 23–4.
497. Ibid.
498. Abū Da'ūd, Ṭahāra, bāb: man qāl yatawaḍḍa' al-junub.
499. Ibid., bāb: fī junub yuṣallī bi-'l-nās wa-huwa nāsin.
500. Ibid., al-mustaḥāḍa; man qāl tada' al-ṣalāt fī 'iddat il-ayyām.
501. Ibid., bāb: idhā aqbalat il-ḥayḍa tada' 'l-ṣalāt.
502. Ibid., al-tayammum. (He confused two men called 'Abdallāh.)
503. Ibid., al-mustaḥāḍa, bāb: yaghshāhā zawjuhā.
504. Ibid., al-manāsik, bāb: mā yalbas al-muḥrim.
505. Al-Tirmidhī, *Sunan*, 10 vols, Cairo, 1350–3/1931–4, 1, p. 114. Ṭahāra, bāb: al-wuḍū' min mass il-dhakar; bāb: tark al-wuḍū' min al-qubla.
506. Abū Da'ūd, bāb: al-wuḍū' min al-qubla.
507. Ṣiddiquī, p. 112.
508. *'Ulūm al-Ḥadīth*, p. 34.
509. Al-Qāsimī, *Qawā'id al-taḥdīth*, Cairo, 1380/1961, p. 247.
510. Ṣiddiquī, p. 123.
511. Qāsimī, p. 248.
512. Ibn Ḥajar, *Tahdhīb al-Tahdhīb*, 12 vols, Beirut, 1968, 9, p. 513.
513. *Muslim Studies*, 2, p. 236.

514. *'Ulūm al-Ḥadīth*, pp. 16, 18.
515. Mālik, *Muwaṭṭa'*, bāb: al-wuḍū' min mass il-farj.
516. *Muwaṭṭa' Muḥammad*, p. 35.
517. *Umm*, 1, p. 15.
518. Abū Da'ūd, Ṭahāra, bāb: al-wuḍū' min mass il-dhakar.
519. Al-Khaṭṭābī, *Ma'ālim al-Sunna*, 4 parts in 2, Aleppo, 1351/1932, 1, pp. 65–6.
520. Ibid., p. 66.
521. Ibid.
522. Tirmidhī, Ṭahāra, bāb: al-wuḍū' min mass il-dhakar.
523. Loc. cit., p. 15.
524. Al-Ḥāzimī, *Kitāb al-I'tibār*, Hayderabad, 1319–59/1901–40, pp. 39–45.
525. It was, in fact, a book, the celebrated *Ṣādiqa*; cf. Dārimī, op. cit., 1, p. 105, no. 502; *Muslim Studies*, 2, p. 23.
526. Cf. Q 2.282.
527. Ibn abī Ḥātim, *'Ilāl al-Ḥadīth*, 2 vols, Cairo, 1343/1925, 1, p. 48, no. 111.
528. Muslim, Ṣayd, bāb: ibāḥat al-ḍabb.
529. Ibid., 3.
530. Ibid., 4.
531. Ibid., 5.
532. Ibid., 6.
533. Ibid., 7.
534. Ibid., 8.
535. Ibid., 9.
536. Ibid., 10.
537. Ibid., 9.
538. Ibid., 10.
539. Ibid., 12.
540. Ibid., 14.
541. Ibid., 15.
542. Ibid., 16.
543. Ibid., 17.
544. Ibid., 18.
545. Bukhārī, Dhabā'iḥ wa-'l-ṣayd, bāb: luḥūm al-ḥumur. Note that Ibn 'Abbās is said to have rejected the report on the basis of Q 6.145.
546. Muslim, al-Ṣayd wa-'l-dhabā'iḥ, bāb: taḥrīm akl laḥm al-humur al-insiyya, 12.
547. Bukhārī, loc. cit., al-dajjāj.
548. Ibid., Ayyām al-Jāhiliyya, 4.
549. *Mukhtalif*, p. 255.
550. Ibid., p. 310.
551. Ibid., p. 314.
552. Mālik, *Muwaṭṭa'*, Nikāḥ, jāmi' mā jā'a fi-'l-raḍā'a.
553. *Collection*, p. 232.
554. Bukhārī, bad' al-khalq, bāb: ṣifat al-nabī.
555. Ibid., Buyū', 1.
556. Ibid.
557. Ibid., 'Ilm, bāb: kitābat al-'ilm; cf. al-Dārimī, 1, p. 103.
558. Al-Ṭabarī, *Tafsīr*, 1, pp. 77–9.
559. Ibid., 1, pp. 29, 91–2; cf. Bukhārī, Tafsīr; Q 74.

560. Muslim, al-Salām, bāb: lā ʿudwā etc.
561. Bukhārī, Tafsīr, Q 9.80.
562. Muslim, Introduction, bāb: al-taḥdhīr min al-kidhb ʿalā rasūl illāh.
563. *Kifāya*, p. 102.
564. Ibid.
565. Muslim, loc. cit.
566. Ibid.
567. Ibid.
568. *Mukhtalif*, p. 40; cf. *Kifāya*, p. 102.
569. Bukhārī, Adab, man summiya bi-asmā' al-anbiyā'.
570. Nawawī, op. cit., p. 92.
571. Ibid., p. 93.
572. Muslim, Introduction, al-kashf.
573. Nawawī, loc. cit., p. 95.
574. Ibid.
575. *Kifāya*, p. 37.
576. Abū Da'ūd, kitāb al-sunna, 2.
577. Bukhārī, ʿalāmāt al-nubuwwa.
578. Al-Ḥāfiẓ al-Nīsābūrī, *Kitāb maʿrifat ʿulūm al-Ḥadīth*, Cairo, 1937, p. 2.
579. *Introduction to Islamic Thought and Theology*, trans. A . and R. Hamori, Princeton, 1981, pp. 69–70.
580. Now being ably continued by Dr G. H. A. Juynboll. See his *Muslim Tradition*, Cambridge, 1983.
581. Ṭayālisī, 1, p. 302.
582. Ibid.
583. Ibid., p. 303.
584. *Ikhtilāf*, p. 244.
585. Mālik, *Muwaṭṭa'*, Ashriba, al-ḥadd.
586. Ṭayālisī, 1, p. 303.
587. Mālik, *Muwaṭṭa'*, ʿUqūl, mā jā'a fī ʿaql al-aṣābiʿ.
588. *Umm*, 7, p. 282.
589. *Ikhtilāf*, pp. 17–18; *Risāla*, p. 423.
590. *Risāla*, p. 39.
591. The order of the four sources varies: ibid., p. 508.
592. Ibid., p. 460.
593. Ibid., p. 189.
594. Mālik, *Muwaṭṭa'*, Zakāt, al-zakāt fi-'l-ʿayn min al-dhahab wa-'l-wariq.
595. *Risāla*, p. 527.
596. Ibid., p. 461.
597. Ibid., p. 772.
598. Ibid., p. 774ff.
599. Ibid., p. 472.
600. Ibid., p. 403.
601. Ibid., p. 413ff.
602. Ibid., p. 396.
603. Ibid., p. 461.
604. Ibid., pp. 84, 172ff.
605. Ibid., p. 422ff.
606. For example, *Umm*, 7, p. 199: al-tamattuʿ fi-'l-Ḥajj.
607. For example, Ibid., p. 248.

608. Ibid., p. 258.
609. *Muwaṭṭa' Muḥammad*, p. 91.
610. Op. cit., 1, p. 33.
611. Op. cit., 1, p. 13, bāb: ta'ẓīm ḥadīth rasūl allāh.
612. Op. cit., pp. 19–20.
613. Ibid., p. 59.
614. *La'ālī*, 1, p. 213ff.
615. Ibid., p. 214.
616. Mālik, *Muwaṭṭa'*, Aqḍiya, al-qaḍā' bi-'l-yamīn wa-'l-shāhid.
617. *Muwaṭṭa' Muḥammad*, p. 301.
618. *Umm*, 6, p. 273ff.
619. *Risāla*, p. 171; cf. Mālik *Muwaṭṭa'*, 'Uqūl, mā jā'a fī mīrāth al-'aql; Abū Da'ūd, Dīyāt, dīyāt al-a'ḍā'.
620. Mālik, *Muwaṭṭa'*, Ṣalāt, ṣalāt al-khawf; *Risāla*, pp. 184–5.
621. Muslim, Ṣalāt, ṣalāt al-khawf.
622. Ibn Māja, Ṣalāt, ṣalāt al-khawf.
623. *Risāla*, p. 288, n. 4; p. 286, n. 4.
624. Ibid., p. 377.
625. Ibid., p. 379.
626. Ibid., pp. 461–3.
627. Ibid., pp. 462–4.
628. Ibid., pp. 466–7.
629. Ibid., pp. 458–9.
630. Ibid., p. 460.
631. Ṭabarī, *Tafsīr* (ed. Shākir), 3, p. 438.
632. *Mukhtalif*, p. 261ff.
633. Tirmidhī, Ṣalāt, mawāqīt al-ṣalāt.
634. Bukhārī, Ṣawm, bāb: man afṭar fi-'l-safar li-yarāhu 'l-nās.
635. *Durr*, 1, p. 190.
636. See J. Burton, *Abū 'Ubaid al-Qāsim b. Sallām's Kitāb al-nāsikh wa-'l-mansūkh*, Gibb Memorial Trust, 1987, p. 127.
637. *Fatḥ al-Bārī*, 5, p. 79.
638. Bukhārī, Zakāt, bāb: al-'ushr fīmā yusqā min mā' al-samā'.
639. *La'ālī*, 1, p. 173.
640. Ibid., pp. 266–8; cf. ibid., p. 341: 'No prophet was granted any miracle, but that Muḥammad was granted a similar, or even more compelling sign'.
641. The foregoing statement was credited to Shāfi'ī.
642. Ibid., p. 101.
643. Ibid., p. 121.
644. Ibid., p. 163.
645. Ibid., p. 204.
646. Ibid., p. 251.
647. Ibid., p. 218.
648. Ibid., p. 282.
649. Ibid., p. 301.
650. Ibid., pp. 317, 321, 334.
651. Ibid., p. 337.
652. Ibid., p. 391.
653. *'Ilal*, p. 103.
654. Bukhārī, Adab, 13.
655. Tirmidhī, 'Ilal, 5, p. 744.

656. *'Ilal*, p. 122.
657. Tirmidhī, loc. cit.
658. Ibid., p. 745.
659. Ibid.
660. Ibid., p. 746.
661. Ibid., p. 754.
662. Ibid., p. 755.
663. Ibid.
664. Ibid.
665. Ibid., p. 746.
666. *Kifāya*, p. 205.
667. Dārimī, 1, p. 101, no. 481.
668. Tirmidhī, loc. cit., pp. 751–3.
669. Ibid., p. 753.
670. Ibid., p. 754.

Glossary

Abbasids	The second Quraysh-based Islamic dynasty claiming descent from the Prophet's uncle, al-ʿAbbās. Centred in Baghdād, the Abbasid caliphate ruled for five centuries, 750–1258, until overwhelmed by the Mongol invaders.
ʿadāla	Abstract noun: probity, honesty, manliness and observance of all the ordinances of the faith are the qualities that must be demonstrated by one whose testimony is acceptable in an Islamic court and in the transmission of acceptable *ḥadīth*s. Thus, the cognate adjective, *ʿadil*.
Allāh	The name of God employed by Arabic-speaking Christians, Jews and Muslims.
Allāt	A female lesser deity, one of 'the daughters of God'.
Anṣār	The converted Yathribites who prepared the first base in which Muḥammad could operate freely.
ʿĀshūrā'	The tenth day of the tenth month. Technically, a fast-day corresponding to 'the Day of Atonement'. Later, the tenth day of the first month, Muḥarram, on which is commemorated the martyrdom of the Prophet's grandson, al-Ḥusayn b. ʿAlī.
athar	Synonym of *khabar*, or *ḥadīth*, but usually reserved for a report from the Companions of the Prophet.
Badr	Site of the Prophet's first major military success against the Makkans in AD 624.
caliph	Arabic *khalīfa*, a successor to the Prophet's political leadership of the community.
Companion	A contemporary of the Prophet who strove for the success of Muḥammad's mission.
ḍābiṭ	Precise, accurate in reproducing reports.
ḍaʿīf	Imprecise, inaccurate or careless in reporting.
'daughters of God'	Lesser female deities regarded as intercessors with God: al-Lāt, al-Manāt and al-ʿUzzā (mentioned in Q 53, 19–20).
dhu 'l-Ḥulayfa	The way-station for pilgrims from Madīna, six miles out on the Makka road.
evil eye	The power to harm a thing one covets by looking at it enviously.
fatra	An interval such as that between any two prophets, or between reception of revelation and its public delivery.
fatwā	An authoritative pronouncement on a specific point of law delivered by a qualified expert, a *muftī*.
fiqh	'Comprehension' specifically of the revealed word of God or of His Prophet, cf. Q 9.122, whence, technically, the branch of learning concerned to understand and relay the revealed law. Experts are known as *fuqahā'* (singular *faqīh*).
ghusl	The major ritual ablution necessary to renew the ritual purity following menstruation or sexual intercourse.

ḥadīth	Any report, whether oral or written. Technically, a report of legal or religious significance.
Ḥadīth	The science or literature of the Islamic tradition.
ḥāfiẓ	A transmitter of *ḥadīth*s endowed with excellence of memory.
ḥajj	The religious pilgrimage to the holy sites in and around Makka to be undertaken at least once in one's lifetime during the first ten days of the last month of the Muslim year, *dhu 'l-ḥijja*.
ḥasan	'Fair', 'comely'. Technically, a report whose transmitters are not all of the highest grade in respect of excellence of memory and power of recall.
Ḥijāz	A barrier, the great mountain range separating the interior from the low-lying coastal plain of the Red Sea; by extension, the province in which both Makka and Madīna are situated.
hijra	The absolute renunciation of family, clan, tribal and homeland ties and loyalties, together with the abandonment of property, whence *muhājir*, one who associates with another in such renunciation.
ʿifrīt	A demon, usually malevolent.
ihlāl	A binding, solemn declaration of intent to undertake a work of piety, such as a pilgrimage or an *ʿumra*.
iḥlāl	Discharge from the foregoing on completion of all formalities undertaken, whence *muḥill*, *ḥalāl*.
iḥrām	The formal assumption of all restrictions associated with the performance of sacred acts such as prayer, fasting or pilgrimage; whence *muḥrim*, *ḥarām*, the one under such restrictions.
ijāza	A licence; permission granted by a master to his pupil to disseminate in the master's name the learning acquired from him. Such a licence may be granted in respect of a single work, or it may be unrestricted, permitting transmission of all that is ascertained to be the teacher's stock of learning, whether acquired directly or indirectly from another. The *ijāza* transferable to a third, competent party is known as *ijāzat al-ijāza*. Among later abuses, condemned by the scholars, was the granting of this type of licence to persons as yet unborn. The legitimacy of licensing absent persons or infants was debated.
ʿilla	'Cause, reason'; the shared element that permits two things to be viewed analogically. For example, the capacity to intoxicate brings any beverage under the ban on the consumption of alcohol. 'Sickness, ailment'; any consideration which impairs the 'health' (*ṣiḥḥa*) or 'soundness' of any *ḥadīth*.
imām	Leader at the ritual prayer, whence, by extension, leader of the political community of the Muslims. In both cases, the office is known as *imāma*.
īmān	Total intellectual commitment to the dogmas of Islam, whence *mu'min*, 'sincere believer'.
irsāl	'Sending forth'; technically, the utterance of a report lack-

ing 'the bridle' or restraint of adequate formal attestation. It normally refers to a report from a Successor about the Prophet which fails to name the Companion intermediary.

Islām — 'Submission' to the Prophet. It may refer to the merely outward profession of faith which lacks full internal conviction, Q 49.14.

isnād — 'Leaning against'; the attestation of any report indicated by the complete listing of transmitters of each generation, whence *musnad*, adequately attested.

jāmiʿ — Comprehensive; a collection of *ḥadīth*s that covers the principal topics: religious dogma; laws or *sunan*; exhortations to reflection on the 'four last things' (death, judgment, Heaven, Hell); Muslim social etiquette; Quran commentary; history and biography; political crises; merits (*manāqib*) and demerits (*mathālib*) of persons or places. In addition to the major collections of al-Bukhārī and Muslim, al-Tirmidhī's *Sunan* is frequently referred to as a *jāmiʿ*.

jinn — 'Invisible', hence supernatural, beings thought to be the offspring of demons.

kaʿba — 'A cube'; the temple of cubic structure in the centre of Makka, known as 'the house of God'.

Khārijī — (plural Khawārij) 'a deserter, seceder'; the name given to several strict puritanical sects descended from those who abandoned ʿAlī's cause on his agreeing to arbitration of his differences with Muʿāwiya. They raised the questions of the nature of 'faith' and of the effect on 'faith' of the commission of sin.

Khaybar — A Jewish settlement in the vicinity of Madīna, taken after a siege in AH 7/AD 629.

al-Manāt — See 'daughters of God'.

maqṭūʿ — 'Broken off'; used of a *ḥadīth* in whose *isnād* a gap is detectable so that it does not reach its putative source, normally the Prophet, in an unbroken connection. Some use *munqaṭiʿ* as a synonym of *maqṭūʿ*, but the former term is more commonly used of any break at any point in the *isnād*.

marfūʿ — 'Raised', used of a *ḥadīth* which involves the Prophet's authority. Hence *rafaʿ*, 'to raise'.

al-Marwa — One of a pair of hillocks, the other being al-Ṣafā, between which the pilgrim proceeds in the course of the *ḥajj* or *ʿumra*. The ritual is termed *saʿy*.

matn — 'The back' or 'the body'; the substantive content of any *ḥadīth*, whether oral or written.

mawḍūʿ — 'Composed'; a spurious or fabricated *ḥadīth*.

mawqūf — 'Halted'; a report which stops short of reaching the Prophet and thus involving the authority of a Companion or later figure.

muḥrim — One who, undertaking to perform a ritual act, assumes all the restrictions attached to the sacral condition.

muḥṣan — Liable, in the event of adultery, to the penalty of death by stoning. The minimum conditions which establish *iḥṣān*

	are: liberty, marriage and the consummation of marriage. Others add being Muslim.
munkar	'Unrecognised'; of a *ḥadīth*, unacknowledged.
munqaṭiʿ	See *maqṭūʿ*.
mursal	Reported as from the Prophet by a Successor, but lacking identification of the Companion informant.
muṣannaf	Arranged according to the topics of interest in law.
Musaylima	A contemporary and rival of the Prophet.
musnad	'Supported'; having a complete *isnād*; a collection of *ḥadīth*s arranged according to the informants.
muttaṣil	'Connected up'; having an unbroken *isnād*.
mutʿa	'Enjoying'; used of the combination of an *ʿumra* with a *ḥajj* on a single visit to Makka, alluded to in Q 2.196. The term is also used of temporary marriage in return for a stipulated fee, said to be referred to in Q 4.24. Supported by the Shīʿa, temporary marriage is abominated by the Sunnīs.
Muʿtazila	The collective name given to systematic theologians influenced by ancient Greek metaphysics. They united in insistence on the freedom of the human will and on the createdness of the Quran to emphasise the justness and the oneness of God, and demanded a role for reason in working out the elements of Islamic belief and principles.
naskh	The generic title of a number of theories concerned with apparent conflict of Quran verses, or of Quran with *ḥadīth*s, or of one *ḥadīth* with another. Three main applications of this principle will be found in the literature on 'the sources of law': alleged omissions from the Quran based on the interpretation of verses that appear to refer to the possibility of the Prophet's 'forgetting'; the alleged abrogation of certain Quran verses, or of certain *ḥadīth*s; the claim that certain rulings of the law originated in verses allegedly revealed, but since 'withdrawn' from the Quran texts.
niyya	'Intent'; the formal declaration of intent necessary to the validity of any legal or ritual act.
rakʿa	A single cycle of actions and words, different combinations of which constitute ritual prayer at various hours.
rāwī	A transmitter of reports, written or oral.
ra'y	'View'; the considered, judicious opinion of a qualified scholar. Later, the term was used pejoratively to imply 'mere opinion', as opposed to adherence to the *Ḥadīth*.
riwāya	A transmission.
sabab	'Cause'; the specific historical situation claimed to have led to the revelation of a particular Quran statement, or the institution of a given ruling by the Prophet. The plural is *asbāb* (*al-nuzūl*).
Ṣafā	See al-Marwa.
ṣaḥīḥ	'Of sound health'; the highest grade of *ḥadīth* in whose *isnād* figure the highest grade of transmitters.
ṣalāt	Prayer, whether obligatory (*farīḍa*) or supererogatory (*nāfila*, *sunna*), the latter the opposite of *wājib*, 'required'.
sanad	'Prop', whence *isnād*, *musnad*.

shaykh	'An elderly man'; scholar or teacher of *Ḥadīth*.
shīʿa	'Party', as in *shīʿat ʿAlī*, the supporters of ʿAlī, or *shīʿat Muʿāwiya*, supporters of Muʿāwiya b. abī Sufyān, ʿAlī's rival for the leadership.
Successor	Any member of the generation following that of the Prophet and his contemporaries, his Companions. Those who met any of the Companions are the senior Successors; those who met none are the junior Successors.
sunna	'Way'; 'Path', hence use, wont or custom of any group of Arabs. The plural is *sunan*.
sunnī	Of or pertaining to *sunna*, especially the *Sunna* of the Prophet. Used in conscious opposition to Shīʿa, Shīʿī. There being no ecclesia or centralised magisterium, the translation 'orthodox' is inappropriate. To the Muslim 'unorthodox' implies heretical, *mubtadiʿ*, from *bidʿa*, the contrary of *sunna*, and so 'innovation'.
tadlīs	'Fraud'; dissembling by giving the impression of being able to report from a person whom one has not however met, or, if having met him, not heard from him what one purports to transmit as being his words. It is also used of disguising the name of an informant, with the probable intent to mislead. One who practises *tadlīs* is a *mudallis*.
ṭahāra	Ritual purity required for the performance of ritual acts; whence *ṭāhir*, being in the requisite state.
taṣḥīf	Inadvertently altering the sense of a text by having misread it, or, in the worst case, deliberately misrepresenting both wording and meaning. Connected with *taṣḥīf* (from *ṣaḥīfa*, the written page) is the misrepresentation, inadvertent or otherwise, which results from confusing consonants (*ḥarf*, *ḥurūf*) of similar shape, *taḥrīf*. Innocent *taḥrīf* was occasioned by the use of an inadequate notation lacking the necessary diacritics.
ta'wīl	Interpretation that goes beyond the letter of a text in search of the spirit of the ordinance. Contrasts with *tafsīr*, interpreting precisely what is in the text its *ẓāhir*.
thābit	'Firm'; said of one who is a competent transmitter of precisely what he heard.
thayyib	Non-virgin by virtue of a current or a previous marriage that was consummated. Thus, married, or widowed or divorced.
thiqa	Entirely trustworthy and reliable as a transmitter.
Tora	The Pentateuch or the five books of Moses.
Uḥud	A mountain near Madīna, scene of the Prophet's second major military confrontation with the Makkans.
Umayyads	The descendants of Umayya b. ʿAbd Shams, founder of one of the clans of Quraysh. The name was given to the dynasty founded by Muʿāwiya b. abī Sufyān, who ruled Islam from their capital, Damascus, 661–750.
umma	An independent congregation, nation or dispensation.
ʿumra	The shortened form of the visitation of the Kaʿba which may be performed at any time of year.
ʿUzayr	A figure said to have been deified by the Jews, Q 9.30.

al-'Uzzā	One of the three 'daughters of God'.
wādī	A dry river-course.
wuḍū'	The lesser ablution; details at Q 5.6.
Yathrib	The former name of the settlement later known as Madīnat al-nabī, 'where the Prophet administered his law', later abbreviated to Madīna.
zakāt	The tax on property, livestock, agricultural produce, or specie, introduced by the Prophet.

Bibliography

Abbot, N., *Studies in Arabic Literary Papyri*, II, Chicago, 1967.
Aḥmad b. Ḥanbal, *Musnad*, 6 vols, Beirut, 1389/1969.
ʿAlī b. ʿAbdallāh (al-Madīnī), *ʿIlal al-Ḥadīth wa-maʿrifat al-rijāl*, ed. A. M. A. al Qalaʿjī, Aleppo, 1400/1981.
Ibn al-ʿArabī, *Aḥkām al-Quran*, 4 vols, Cairo, 1376/1957.
—— *Sharḥ Ṣaḥīḥ al-Tirmidhī*: see al-Tirmidhī.
al-Baghdādī, *al-Kifāya fī ʿilm al-riwāya*, Hayderabad, 1357/1938.
—— *Taqyīd al-ʿilm*, ed, Y. al-ʿIshsh, Damascus, 1974.
al-Bukhārī, Muḥammad b. Ismāʿīl, *al-Ṣaḥīḥ*.
Burton, J., 'Those are the high-flying cranes', JSS, 15, 2, 1970.
—— 'The meaning of iḥṣān', JSS, 19, 1, 1974.
—— *Collection of the Qur'ān*, Cambridge, 1977.
—— 'The interpretation of Ḳ 87:6–7', *Der Islam*, Band 62, Heft 1, 1985.
—— *Abū ʿUbaid's Kitāb al-nāsikh wa-'l-mansūkh*, Gibb Memorial Trust, Cambridge, 1987.
—— *The sources of Islamic Law*, Edinburgh, 1990.
al-Dārimī, *Sunan*, 2 parts in 1, Cairo, 1387/1966.
ʿAbdallāh b. abī Da'ūd, *Kitāb al-Maṣāḥif*, ed. A. Jeffery, Cairo, 1355/1936.
Abū Da'ūd (Sulaymān b. al-Ashʿath), *Sunan*, 2 parts in 1, Cairo, 1348/1929.
Abū Da'ūd (al-Ṭayālisī), *Manḥat al-Maʿbūd*, 2 parts in 1, Cairo, 1372/1952.
Encyclopaedia of Islam, 1st edn, 4 vols, E. J. Brill, Leiden, 1913–34.
al-Ghazālī, *al-Mustaṣfā*, 2 vols, Cairo, 1322/1904.
Goldziher, I., *Muslim Studies*, 2 vols, trans. C. R. Barber and S. M. Stern, London, 1971.
—— *Introduction to Islamic Theology and Law*, trans. A. and R. Hamori, Princeton, 1981.
Guillaume, A., *Islam*, Harmondsworth, 1954.
——*The Life of Muḥammad*, Oxford, 1955.
al-Ḥāfiẓ al-Nīsābūrī, *Kitab Maʿrifat ʿulūm al-Ḥadīth*, Cairo, 1937.
Ibn Ḥajar, *Fatḥ al-Bārī bi-Sharḥ al-Bukhārī*, 17 vols, Cairo, 1378/1959.
—— *Tahdhīb al-Tahdhīb*, 12 vols, Beirut, 1968.
Ibn abī Ḥātim, *ʿIlal al-Ḥadīth*, 2 vols, Cairo, 1343/1925.
Ibn Ḥayyān, *al-Baḥr al-Muḥīṭ*, 8 vols, Riyāḍ, 1969.
al-Ḥāzimī, *Kitāb al-Iʿtibār*, Hayderabad, 1319–59/1901–40.
Juynboll, G. H. A., *Muslim Tradition*, Cambridge, 1983.
al-Khaṭṭābī, *Maʿālim al-Sunna*, 4 parts in 2, Aleppo, 1351/1932.
Mālik b. Anas, *al-Muwaṭṭa'* (al-Shaybānī, *Muwaṭṭa' Muḥammad*).
Muslim, b. al-Ḥajjāj, *al-Ṣaḥīḥ*.
al-Nawawī, *Sharḥ Ṣaḥīḥ Muslim*, on margin of: al-Qasṭallānī, *Irshād al-Sārī li-Sharḥ Ṣaḥīḥ al-Bukhārī*, 12 vols, Cairo, 1326/1908.
Patton, W. M., *Ahmed b. Hanbal and the Mihna*, London, 1897.
al-Qāsimī, *Qawā'id al-Taḥdīth*, Cairo, 1380/1961.
al-Qurṭubī, *al-Jāmiʿ li-Aḥkām al-Quran*, 20 parts in 10, Cairo, 1369/1950.
Ibn Qutayba, *Ta'wīl mukhtalif al-Ḥadīth*, Cairo, 1387/1966.
al-Rāzī, *al-Tafsīr al-KabIr*, 32 parts in 16, Teheran, 1970.

Robson, J., 'The *isnād* in Muslim tradition', *Trans. Glasgow University Oriental Society*, xv, 15–26.

Saḥnūn, *al-Mudawwana al-Kubrā*, 16 parts in 6, Baghdad, 1970.

Ibn Saʿd, *Kitāb al-Ṭabaqāt al-Kubrā*, 8 vols, Beirut, 1380/1960.

Ibn al-Ṣalāḥ, *ʿUlūm al-Ḥadīth*, Madīna, 1386/1966.

Schacht, J., *Origins of Muhammadan Jurisprudence*, Oxford, 1950.

Serjeant, R. B., 'The sunna jāmiʿa pacts ...', *BSOAS* 41, part 1, 1978.

al-Shāfiʿī, *Kitāb al-Umm*, 7 vols, Cairo, 1321/1903.

— *Risāla*, Cairo, 1358/1940.

al-Sibāʿī, M., *al-Sunna*, Damascus/Beirut, 1398/1978.

Siddiquī, M. Z., *Ḥadīth Literature*, Calcutta, 1961.

al-Suyūṭī, *al-Durr al-Manthūr fī tafsīr al-Maʾthūr*, 6 vols, Cairo, 1314/1896.

—— *al-Laʾāli al-maṣnūʿa fi-ʾl-aḥādīth al-mawḍūʿa*, 2 vols, Cairo, 1352/1933.

—— *al-Itqān fī ʿUlūm al-Quran*, 2 parts in 1, Cairo, 1354/1935.

—— *Tanwīr al-Ḥawālik, Sharḥ ʿalā Muwaṭṭaʾ Mālik*: see Mālik.

al-Ṭabarī, *Jāmiʿ al-bayān ʿan taʾwīl āy al-Quran*, 30 parts in 12, Cairo, 1321/ 1903.

—— Ditto, 15 vols, (ed. Shākir), Cairo, 1374/1955– .

—— *History*, vol. vi, *Muhammad at Mecca*, trans. W. M. Watt and M. V. McDonald, New York, 1988.

al-Thaʿālibī, *al-Jawāhir al-Ḥisān fī Tafsīr al-Quran*, 2 vols, Algiers, 1323/1905.

al-Tirmidhī, *al-Ṣaḥīḥ*, 10 vols, Cairo, 1350/1931 (with *Sharḥ Ṣaḥīḥ al-Tirmidhī* of Ibn al-ʿArabī, q.v.).

—— *ʿIlal al-Ḥadīth, Ṣaḥīḥ al-Tirmidhī*, 5 vols., Cairo, 1356–85/1937–65, vol. 5, pp. 736–63.

Watt, W. M., *Muhammad at Mecca*, Oxford, 1953.

Wensinck, A. J., *Concordance et indices de la tradition musulmane*, 8 vols, E. J. Brill, Leiden, 1936–88.

Further Reading

GENERAL AND REFERENCE WORKS

Arnold, T., and Guillaume, A., *The Legacy of Islam*, Oxford, 1965.
The Encyclopaedia of Islam, 1st ed., 4 vols and supplement, Leiden, 1913–42.
Gibb, H. A. R., *Muhammedanism*, London, 1949.
Guillaume, A., *Islam*, Harmondsworth, 1954.
Hughes, T. P., *A Dictionary of Islam*, London, 1935.
Schacht J., and Bosworth, C. E., The Legacy of Islam, Oxford, 1974.

THE PROPHET

Guillaume, A., *The Life of Muḥammad*, Oxford, 1955.
Muir, W., *The Life of Muḥammad*, London, 1877.
Rodinson, M., *Muḥammad*, London, 1971.
Watt, W. M., *Muḥammad at Mecca*, Oxford, 1953.
— *Muḥammad at Madina*, Oxford, 1956.
— *Muḥammad, Prophet and Statesman*, London, 1961.

THE QURAN

Bell, R., *An Introduction to the Quran*, Edinburgh, 1954.
Burton, J., *The Collection of the Qur'ān*, Cambridge, 1977.
Merchant, M. V., *Quranic Laws*, Lahore, 1947.
Roberts, R., *The Social Laws of the Quran*, London, 1925.
Watt, W. M., and Bell, R., *Introduction to the Quran*, Edinburgh, 1977.

THE ḤADĪTH

Christopher, J. B., *The Islamic Tradition*, New York, 1972.
Goldziher, I., *Muslim Studies*, 2 vols, trans. C. R. Barber and S. M. Stern, London, 1971.
Guillaume, A., *The Traditions of Islam*, Oxford, 1924.
Juynboll, G. H. A., *Muslim Tradition*, Cambridge, 1983.

ISLAMIC LAW

Coulson, N. J., *A History of Islamic Law*, Edinburgh, 1964.
Schacht, J., *An Introduction to Islamic Law*, Oxford, 1964.

ISLAMIC JURISPRUDENCE

Burton, J., *The Sources of Islamic Law*, Edinburgh, 1990.
Goldziher, I., *The Ẓāhirīs*, ed. and trans. W. Behn, Leiden, 1971.
Khadduri, M., *Islamic Jurisprudence* (trans. of Shāfiʿī's *Risāla*), Baltimore, 1961.
Schacht, J., *The Origins of Muhammadan Jurisprudence*, Oxford, 1950.

LAW AND THEOLOGY

Goldziher, I., *Introduction to Islamic Theology and Law*, trans. A. and R. Hamori, Princeton, 1981.
MacDonald, D. B., *The Development of Muslim Theology, Jurisprudence and Constitutional Theory*, Beirut, 1965.

THEOLOGY

Watt, W. M., *Islamic Philosophy and Theology*, Edinburgh, 1962.
— *The Formative Period of Islamic Thought*, Edinburgh, 1973.

WORKS WRITTEN FROM AN ISLAMIC PERSPECTIVE

al-Azami, M. M., *Studies in Early Ḥadīth Literature*, Riyāḍ, 1976.
— *On Schacht's Origins of Muhammadan Jurisprudence*, Riyāḍ, 1985.
Siddiqui, M. Z., *Ḥadīth Literature*, Calcutta, 1961.

ARTICLES

The late Professor James Robson published a series of articles on different aspects of *Ḥadīth*. Unhappily, his studies were never integrated into a monograph, but the articles still remain of interest and value to the student of *Ḥadīth*.

'The Material of Tradition', *Muslim World*, vol. 41, 1951, pp. 166–80; 257–70.
'Tradition: Investigation and Classification', *Muslim World*, 41, 1951, pp. 98–112.
'Muslim Traditions: the Question of Authenticity', *Memoirs and Proc. Manchester Lit. Philosophical Society*, vol. 93, 1951–2, pp. 84–102.
'The *isnād* in Muslim Tradition', *Glasgow University Oriental Society Transactions*, vol. 15, 1953–4, pp. 15–26.
'Ibn Isḥaq's Use of the *isnād*', *Bull. J. Rylands Lib.*, vol. 38, 1955–6, pp. 449–65.
'The Form of Muslim Tradition', *GUOST*, vol. 16, 1955–6, pp. 38–50.
'Varieties of the *ḥasan* Tradition', *Journal of Semitic Studies*, vol. 6, 1961, pp. 47–61.
'Traditions from Individuals', *JSS*, vol. 9, 1964, pp. 327–40.
'Standards Applied by Muslim Traditionists', *BJRL*, vol. 43, 1961, pp. 459–79.
'The Transmission of the Ibn Māja's Sunan', *JSS*, vol. 3, 1958, pp. 129–41.
'The Transmission of Nasā'ī's Sunan', *JSS*, vol. 1, 1956, pp. 38–59.

Also of Interest

Schacht, J., 'A Revaluation of Islamic Traditions', *Journal of the Royal Asiatic Society*, 1949, pp. 143–54.
Sprenger, A., 'On the Origin and Progress of Writing Down Historical Facts among the Musulmans', *Journal of the Asiatic Society of Bengal*, vol. 125, 1856, pp. 303–29.
Horovitz, J., 'The Earliest Biographies of the Prophet and their authors', *Islamic Culture*, vol. 1, pp. 535–59; vol. 2, pp. 22–50, 164–82, 495–526.

Index

INDEX OF QURANIC REFERENCES